"Daniel B. LeGoff, the inventor of LEGO®-based therapy, has provided a colourful set of case studies to help teachers and clinicians get a real feel for how to implement this playful and non-stigmatizing intervention with kids with autism. LEGO®-based therapy harnesses their strong drive to systemise to help them learn how to socialise. It is also intrinsically rewarding for such kids. As such, it is a pleasurable experience for both the therapist and the child."

*– Professor Simon Baron-Cohen, Director,*
*Autism Research Centre, Cambridge University, UK*

*by the same author*

**LEGO®-Based Therapy**
How to build social competence through LEGO®-based Clubs
for children with autism and related conditions
*Daniel B. LeGoff, Gina Gómez de la Cuesta,*
*GW Krauss, and Simon Baron-Cohen*
ISBN 978 1 84905 537 6
eISBN 978 0 85700 960 9


*of related interest*

**Building Language Using LEGO® Bricks**
**A Practical Guide**
*Dawn Ralph and Jacqui Rochester*
*Foreword by Gina Gómez de la Cuesta*
ISBN 978 1 78592 061 5
eISBN 978 1 78450 317 8

# HOW
# LEGO®-BASED
# THERAPY FOR
# AUTISM WORKS

## LANDING ON MY PLANET

### DANIEL B. LEGOFF

Jessica Kingsley *Publishers*
London and Philadelphia

First published in 2017
by Jessica Kingsley Publishers
73 Collier Street
London N1 9BE, UK
and
400 Market Street, Suite 400
Philadelphia, PA 19106, USA

*www.jkp.com*

**Library of Congress Cataloging in Publication Data**
A CIP catalog record for this book is available from the Library of Congress

**British Library Cataloguing in Publication Data**
A CIP catalogue record for this book is available from the British Library

ISBN 978 1 78592 710 2
eISBN 978 1 78450 290 4

Printed and bound in Great Britain

MIX
Paper from
responsible sources
FSC
www.fsc.org   FSC® C013056

# DISCLAIMER

*LEGO®, the LEGO logo, the Brick and Knob configurations and the Minifigure are trademarks of the LEGO Group, which does not sponsor, authorize or endorse this book.*

# CONTENTS

# INTRODUCTION

After the release of the LEGO®-based therapy manual a few years ago (LeGoff *et al.* 2014), the main reason for following up with this book was to provide anyone interested in this therapy more of the clinical and anecdotal background details that led up to the final form of LEGO-based therapy. This is the story behind the data and methodology. The treatment manual was developed to establish that there was a method involved in running LEGO-based therapy groups, and that this method was both effective in improving social and communication skills in children and adolescents with autistic conditions, and that it was replicable. My experience with these groups started in the mid-1990s, well before the publication of the first outcome study (LeGoff 2004), and that history has not been described anywhere in the literature on LEGO-based therapy. I have previously written that there was no theoretical rationale or framework that led to the use of LEGO as a therapy tool for the treatment of autism. LEGO-based therapy was not based on a specific body of research literature or a particular theory about autistic conditions. It was a treatment developed by the children themselves. I wouldn't even call myself a facilitator, except that I paid for the LEGO and the space that allowed this to happen.

With the manual, I had more than mixed feelings. I resisted it. I just wanted to give the kids LEGO and a place to meet where they could communicate and socialize. I didn't want to have a bunch of therapists interfering. The core concept was so simple and straightforward it seemed like no one would need a manual. Get children who have autism and enjoy LEGO together and offer them LEGO-based activities which require interaction and collaboration. That's it. With some coaching from the sidelines, they engaged in their own therapy. The effect was like an emergent property: hydrogen and oxygen alone do not predict the properties of water. Autism and LEGO® do not predict what happened in my office. In reviewing the process, there did seem to be some details that needed explicating.

One of the issues I wanted to emphasize in writing this book was the unique qualities, personalities, life-stories and creative genius of the participants. As with all children today who carry a diagnosis of autism, knowing their diagnosis does not diminish their uniqueness or personality. Autistic characteristics are just features which can be more or less disabling, but which are embedded within unique and unpredictable personalities and life histories. It was the stories about uniqueness and creativity which were missing from the manual, and in the end, it was these children's capacity for creativity that resulted in a successful treatment approach.

With regard to the designation of this population, which has undergone a number of changes – from Kanner to Asperger to the *Diagnostic and Statistical Manual of Mental Disorders* (DSM) and then the *International Statistical Classification of Diseases and Related Health Problems* (ICD) – they've labeled these kids everything except what they are: unique, brilliant, innovative. The Pervasive Developmental Disorder (PDD) category had been introduced as a diagnostic entity in the American Psychiatric Association (APA)'s fourth edition of the *Diagnostic and Statistical Manual of Mental Disorders* (DSM-IV). The pervasive developmental disorders at that time also included Autistic Disorder, Rett's Disorder, Disintegrative Disorder and the vaguely defined Pervasive Developmental Disorder, Not Otherwise Specified (PDD-NOS). Prior to the changes in the diagnostic criteria for autistic conditions, autism (or autistic psychopathy) was considered a rare and virtually untreatable condition. It had the ominous overtones of childhood schizophrenia. This negative profile and prognosis for autism was made even more terrifying to parents by the realities of the outcomes at that time: lifelong disability, institutionalization, impenetrable social aloofness, and unpredictable and often self-injurious behavior. Asperger's Disorder was a much more hopeful diagnosis, characterized by eccentricities, like collecting interesting things, and not being good at basketball or football, and not good at cocktail conversations. There were many difficult features, like the lack of empathy (if someone has a scientific definition of empathy, I'm willing to hear about it), and the maddening lack of eye contact – but these were trivial compared to the devastating impact of full syndrome Autistic Disorder, or the similarly severe Rett's Disorder or Disintegrative Disorder.

There were immediate effects of expanding the autism diagnosis into a separate category and including the milder forms of Pervasive Developmental Disorders (PDD-NOS and Asperger's). These effects became even more evident with the introduction of the "autism spectrum" concept, which officially replaced Pervasive Developmental Disorders in the DSM-5 (APA 2013). The first impact was reflected in the epidemiology – the incidence and prevalence rates of autistic conditions increased dramatically, from about one in 1000 children to closer to one in 100 – a ten-fold increase – over a period of about ten years. In other words, autism went from being a rare childhood disorder to being a household term, commonly referred to in the media as an epidemic, and spawning a massive healthcare and educational reform movement, in less than one generation.

During this time, there was a scramble to meet the educational and treatment needs of this growing population of children and their families. Little was known about the longer-term outcomes. Adult functioning, quality of life, sexuality, community integration, voters' rights. What is life like for an adult with autism? What are we going to do with a massive number of adults with autism? The statistics were up to one in 68 male children. That was hundreds of thousands of people. We had no infrastructure for that. It just wasn't in the textbooks in any substantial context. Naturally, there was a "boom" quality about the research and clinical programs that sprang up in the US and other countries during that decade. Early diagnosis and access to "evidence-based" interventions (mostly, those based on applied behavior analysis, or ABA) were the rallying cries of county, state and federal agencies and, soon, fundraising and grant agencies as well.

Scientific and clinical research focused on biological or genetic causes of autistic conditions (Eric Courchesne's work was seminal in this area, as well as the usual over-layer of "review" literature) increased dramatically, and then found its way into the public media. As the dust settled on the autism eruption, it became apparent to many of us that there had been a permanent change in the landscape of children's health and education.

It was around the time of this rapid expansion in incidence, increase in public awareness and rally for services that I graduated from my post-doctoral fellowship in Honolulu, and went to work for the State of Hawaii and their Department of Health's Child and Adolescent Mental Health Division (CAMHD). A few of my colleagues in the CAMHD and early intervention services programs were aware of and were interested in the growing PDD population, but it was not a popular topic. Oppositional, conduct disordered and attention deficit hyperactivity disordered (ADHD) populations were larger and, historically, took up more of the state's resources than autism and other developmental disabilities did. The PDD group was also perceived less optimistically in terms of intervention outcomes. Medication and some parent counseling could turn a kid with Oppositional Defiant Disorder (ODD) or ADHD around and get him or her going in the right direction. PDDs, and autistic disorder in particular, were considered a lifelong struggle. Of course, no one was quite sure what to make of Asperger's Disorder, and some of my colleagues weren't sure it even existed. Psychiatric colleagues insisted that Asperger's was just the early onset of a schizoid or schizotypal personality disorder.

LEGO®-based therapy was not a derivative of some other theory-based intervention approach. No clinical literature focused on social development in autistic children guided LEGO-based therapy. Skill-streaming (McGinnis and Goldstein 1997) and Gray's Social Stories™ were then published (Gray 1994), but I was struggling to find them useful in my work. The children did not spontaneously engage with any activity introduced in these approaches. You could use some other enticement – being playful and engaging or offering some other reward – to get a child to come with you from the waiting room to the therapy area, but it was very exceptional that a child, especially one with autism, would eagerly come from the waiting room. In the case of LEGO® therapy, it was difficult to get them to stay in the waiting area, and they would pull away from their parents and go running into the therapy room.

Before LEGO therapy, there was almost nothing in my playroom that encouraged them to come with me from the waiting room other than just playing with me – usually me, physically. (I'm not a hands-off kind of therapist. I pick kids up and play with them, tickle them, chase them down the hall, let them jump on me.) My playroom was well stocked: water table, sand-tray, puppet theater, clay, painting easel, Barbies, Matchbox cars, dress-up clothes, light sabers and swords... I had the entire toy department in my playroom. But it was LEGO that drew them in. If a kid with autism scanned my playroom and saw LEGO, that's where they went. Non-autistic clients might try out the dresses and hats, sketch a bit on the easel, check out the action figures, splash around with the water table, but the kids with autism went straight for the LEGO. So then we built LEGO together, even if they didn't have any language and didn't make eye contact. If there was some LEGO in the room, we had a basis for connection. Better than Skittles or m&m's: "Hey, let's play LEGO!", and off we went.

At the time, there was a growing literature on utilization of peers in educational settings to help with autistic behavior change and social development. Although I read and followed the research on peer-mediated behavioral strategies in the classroom, and used these methods when I consulted with educators working with students with autism, these approaches weren't directly applicable to an outpatient clinic setting. I did borrow some of the LEGO-based therapy methodology from people like Phillip Strain and Frank Kohler (Kohler *et al.* 1997), and Robert and Lynn Koegel (Koegel and Koegel 1995). I also become aware of the Division TEACCH literature out of the University of North Carolina, started by Eric Schopler and Gary Mesibov (e.g. Schopler and Mesibov 1992), which was directly relevant to the population I was working with. Unfortunately, as with the work of McGinnis and Goldstein (1997), the literature was much more focused on classroom-based strategies, rather than on interventions that were appropriate for outpatient settings in which the participants were available for an hour or two per week, not all day, five days per week.

These researchers did emphasize a sensible approach to autism interventions – not the 40+ hours per week that was involved with Lovaas-style early intensive behavioral intervention (EIBI) programs – including utilization of peers and natural settings, which was important to me since these features promoted generalization and long-term benefits. It was with these influences in mind that I encountered the first opportunities to create a group therapy that used a natural play context, and the use of peers as a source of influence on the individual's social development.

From the outset, I was aware that social development was the key issue for children with autistic conditions. As much as they might make progress academically and improve in terms of their behavioral issues, if they weren't more socially responsive, they weren't going to have good long-term outcomes. The problem I had with approaches that were just behavioral or adult-initiated insight-oriented (Comic Strip Conversations, Social Stories™) was that there didn't seem to be a path from the therapy to independent coping. When I used these therapies, the clients didn't seem to be moving on from reliance on adults – parents, teachers, therapists – to being independently more appropriate and more functional in social settings. In fact, in terms of adult dependence, most of the kids with autism I was working with were worse off after the initiation of services. This was especially the case with behavioral strategies. The children were more dependent on adults after the therapy than they were before. They might be more appropriate, and cooperative, but they were also more dependent, less creative and less spontaneous. I wanted an approach that could provide corrective feedback and shape social communication and interaction that also saved the creative uniqueness and spontaneity of these children.

Aside from being an intervention that required a small time commitment, what also appeared to make LEGO®-based therapy interesting was the sustained creative process involved.

It has been my experience that the weakness of many treatment approaches, aside from dependence on adults, was the lack of sustained engagement and opportunity for self-expression. Doing therapy and consulting on the classroom management strategies used with different groups of children with varying mental health issues over the years had convinced me that, for most children, the key to a successful therapeutic experience was bringing out the child's own creativity and engagement with life. For most of my training and early years of clinical practice, I focused on being able to quickly establish a rapport and then a treatment alliance with children and their families by encouraging this kind of playfulness and creativity.

This seemed to me to be a key issue in the poor outcomes for so many of the treatment approaches being utilized at the time, whether they emphasized the development of verbal insights about social situations, or focused on rehearsal of socially appropriate behaviors, mannerisms and scripts. The child with autism was not given much opportunity to initiate or even participate in a spontaneous way, and thereby contribute and become personally invested in the outcome. Even when they had a connection with the therapist, there was little motivation to do the difficult work of changing how they behaved in the world – the classroom, the community, the home – because the changes in the therapy didn't come from them – they were just doing as they were told. It reminded me of bad coaching – the coach did all the work, showed off their skills, and never let you have the ball.

What I was consciously attempting to do by using LEGO® materials with individual clients, and then in small groups, was to help bridge not just the gap between them and me, but also that empty space that existed between them and their own achievements. It didn't matter that they didn't make eye contact with me, or their parents or teachers, or even their peers, unless there was some other motivating factor – a need to share something, a non-social motivation. LEGO provided a conduit for social connection in a deeper way. They were contributing a unique element of an unspoken, deep element of human need – to be a part of joint effort. In doing so, simultaneously they also engaged their creativity and prosocial interests. They not only wanted to share LEGO® materials with each other, but they wanted to do so efficiently, and with a goal in mind: a joint purpose, a shared accomplishment. This experience, to me, was at the core of the LEGO-based therapy experience.

Needless to say, much of the credit of what was successful in LEGO therapy was due to the LEGO Company products, which I'm sure most of my readers are well aware of. The fact that LEGO products were invariably novel and the toy company clearly had its finger on the pulse of children's creative fantasies and fascination sustained many participants' interest in the groups. In fact, many participants continued to participate in the groups long after they had formally "graduated" from the groups, and were deemed to have social and communication abilities above their age peers – they didn't care about the therapy, they just enjoyed the LEGO group process too much to quit.

I will end this introduction with a comment about the details of the case histories. They are based on actual cases, but of course the names and specific details have been changed to protect their privacy. In some instances, I have used some fictional leeway in fleshing out conversations and events in order to help give a more detailed and less dry, fact-oriented material. This content is included in order to give a better subjective, real-life feel to the cases, and no attempt was made to exaggerate or distort the true nature of the clinical interventions or outcomes. As much as possible, I've tried to include all the bumps and blemishes that were part of the process of developing LEGO-based therapy, and working with this group of children. In some cases, case history information has been combined so that some of the histories represent events and experiences from more than one child. Aside from these superficial changes, and the use of recreated conversations (to the best of my recollection) that are very close to what was actually said, the case histories and the therapeutic interventions described are accurate and true. I will apologize in advance to some individuals who may recognize themselves here, or their family members, in an unflattering light, or who may experience painful reminders of difficult times. It was a learning experience for us all, and hopefully now these experiences can also help others who may be having similar life experiences and challenges.

# AARON

## INITIAL CONTACT

I met Aaron for the first time at my private office in Honolulu. He was eight years old, and was referred to me directly by his parents, Jim and Louise, at the recommendation of their pediatrician due to some concerns about his behavior at school. His teacher had told them Aaron was unpredictable and impulsive at times; and that he seemed to be a loner and wasn't making friends. Aaron's parents had moved to Hawaii from Oregon when Jim had taken a job as a marine biologist at the University of Hawaii in Manoa. This had seemed like a dream-come-true for them. Louise was an elementary school teacher, and she was quickly able to find work nearby at what would be Aaron's school in Manoa Valley. Jim taught classes at the university and had a research lab across the island on the windward shore. Aaron was three when they moved, and he was four and still in preschool when his younger sister, Lani, was born. Aaron's parents remembered this as a blissful time; they were in paradise.

By the age of five, when Aaron's sister was still a toddler, Aaron's parents had noticed that Aaron seemed different from his peers. He was a cheerful, affectionate boy, clearly attached to them, and curious about and playful with Lani. But, he didn't seem to play the way his friends did, and he seemed very serious, even edgy and irritable at times, in interactions with kids his age. He tended to prefer to play at adult-like activities, which they thought was due to his being a first-born child, and not having other relatives or many friends nearby. At first, they thought it was cute the way he wanted to carry a briefcase full of books like his father, and he started making careful drawings of rocks and seashells he found on the beach. He was especially happy about finding live crabs or mollusks. His father studied mollusks, and was often carrying buckets of them in his car from the field lab to his office. Aaron brought rocks and shells home from the beach, and lined them up on the shelves and window sills in his room, which he called his lab. He put small crabs, clams, opihi and sea urchins in water in the sink, or a bucket outside, and peered at them for hours. He was clearly a very intelligent and serious-minded kid, very much in his father's image.

Aaron's preschool teachers had also noticed that he seemed to have difficulty fitting in with his classmates. He didn't like to sit in group and play games with the others, but would frequently ask to go outside to look for stones, insects, flowers or snails in the play area and surrounding landscape. He would then sketch the plants, flowers and insects he found in a set of notebooks he kept. In Kindergarten, Aaron shared his sketches and notes on the plants and insects he found with his parents and teacher, but was much less interested in his classmates. His teacher told his parents that he was "in his own world" most of the time, and it took a lot of convincing to get him to join the class for most activities, including meals.

Aaron's first grade teacher recognized that Aaron was exceptional, and thought that this, and his recent move to the islands, accounted for his being somewhat aloof and disinterested in group play. He was doing very well with learning, and was ahead of the class in pre-academic areas. He was so far ahead, in fact, that his teachers thought they should recommend that he skip Kindergarten and go into first grade the following year – he was already reading at a second or third grade level, and although his handwriting was large and messy, he was already able to write complete sentences and short paragraphs. Using his father's reference books on indigenous plants and animals, he looked up and recorded in his notebooks the Latin names for the flowers, insects and crustaceans that he collected. He was also adept with using the computer, and his father had given him one of his castoffs as a birthday present.

On a windy day in the spring, when Aaron was in second grade, his class went on an outing to the beach. He had already been introduced to the teacher who would have him in her room in the fall. He told his parents that he liked his new teacher, and wanted to impress her with some shells and maybe a crab from the beach. Soon after the class got to the beach park, and the teachers had made sure everyone had on hats and sunscreen, Aaron took his dip net and bucket and was off on this mission. He searched among the large rocks that made a breakwater for the boat harbor next to the park. His teachers could see his hat poking up from the rocks as he dipped his net and pulled up sea urchins and scrambled after live crabs that scurried over the rocks. The teacher and her aides let him do his thing, and were busy with lunch preparations before they realized Aaron was missing.

While Aaron's teacher stayed with the other students and supervised lunch, the two classroom aides went off to look for Aaron. They searched over the rocks where he was seen last, then up and down the beach. They returned almost an hour later, without Aaron. The teacher and her aides were now very worried, and were at a loss as to what to do. One of the aides spotted a police cruiser and ran over to ask for help. Aaron was in the back of the cruiser. The police were about to take him to the station to meet with a children's services worker. Aaron had not told them his name, or that he had been with his class, or that they were in the beach park nearby. In fact, he had not said a word to them. They had picked him up at the commercial fishing wharf where a local fisherman noticed him exploring the wharf on his own, and had tried to talk to him. Since Aaron wouldn't identify himself, or say where he came from, the fisherman had called the police, assuming that his family were probably tourists from nearby Waikiki, and that he was lost.

Aaron's teacher was relieved, but also upset. She couldn't believe that Aaron had refused to identify himself. The police officer told the teacher that he assumed the boy didn't speak English, or was deaf. When the teacher asked Aaron why he didn't identify himself, or tell the police where he had come from, he said, "They're strangers. I'm not supposed to talk to strangers" His teacher later tried to explain to him that "strangers" did not include the police, but Aaron was adamant that he had done the right thing. "I don't know them, so they're strangers. No one ever said the police could not be strangers." His teacher was struck by how odd his behavior had been. He had wandered off without saying anything, gone to a busy commercial fishing wharf, and then gone with the police quite happily, and got into their car, but hadn't talked to them because they were strangers. She said to Aaron's parents later that day, "I know there is something wrong. Aaron is very intelligent, but that was just off. I don't know what he was thinking." Aaron's parents agreed that he should be evaluated. His mother reassured the teacher that she had not done anything wrong. "It doesn't surprise me that he wandered off. He's always like that. And I never know what he's thinking."

Aaron's father disagreed. He felt that Aaron was just very intelligent, and hadn't had the chance yet to make friends with those with similar interests. He told Louise, "I didn't really have any close friends until I was in college. Or maybe graduate school." He thought Aaron's behavior was not that unusual at all: "He's just not a people person. He likes nature." But he agreed to have their pediatrician and the school psychologist evaluate him for the Child Study Team. Later, he regretted this decision and tried to rescind his permission: "There's nothing wrong with him. They're just going to label him, and put him under a microscope." As his wife pointed out, it was a bit too late to stop that. The school staff were already being carefully observant of Aaron on the playground and during lunch break, and monitored him when he went to the bathroom, or transitioned from the classroom to the library or gym, etc.

Aaron was aware of this, and complained to his parents that the school staff were watching him all the time. His mother explained it was because he had wandered off from the group at the beach. His father was furious, though, and felt that they were singling Aaron out, and felt that some of this was due to racial reasons. He had started to feel there was subtle, or even overt, elements of anti-mainland, and anti-Caucasian, sentiments at the school. "All the teachers are Japanese, most of the kids are local, and there's Aaron. Of course they're singling him out." Aaron's mother disagreed, and felt that Jim was projecting his own issues onto Aaron – that he himself was socially awkward, and had always had difficulty fitting in, and this had nothing to do with the school or the local culture.

The pediatrician who saw Aaron didn't feel there was that much wrong with him, but thought that he might have mild ADHD and recommended a trial of stimulant medication. The school psychologist evaluated Aaron's cognitive and academic functioning, and interviewed Aaron's mother about his development, his behavior at home, and his interests and social functioning. She found that Aaron was functioning in the Very Superior (gifted) range on IQ testing, and that his academic test scores were just as high. He was now at about a fifth grade level in all academic areas, and he hadn't entered third grade yet. She was concerned about Aaron's behavior at school and the reports of his unusual interests and difficulties with peers, though, and mentioned that she thought he might have Asperger's Disorder, which was a new diagnosis at the time. The diagnosis had just come out in the *Diagnostic and Statistical Manual, Fourth Edition* (DSM-IV) a couple of years before, and she was not that familiar with it, but Aaron seemed to show many of the signs of what she had read was being called "the little professor syndrome."

Jim was adamant that they were over-reacting to Aaron's behavior and functioning. He felt that his differences from his peers, and his scientific interests, were entirely due to his high IQ, and he began doing research on the education of gifted children. His mother agreed that Aaron's IQ would make him different from his peers, but she did not feel that that explained his being so aloof, and the incident at the beach: "He was so concrete. If he was that intelligent, he would also have some commonsense not to wander away from his class, and to talk to the police when they came." She felt there had to be something more going on.

Despite Aaron's father's protests, the school district eventually referred him to me for further assessment, and they specifically wanted my opinion about possible Asperger's Disorder. Aaron's parents did research on Asperger's Disorder, and had a long talk with their pediatrician. Jim called a friend at the university who taught developmental psychology and arranged a meeting. They asked questions, and the answers they got were disturbing. Asperger's was a pervasive developmental disorder, a form of high functioning autism. It was considered to be a lifelong, disabling condition that affected the ability to have meaningful relationships and to function independently in the world. This was devastating news to Jim, and as much as he didn't want to believe it – he couldn't believe it – his wife was more convinced. The psychologist, who was a researcher, not a clinician, met with Aaron and recommended that they follow up with the assessment with me.

Aaron seemed content to explore the big playroom while his mother and I talked. He showed an interest in some of the toys and expressive materials, but then he found the LEGO® corner and he stayed there. He zeroed in on a couple of sets which had boats, divers and sharks, including one set with a diving cage. At one point he waved his hand in the air for my attention, and then pointed at the LEGO corner: "Can I?…" I said, "Help yourself." He turned his back on us and sat down, quietly building.

We knew he was listening to us though, as, periodically, during his mother's recounting of events, he would call out a factual correction: "Cephalopods *are* mollusks." His mother was telling me about his interest in marine animals, and the ones that he brought home to study and draw. She was no longer crying, and seemed relieved to be talking openly about the events leading up to the issues at school and the referral to me. She was just explaining how his interest didn't seem normal, that it was extreme and he didn't seem to have a balance. Aaron had ignored her while she talked about the issues with his father, and the arguments about Asperger's. Aaron was focused on building the scene of a LEGO® ocean expedition (from the Divers collection), and on clarifying his mother's factual mistakes: "You can't say squid *and* mollusks, because squid are cephalopods and cephalopods are mollusks."

Louise sighed, "Sorry, Aaron. I thought mollusks were clams and oysters. Alright, it's not really important right now." Aaron came over, stood next to his mother and put his hand on her shoulder. She patted his hand, looked up at him and smiled. Aaron nodded at me, then turned to his mother and said, "Clams and oysters and scallops and mussels are *bivalve* mollusks. But gastropods, like snails, and cephalopods, like squid and octopi, are also mollusks." Then he nodded again and went back to his LEGO building. Louise looked at me, shrugged, and tried to laugh, but the tears were back.

At this point, I could certainly understand the concerns of Aaron's mother and the school staff, and at least during this initial contact, it seemed like Aaron might have Asperger's Disorder. His father, however, had left a message asking to meet with me before I wrote my assessment report. He was still a parent, and this seemed like a reasonable request. Before I'd had a chance to call him back and suggest a time to meet, I received a letter from him and his attorney, threatening legal action if I did not meet with him and include his input in the assessment. This seemed a bit ominous to me – overkill – but I could understand his concern. There was a lot at stake in this evaluation.

Jim arrived early for the appointment, and when I came out to the waiting room, he was pacing by the front desk. He was a tall man, with tousled curly blond hair and a beard, and wearing Khakis and a golf shirt. His glasses were tinted and heavily smudged, so it was hard to see his eyes. He held out his hand and looked down, a gesture I suddenly recognized from Aaron. He didn't respond to my greeting, but looked around the room and said, "Where do we?... You spoke to my wife and you met Aaron. I wasn't... I didn't agree about this evaluation. There's nothing wrong with Aaron. Look, I've done my own research on this. He's just...he's very smart, and he gets nervous with people. With people who don't understand him." Jim looked around the office, sitting on the edge of the chair. "This Asperger's, it's like autism, right? Mild, mild type of autism. But Aaron is not like that. Maybe on paper, you know he doesn't have a lot of friends, but he is very friendly. You met him, right? Well, then you can see, he's not autistic."

## LEARNING THROUGH LEGO®

Aaron was a very objective boy, and when he understood something rationally, he believed it whole-heartedly. Quite often, though, he would balk at my suggestions or insights, saying that he didn't get it, that I was being subjective, or that what I was asking him to do or consider was too hard, or that it wouldn't work for him. For example, we talked about making eye contact when speaking to someone, which he said was too distracting, and he didn't see the point. "What's so important about looking at someone's eyes, or even looking at them at all? I can still hear them." I explained that people looked at each other, especially each other's eyes, as another layer of communication, to convey and perceive emotions and attitudes.

I explained that if a person was interested, or bored, or confused, or angry about what we were saying, we could tell by looking at their face, especially their eyes. Similarly, when people were trying to understand our emotions and how we were responding to them and what was being said, they looked carefully at our faces and eyes. I said, "How would you know, for instance, if someone was bored or confused by what you were saying, if you didn't look at them?" Aaron looked away: "They can just tell me that's boring, or confusing." So I offered: "But most people are too polite to say that. They'll just look away, or get this look" – I showed him a perplexed expression, wrinkled brow, smirk and head-tilt – "which means they don't get it, or maybe they don't believe you." Aaron tried imitating me: "Like this? I don't believe you, Dr. Dan. Not everyone is as polite as you. That's just you, because you're Canadian."

Luckily, I had some recent anthropology research articles on the universality of facial expressions, and was able to show Aaron that many or even most of human emotions are expressed similarly regardless of cultural background. "Aaron, if people didn't benefit from sharing their emotions by making faces, why would we all do it? There's something important about facial expressions, so important that it's not learned, it's innate – most people are born knowing how to express their emotions and how to read other people's emotions through facial expressions." Aaron looked at me carefully, and then he nodded. "Okay, that makes sense. But why can't I do that?" I explained that he could do it, but that it didn't come naturally to him the way it did to some people. Some people can draw what they see, as he did, naturally and well, and other people struggled to do it at all, but they could learn. Aaron was looking down: "So I have to learn faces." I nodded, "Yes, Aaron, and you do that by looking carefully, just the way you look at sea creatures – you notice the details and get to know what they mean, what they tell you about the animal. But you have to look." I leaned down to get into his line of sight. He reached up and touched my face with his fingertips. "You have a good face for that. It's always doing something."

For many aspects of social development, Aaron wanted objective, rational guidelines or rules, which made it hard for him, and me, so I had to emphasize his trust in me, and whenever possible, back up my point of view with some research or rational explanation. Unfortunately, he trusted his father more than me, which is understandable and normal, but Jim was not very supportive about Aaron's therapy at times. At other times, he could be outright hostile. Jim perceived me as an ally of Louise's, and he was skeptical about whether there was anything wrong with Aaron, and whether he needed my help in any way. Jim was skeptical about psychotherapy, and probably for good reasons. The outcome research on insight-oriented therapies wasn't very good, and the pseudo-scientific rationales for it weren't much better – personality theory was often as much art as it was science, and Jim, as a "hard" scientist, knew the difference between the level of prediction and control in chemistry and biology and that in psychology.

In the early phase of therapy, Aaron and I were still working on the treatment alliance – basically, getting him to trust me enough to believe me about things that didn't seem logical – and we talked about communicating, and friendships, and sharing ideas with others in effective ways. Aaron had expressed that a good idea should be accepted regardless of how it was expressed. I told him I wished that was true, but often people who might have great ideas don't get people to listen to them and understand them because they aren't good communicators.

Aaron turned away from me, clearly not interested in this idea himself, and he took a LEGO® pirate ship down from the shelf. He looked over at me and held up the pirate ship, very consciously putting it directly between his eyes and mine. He then raised his eyebrows, and made a magician's gesture with the other hand. "Okay, good," I said. "What are you after?"

"I have an idea," Aaron said, "and I'm trying to communicate it effectively."

I nodded and smiled. "You're doing great so far. I'm paying attention."

He put the pirate ship down on the table in front of me and again made a magician's "ta da!" gesture at the ship with both hands this time, and then he looked at me, smiled, and sat down. He started quickly dismantling the mast and sails of the ship, and quickly added some bricks, doors and windows. Then he fiddled with some minifigures for a while. What he came up with was an updated pirate ship, with modern weapons and a large central cabin, along with a crew who looked like modern pirates, part ninja warriors and part scuba divers. I thought it was a good modification of the pirate ship (which I knew would have to go back to its original condition soon), and showed some imagination. "That's very creative, Aaron. Where did you get the idea for that, which I'm guessing is a modern-day pirate ship?"

"It's not a pirate ship anymore, it's the *Sea Shepherd*! This is Paul Watson and his crew!"

---

I hadn't expected that. Paul Watson and the *Sea Shepherd* were not that widely known at the time. Watson was a former Sierra Club and Greenpeace environmental activist from Vancouver who had become more radical than many of the other activists. He had risked his life in dramatic fashion and had been arrested for interfering with seal hunters and whalers, and had captained the *Sea Shepherd* and other ships to interfere with whalers and fishing vessels that were having a negative impact on marine life, especially sea mammals. Watson was a legend among radical environmentalists, and I had heard a lot about him and had heard him speak at my alma mater, Simon Fraser University, where Watson was also an alumnus. I didn't have to ask how Aaron had found out about Paul Watson and the Sea Shepherd Society. I found out later that Jim was not only a big fan of Watson's, he knew him personally, and had named his daughter, Lani, after Watson's daughter, Lilliolani. Having gotten to know Jim a bit better, I could see why he and Watson would have become friends.

I could see the connection between what we had been talking about – communicating ideas – and Watson's Sea Shepherd Society, but I wasn't sure that Aaron had really intended to make this association. It could have been a coincidence. So I said, "We were talking about how to communicate ideas."

Still fixing some details on the ship, and without looking up, Aaron said, "You were talking about that."

"Right," I said. "And then you started putting together the *Sea Shepherd*."

Aaron was still preoccupied, but as usual, he was listening. "Yep."

"So, what do you think about Paul Watson and his ideas?" I said, helping Aaron with some tricky bits on the boat. Aaron didn't say anything for a while, and then he looked up and scanned the room. He went over to the art area and made a small placard with felt pens and cardboard, on which he wrote: "The *Sea Shepherd*. Paul Watson. A great idea."

I managed to keep the conservationist LEGO® kids from turning the *Sea Shepherd* back into a pirate ship just long enough for Jim to see it. Aaron had told him that he had made something he wanted him to see, but he didn't tell him what it was. When Jim saw the *Sea Shepherd* on the shelf with the other LEGO, he smiled. It was a smile of pure pride and pleasure. I had my camera out ready to take a picture of the *Sea Shepherd*, since it was likely to be recommissioned at some point, so I took a picture of Jim with that smile. Looking at the picture later, I noticed that Jim wasn't smiling at the ship; he was looking at his son, who was standing in front of his creation, wearing the same smile.

Aaron and I were beginning to enjoy each other's company. He put up with my prompting and nagging him about eye contact and body language, and I came to appreciate his unique way of thinking and communicating. He let me change the topic of conversation away from marine biology, and I took pleasure in the way he would slowly find his way back to it. One day Aaron came in and reported on an adventure over the weekend to the Big Island, to watch some volcanic activity, and to make a pilgrimage to the Hawaii Volcano Observatory with his father and Lani. Without saying anything more, Aaron started collecting parts from the bins and assembling them, stopping to think, and then continuing.

"Alright," he said, "but where are we going to get the mirrors?"

---

He said he wanted to make a Dobsonian. This is a type of Newtonian reflector telescope, and the mirrors were the key parts. It was another surprising but natural in-sync moment. I had just met John Dobson, the inventor of this telescope design. He had been visiting the islands, hosted by the Bishop Museum Planetarium. He was staying with a close friend of mine who worked at the Planetarium and had just recently built a Dobsonian telescope at home using materials from the hardware store. Aaron had also met Dobson, with his father and Lani, at the Star Party on the Big Island.

---

I said, "You want to make a real Dobsonian, a working one, out of LEGO®."

"Well sure," Aaron said, "a miniature one. Otherwise, the mirror would be too heavy, especially if you want it to be adjustable."

I knew just enough about the topic to understand that he knew exactly what he was talking about. He knew about the different designs for the support base and the eye piece for viewing the reflected light from the mirrors. And it had to work. He wouldn't put in the effort to build something that was just a replica, or a toy. It had to work, otherwise it was a lie. We ran into a similar situation with the pirate ship/*Sea Shepherd* when he asked me if the model would float. I told him it wasn't designed to float, but as he pointed out, some LEGO boats were designed to float in water, so why wasn't this one? He insisted that we try it, so we put it in the water station sink. It floated in the water tray briefly, and then sank. Then he was upset about the ship's design and wanted to communicate with the LEGO® Company about it. I thought he would just forget about it, but he perseverated about the non-buoyant ship for months.

This was typical of Aaron's thinking at the time. On the one hand, he was clearly brilliant and had a technical reasoning ability well above his age level, yet on the other hand, he was overly concrete and lacked insight about the social uses of language, idioms and social reasoning. He understood rules and principles, but not the pragmatics of applying them in actual situations, or understanding when to apply rules and when they were no longer relevant or appropriate. This thinking style was a daily source of stress for both Aaron and his parents, as well as his teachers and classmates. It was a rich area of discussion for Aaron and me on many occasions, as we struggled to sort out many aspects of normal thinking and behavior – especially in social situations – which didn't seem to follow rules of logic, but which were nevertheless normal, and therefore to be expected and accepted.

Aaron had accepted that he wanted to be liked by others. It was a quality in himself that he struggled with, this issue of having friends and having them show an interest in him. For the most part, he wasn't well motivated. In most situations, what he was thinking about at the moment was more salient and relevant, and therefore more important, than the social context. He also struggled to understand how anyone could think anything different. Based on the facts – and these were singular and omnipotent – and using his version of irrefutable logic, only one conclusion could be drawn. If someone else came to a different conclusion, they were wrong. I had a copy of Ed Young's *The Seven Blind Mice* in which each one of a group of blind mice discovers a different part of a mysterious creature, and they come to different conclusions about what it is, until they share their information and collectively agree that it is an elephant. We read this together, despite Aaron's protests that it was a children's book, not a scientific book. He struggled with the concept that reality was potentially subjective.

Our subsequent discussions about *The Seven Blind Mice* led to my having to raise the bar a bit in terms of the intellectual weight. I was conceding to go along with Aaron's "young scientist" worldview, but at the same time working on his capacity for perspective taking and other "theory of mind" abilities. I introduced him first to the idea that "facts" could be interpreted subjectively, and the basic tenets and arguments of epistemology: that knowledge or facts had different kinds of justifications, and that it was debatable whether one person, or one group of people, could decide for everyone else what the basic justification for facts could be. We also talked about William James and his pragmatic point of view with regard to knowledge, i.e. that facts were valid as long as they were considered to be true from the point of view of the person holding the facts. I tried to help him assimilate these ideas at his own rate, and had to wait sometimes for weeks before some concepts percolated down through his previously unshakable faith in a "naïve realist" point of view. As overly theoretical and abstract as this discussion might seem to others, especially therapists who mistrust "intellectualized" discussions as defensive and un-therapeutic, Aaron definitely had a strong emotional stake in these ideas, and his reaction was anything but intellectualized. He was beginning to have more of a concept of self and others by being confronted by someone (me) who had ideas which were different from his, but at the same time were also logical and consistent with the scientific method.

In the end, Aaron was finally able to concede that there was a time and place when empiricism held sway and all ideas and facts had to concede to the scientific method. Although he would not allow that there was a better way to view the world on the whole, he did admit that outside of the context of a scientific discussion, social reality took over. His experience with other people was consistent with this perspective. In most situations, the rules to play by were social rules, not scientific ones. He also came to realize that he was much better at the game played by the rules of science than he was at the social game, but he did want to continue to play. Once he had achieved this insight, that he wanted to participate in "social-rule" situations – playing games, making friends, being a big brother, being a son, being a student in a classroom – he became interested in learning more about the rules and the skills involved.

I wanted to emphasize for Aaron that the best way to develop a new skill was to identify his own strengths, and then to emphasize these in his approach to a new challenge. I pointed out that he was an excellent observer, and, of course, he agreed. So I recommended that he observe his classmates, and using his natural talent for science, draw some conclusions about the underlying rules of successful social behavior. I explained that psychology was also a science, and was based on observation and deduction just like other sciences. He liked this approach very much. He agreed to pick a couple of his classmates to observe: one whom he perceived as being socially successful or "cool," and one who was definitely unpopular and "not cool." We talked about the markers of being socially successful, such as having a lot of friends who would want to come to your birthday party, regardless of what was happening at the party, just because they liked you. He wasn't sure. He didn't get invited to many parties, and he didn't like having birthday parties himself. I suggested looking for a classmate who most of the other children greeted, or went out of their way to be near or in contact with. "Got it," he said. "That's Luke." Then I asked him about unpopular, uncool kids. "That's easy," he said. "That's me."

Aaron and I decided that since he already had a pretty good idea about what was "not cool," he should focus on observing a kid who was doing well socially, "a cool kid." In particular, he wanted to observe how he interacted with the other students, his words and actions, and how the other students responded. I warned Aaron about "reactance," or the tendency for subjects being observed to react to the observer. Aaron didn't anticipate much of a problem here: "Everyone ignores me, especially Luke." Aaron did try to be inconspicuous about it though, and he was able to make some useful observations which he shared with me the next week.

Aaron had observed Luke carefully. He noticed the way he dressed, which was invariably in a faded t-shirt, surfing shorts and "slippahs" (flip-flops). He never wore a collared shirt, long pants or socks. He also kept his hair cropped short, and he carried a backpack slung low over his shoulders, with the bag straps elongated, not tugged up. He was usually on time, but not always, and he was usually cheerful. "He never gets upset. Even when something happens, like someone sat in his place at lunch on the lanai. He didn't even notice." I suggested that he might have noticed, we couldn't tell, and that that was an important observation. "He must have at least noticed that someone was sitting where he usually sits, but he didn't care enough to get upset about it," I said.

"Yeah," Aaron said. "He just went and sat somewhere else."

I followed up: "And you said sometimes he's late, right? Does he get upset about that?"

Aaron thought about it. "No. He just comes in and sits down like nothing."

"So," I said, "would you say, maybe he's flexible, or accepting?"

"Ah, this is the deduction part. He does seem to be flexible. He is also accepting. He doesn't care about some things, like what he has for lunch. If he doesn't like it, he'll trade for something else, or he'll just eat it anyway."

"Okay, that's cool," I said, "Did you notice anything else? What about what he said to the other kids?"

"He talks Pidgin to them, but he speaks in English to the teacher. Everyone says hi to him, and he says hi back," Aaron reported.

"Do they all say hi to each other?" I asked.

"No, sometimes hi, but mostly they say, 'Yoh,' and 'Howzit,' or they say their name in a silly way, like Luuuuuke! Or they say 'sup brah,' or 'sup cuz.' You know, local. And a head nod, with the eyebrows."

Aaron was definitely making the right observations. He kept at it for a couple more weeks, watching Luke, and then another student, who was a friend of Luke's, Kai, who was different from Luke, but also popular and well liked. Unfortunately, although Luke had not noticed Aaron watching him, he did pick up on it when Aaron started observing Kai. In local Hawaiian culture, probably even more so than with typical mainland social settings, looking at someone, and especially making eye contact, is considered intrusive or hostile. If Aaron had been older, it's likely that his observing Kai directly as he did might have sparked an altercation. As it was, Aaron had noticed Luke scowling at him, and he and Kai whispered together, looking at Aaron with indifference. I pointed this out to Aaron and told him it was now time to stop observing and act – participate.

"Like how?" he said.

"Like they do. Say 'howzit,' or 'sup.' You have to be friendly now, or you are going to be in trouble with the two most popular boys in your class."

Aaron understood the implications. He could no longer be apart from them, and so he was going to have to join them. This idea was frightening to him at first, and he seemed overwhelmed. "Will I have to dress like them? No socks? Loosen my backpack? What about recess? I don't know if I'm ready for this." I reminded him he probably shouldn't change himself overnight, but he could start with small changes and work on it slowly. He agreed to start with wearing slippahs to school, and to make an effort to greet his classmates as they did. I reassured him: "You don't have to say 'howzit' to everyone, just Luke and Kai. Don't worry, they're nice kids. They'll say 'howzit' back, and the other kids will notice."

Aaron made a sincere effort, and he wasn't disappointed. Luke and Kai acknowledged him, and they didn't seem hostile to him. He invited another boy, Michael, to come over and play at his house after school. With his mother's support, a playdate was arranged, and Michael came over to play. Things did not go perfectly smoothly – Michael wanted to know if Aaron had a Gameboy® or other electronic games, and they settled on watching some cartoons on TV, but Aaron was quickly bored with that. He showed Michael his aquarium at home, and his collection of books about marine life, and Michael was receptive. He especially liked a book about sharks, and asked if he could borrow it. This was tricky for Aaron. He begrudgingly agreed, but he wanted Michael to return the book at school the next day. Michael agreed, but he was cool about it.

"So," I asked, "what do you think Michael felt about you wanting the book back the next day?"

Aaron was uncomfortable with the whole topic. "What difference does it make? It's my book!"

I reminded him that we were playing by social rules here, and part of that game was trying to guess what another person might think or feel.

"Alright," Aaron groaned. "He feels... I don't know."

I said, "You're a scientist, Aaron. Why did you tell Michael you wanted the book back the next day?"

Aaron didn't hesitate: "Because he might lose it, or wreck it."

I probed, "So, you didn't trust him to look after your book."

"No," he said, "I didn't trust him."

"Hmm, so do you think Michael might have known you didn't trust him?"

Aaron looked at me, frustrated. "How would he know that?"

"He would have deduced it, Aaron. People can do that, even non-scientists. And how would he feel about you not trusting him with your book?"

"How would he feel? He felt like I don't trust him."

"Okay, that's a good start," I nodded, encouraging him. "Do you think he liked you more or less because you didn't trust him?"

"Nah. He wouldn't like it. It means I think he can't be trusted. I shouldn't have said it. But I didn't want to lose that book."

We were definitely getting at the nature of social relationships. "That would have been a hard one for me, or anyone, Aaron. I think you handled it pretty well. You lent him the book, but you wanted it back right away. That was a compromise. You took a risk so that you could start a relationship."

"Yeah," Aaron said. "I did!"

## JOINING OTHERS

It was soon after this session that Aaron began showing more interest in the creators of the other LEGO® sets and freestyle creations that had begun appearing on the shelves in the LEGO corner. He had previously made comments about the creations themselves, but now he started making comments and asking questions about the children who had built them. A new UFO set appeared, an elaborate horseshoe-shaped space craft, with an alien pilot and a robot-like droid, and Aaron seemed fascinated by it: "You know, interplanetary travel would be impossible in something like this," he said, gently holding it up. "But it is cool." This got me interested: Aaron was expressing that something that was, in his mind, patently impossible and based on imaginative mythology could be, at the same time, cool. Then he asked about the creator, "Why did they build this? Do they believe in aliens?"

"I don't know," I said. "Do you have to believe in aliens to build an alien LEGO set?"

"Nah," he said, studying the set, opening the glass hatch and taking out the alien pilot, "but I can see why they liked it." He put it down carefully and looked at it closely. "I would like to fly in space. But you wouldn't need a ship like this. Aerodynamic. There's no air resistance in space, so it could be any shape. But this just looks... cool. They did a good job building it, whoever made it."

"Another boy, like you. About the same age," I said. "He liked your telescope." We had eventually gotten his telescope built, using light-weight cosmetic mirrors, and it had joined the other freestyle creations on the shelf.

"Oh yeah?" Aaron looked at me. "What did he say? Did he try it out?"

"Don't worry," I said, "he was careful with it. And he said the same thing you did. In fact, he said it was 'Very cool,' and he asked if I had made it."

Aaron looked excited and said, "What did you tell him?"

"I told him I had nothing to do with it. I said another boy, you, had made it, and that it was all your idea, using the Dobsonian design, the mirrors and everything."

"Was he impressed? I bet he was impressed. Did he know what a Dobsonian was?"

"Nope. He didn't know about Dobsonian scopes, but he does now. In fact, he said he wanted to get one. And yes, Aaron, he was very impressed."

A week or so later, I came out to the waiting room and Aaron was talking to this same boy, Sam, in the waiting room. Aaron was waiting for his appointment with his mother, and Sam was waiting to leave, but his father was late picking him up. Sam was playing with a Gameboy® while Aaron looked over his shoulder. Aaron looked up and raised his hand, then looked down at the Gameboy® in Sam's hands. He said something to Sam, and Sam replied without looking up. Later, Aaron asked me if that boy also built with LEGO®, which sets he had built, etc. The following week, Sam and Aaron were in the waiting room together again, and this time both had brought LEGO creations from home. Sam had brought a new submarine set from the Divers series, which included a couple of divers and a stingray minifigure, and Aaron had brought his own freestyle version of the *Sea Shepherd*, which was large and very elaborate, with an onboard crane and lifeboats (using the hull from another boat, which did in fact float).

They were both very excited and were talking rapidly over the top of each other. Both mothers were standing nearby with stunned but not displeased expressions. Aaron was giving Sam a quick history of the *Sea Shepherd* and Paul Watson, while Sam was telling Aaron about deep sea exploration and searching for lost treasure in the Caribbean. It was not exactly a conversation, but it was definitely a meeting of minds. Aaron was just launching into the scuttling of Japanese whalers, and Sam was on to gold treasure lost in the Caribbean from Spanish ships, when I tried to interrupt them. It took a few minutes for them to register that I was there and wanted their attention. Aaron noticed me first, and was excitedly holding up the

*Sea Shepherd* for me to see (I had already seen Sam's submarine). "Look, Dr. Dan," he said, "I made my own version." Sam started telling me about Aaron's ship. "It's the *Sea Shepherd*," he said, "complete with a minifig version of its captain, the modern-day eco-pirate, Paul Watson, and minifig crew of whaling ship scuttlers. Neat huh?" I thanked Sam for his explanation, and then Aaron looked at Sam's submarine: "They have deep sea exploration subs like that at the research station where my dad works. He's a marine biologist." Sam gave him a drop-jaw look: "What? Your dad is a marine biologist?"

"Yes," Aaron said. "I'm going to be one, too."

I could tell Sam was about to get overexcited and we'd be there all day, so I moved Aaron along towards the playroom. Sam had just started sharing about his plans to explore the bays around Manila in the Philippines for lost Spanish treasure when Aaron and I backed out of the waiting room. Aaron sat in the playroom still holding his *Sea Shepherd*, and looked back through the window towards the waiting area. We could see Sam talking excitedly in the waiting room to Aaron's mother, holding his hands up in the air to explain something apparently big and important. Aaron looked at me and said, "You know, Dr. Dan, that kid is from my planet."

After that meeting, I decided it would be good for both Aaron and Sam to get together and share their interests and enthusiasm, especially about LEGO®. I knew I would have to structure the interaction in some way, otherwise it would be a free-for-all, like it was in the waiting room, and they were likely to clash eventually if I just let them interact without it. I also wanted to create an opportunity for them to interact reciprocally and to have an experience of shared accomplishment. I realized at the time that this was an important aspect of social development that was missing from many of these kids' lives. Most of them didn't play sports, and didn't have much in common with their peers. I wanted to set up a situation that would give them that experience of being on the same team, or collaborating. So I approached each of their mothers and asked them if they would mind if I saw Sam and Aaron together. They were both excited about the idea, and, in fact, Aaron's mother had wanted to invite Sam over for a playdate, but I asked her to hold off for now. I wanted to use this precious opportunity carefully, and manage the interaction myself before considering letting them go off on their own.

Aaron and Sam's meeting in the waiting room, and their subsequent combined sessions during which we worked together on LEGO® building, was the start of LEGO Club. It was also the final signal to me that there was something about LEGO which appealed to this particular type of kid – Asperger's Disorder, PDD or High Functioning Autism (HFA), ASD – it didn't seem to matter too much what they were called in the formal nomenclature. They were a recognizable group: eccentric, pedantic, socially awkward, rigid, brittle and often brilliant. They were as frustrating as they were delightful, and as Aaron and Sam were just beginning to show me, they had a great capacity for insight and change, even when they were sure they didn't. It was also the start of a parallel support network. Sam and Aaron's mothers became close and developed a supportive relationship very quickly. They were of much greater help to each other than I could ever have been. I'll discuss this initial dyad group and the support process that emerged after we meet Sam.

# SAM

## INITIAL CONTACT

The first time I met Sam, I heard him before I saw him. I could hear a loud, raspy voice in the waiting room, all the way down the hall to my office. He was making goofy sounds and using cartoon-like voices. I was used to there being mayhem in the waiting room, so this wasn't a surprise. When I got to the waiting room, I could see his mother, who was seated on the couch, laughing. She waved at me, and pointed across the room where there were two young children, barely more than toddlers, watching a puppet show being staged from inside a large ball pit. The loud, comical voice coming from the ball pit was Sam's.

Sam had been referred to me by an attorney on behalf of his parents who were involved in a lawsuit against a children's recreational program. The referral letter had indicated that Sam had been "possibly abused" in a bathroom there, and that the family was seeking information about how Sam might have been affected by this. I had training and experience with the effects of trauma and abuse in children, and a colleague of mine who had been contacted before me suggested they have me get involved since there was a question as to whether Sam might also be autistic.

---

This was my first involvement in a case in which a child with autism had been the victim of abuse, and sadly, it was far from being my last. As I learned over the following years, children with autistic conditions are vulnerable to abuse, both physical and sexual, at least in part due to their difficulties with understanding social situations. They had no protective radar for socially dangerous or inappropriate situations. They were also vulnerable because of their communication difficulties, and those who would victimize children often took advantage of the fact that they might not be identified because of this communication barrier. Finally, children with autism can also be unpredictable and demanding, creating unexpected frustrations, especially in adults and other children who are not familiar with their rigidity, or incomprehension, and at times, their fearlessness in response to threats or warnings.

Sam's mother, Maxine, wanted me to get to know Sam a bit first. In the waiting room, she heaved herself up from the couch, straightened her muu-muu and introduced herself as Max. "Auntie Max to those two," she said, gesturing at the two toddlers. "My baby sister's." Since Sam appeared to be already occupied, I asked Max if she would like to come in and talk to me first. I went over to the ball pit and announced that I would be in my office down the hall speaking to Auntie Max. The toddlers ignored me, fixed on the puppets, who stopped their action and appeared to look around. "Who's that?" a gruff voice said from the ball pit. "I'm Dr. Dan, Sam." The puppets looked at each other. "Who he talking to?" the voice said, and his cousins squealed with delight. "I'll come and get you in a minute," I said, and the puppet show continued.

"He's great with them," Max said in my office, "but he has always been good with the little ones. Not so much with keiki his age. He's always trying to be silly." She stopped and sniffled, so I reached for the tissue box. Max took the tissues, and sighed a long, sad sigh. "He has such a good heart. You know? He loves everybody, tries to make them laugh, and he trusts everybody. But he doesn't know how to act sometimes. He says the wrong thing, not because he's mean or hurtful, he's just different. The school teachers, and they told us he maybe had ADD or whatever. The pediatrician said maybe he's got that kind of autism, what's it, Heisenberger's? Something like that."

I said, "Asperger's?"

"Yes!" Max nodded and pointed at me like we were playing charades. "Yes, Dr. Dan. Asperger's. We don't know, my husband and I, about this. He has one older sister in high school, Kealani. I had her when I was very young, about her age. She's very smart, and lots of friends. This one? He's smart all right, but the kids are mean to him. You know? He doesn't get picked to play. No playdates.

He's clumsy, can't play soccer or baseball. But he loves the water. Not the ocean, though. He won't go in the ocean, so we took him to the Y. We figured he would make some friends there. But now this!" She put her head back, then took a deep breath: "Okay, okay. So, what you want to know?"

I interviewed Max about Sam's developmental history, asked about extended family, and was asking her about Sam's educational experiences when Sam appeared at the door. "Did you forget about me, Dr. Dan?" he said, cheerfully. Sam had thick, mussed black hair and large, almond-shaped dark brown eyes. He was dressed in his school uniform, a light blue polo shirt, blue pants and black sneakers.

We talked together about Sam's experience of school. He was aware that his teachers were not that happy with him. "I try my best but I'm always in trouble." He also knew that they had discussed the possibility of his having ADHD with his mother. "I don't have a problem with paying attention. I think my attention span is just too long, not too short. I get interested in something and I just want to keep on with it, but then we just move on to something else, or it's recess or lunch, and I'm like, *what?* What are we doing now?" His test scores were usually very good though, and he was diligent about his homework, even when he found it boring. "I do everything they tell me, even when I think it's dumb. Like we have math problems to do, like multiplication. Okay, multiply five times six, thirty, yep, got it. Then we do six times five, alright thirty again, got it. So then, thirty divided by five. Duh, six. And thirty divided by six? Five?" Sam opened his mouth and stuck out his tongue. "No, wait, so then we go to what's five plus five plus five, you know six times. Families of facts, they call it. Math families of facts. It's so dumb! But I do it."

I asked Sam if he ever did his homework with other kids. "Sometimes I do homework with Kea, but we just sit together. We don't work together. But then she gets mad and screams at me. You should be seeing my sister, doc. She's loco." He twirled his finger around his ear and stuck his tongue out again, eyes crossed.

Max said, "Sometimes Sam can be a little...hyper. High on the volume."

"Mom, that's a nice way of saying loud. I know I'm *loud*, but I can't help it..."

"It gets on his sister's nerves. She's been very kind to him, really," Maxine said.

"Well, she threatened to kill me on a plane once," Sam replied.

Sam eventually admitted that he didn't have friends, and he didn't get along very well with his sister, or her friends, mainly because they found him annoying. "I'm loud, and I get excited, and then I talk too much. But everyone in our house talks too much. Have you heard my mom on the phone? She never stops, talk, talk, talk." But, I pointed out, his mother had close friends, and so did his sister. Sam stopped and thought about this, and he looked at his mother and back at me. "Is *that* what this is about?"

I asked Sam what his mother had told him about coming here to see me. He said she had told him it was to help him at school; his teachers were concerned about him, and thought he could be doing better. "I thought I was coming here to get Ritalin or whatever," Sam said. I said that was still a possibility, but first we needed to do some more assessment, and that he and I needed to spend some more time together. "Okay, cool," he said. "Just me and the doc!"

I had Sam complete some neuropsychological testing, including measures of intelligence, attention and concentration, executive functioning and academic achievement, and then some projective tests and other personality measures. He did very well on all the cognitive measures; in fact, he had an overall IQ in the Superior range. His attention, concentration, processing speed and executive functions were also well above average, however, so there was no evidence of ADHD, at least on these standardized tests. The main feature of the projective and personality testing was his verbosity – he gave overly detailed and overly elaborated responses about everything – and that he otherwise denied (or perhaps, really didn't have) any conflicts or worries or issues. He was a fairly happy and well-adjusted person, just a bit naïve and seemingly unaware that other people might find him off-putting, or that they might not be as cheerful and positive as he was. His mother also completed the Gilliam Autism Rating Scale (GARS), and Sam's scores were elevated on all subscales, with an overall "Autism Quotient" well into the clinical range, indicating a high likelihood of an autistic disorder. Given his IQ and language development, the most likely diagnosis was Asperger's Disorder.

Eventually, Sam and I got a chance to talk about what happened at the recreational program. I didn't want to push the topic on him, so I was waiting for a natural opportunity, or I thought he might bring it up. While we were looking at Thematic Apperception (TAT) cards, he looked at one card that depicts an ambiguous situation with what appears to be an older man and an attractive younger woman, and the man is smiling at her in a way that could be leering. Sam said, "He's kind of creepy. Suspicious." I agreed, but I asked him what about the picture made him think so. "Just the way he's looking at her, like he's hungry and she's pie." I thought this was an excellent interpretation, and asked him if he had any more feelings about it. He looked confused for a second, and then sad. "I guess my mom told you about what happened. I asked her not to, but she goes around telling people about it." He shook his head and looked down.

"Yeah," I said, "she told me. Do you want to talk about it?"

"Well, I feel like I've already talked about it enough. I didn't think it was such a big deal, then it became a big deal. I was just there in the bathroom, getting dressed, and this man came over and talked to me. I've seen him there before. He was just wearing a towel, and being friendly – but he was looking at me like the guy in the picture. Then his, you know," he pointed at his crotch, "he was getting a woody. I was like, what? Gross. Then he said he wanted to give me a hug, he tried to hug me, with only a towel on, and his thing sticking out. I just grabbed all my stuff and got out of there."

We talked about the incident a few times after that, and he didn't seem to have been particularly traumatized, although it was a painful and confusing experience, especially for a kid like Sam who was normally so trusting and transparent. He could never lie, or keep a secret. It wouldn't even occur to him that he could lie, since he tended to blurt out virtually every thought he had. He also had little insight that people could be otherwise, so he saw no reason for having secrets. Luckily then, Sam did not feel a sense of shame about what happened, or a need to keep it from people, although he did find it uncomfortable to talk about, since he did have a sense that some topics were inappropriate or private.

I told Max that I didn't think that Sam had suffered any long-term harm from the incident. I did think there was a reasonable chance that he had Asperger's Disorder, however. I explained a bit about the diagnostic criteria and the history of the diagnosis. Max was puzzled because, as she pointed out, Sam was so sociable and loving. I told her that, in my experience, it was a common misunderstanding that people with autism or Asperger's were not sociable or motivated to have relationships. Some are more withdrawn, I explained, as if they were in the world by themselves, but many of them just don't quite know how to go about it. They're clumsy with people. Sam's blunt, matter-of-fact manner and his loudness suggested that he didn't have a sense of how he was coming across, or didn't care, and that was hard for his peers to understand and accept.

"But, he's very sensitive," Max said, getting choked up with tears. "He wants friends so badly, and they are so mean to him. Even the teachers can be mean. I wish I could be with him at school and...grrr!"

"You want to protect him. Of course, you're his mother, and he tells you everything," I said. I told her I could have some input with his teachers and the school administration, but we had to diagnose him first. Then it would be on the table and agreed upon by us and his school that he had a recognized disability and they couldn't discipline him for it, and might even be willing to help. She explained that it was a private school, and she wasn't sure that they would be all that supportive about Sam having a disability, especially one that was rare and virtually unheard of. At the time, this was new territory for both private and public schools, and I wasn't sure how the school administration would react either.

"Okay," I said, "I think we can agree that Sam is socially awkward, he doesn't make friends and he sticks out in social situations. But what about his interests? Unusual preoccupations? Is he obsessed with anything?"

Max didn't hesitate: "Pirates."

"Pirates?" I said. I hadn't heard a lot about pirates yet from Sam. "Yes!" Max said. "We tell him not to talk about that outside of home. We made that rule because it was driving everybody crazy. Once he gets started, he just gets all wound up and won't stop. You should see his room. He's got pirate stuff all over. Not just movie pirates, either, real pirates and treasure. He likes that more than anything, that's all he wants to think about and read about."

Max told me that she could recall Sam's first Hallowe'en when he dressed like a pirate, and then kept wearing the costume for months afterwards. She eventually tried to throw out the hat and the eye patch and the plastic hook and sword, but Sam dug them out of the trash. He wanted story books about pirates and wouldn't let them read him any other kind of story books. He watched shows about pirates on TV, and watched pirate-themed movies on the VHS player over and over until the tape broke or jammed. In the Peter Pan stories, he identified with Captain Hook. Later, Sam started reading about modern-day treasure exploration and recovery, and then about modern-day pirates in Africa. "It didn't help that his father is in the business, sort of. He's obsessed with this stuff, too."

It turned out that Sam's father, after years working as an underwater welding contractor on a salvage tug in and around Pearl Harbor, had started his own business in marine salvage and recovery. Now he had built a lucrative business recovering artifacts from wrecked ships all over the Pacific Rim, and it was no secret that he planned to one day have his only son join the business with him. It wasn't hard to understand how Sam's preoccupation with pirates and treasure had started or how his father's interest and his business had fueled the flames of what had become an all-encompassing passion for Sam. Max sighed, "They're both nuts. Kea and I have to put up with it, or we tell them to go to Poppy's study." The study was Sam's father's home office, apparently a mini-museum of marine salvage artifacts, maps and books on international wrecks and recovery.

This all sounded rather familiar. I had had the experience with a number of other clients with Asperger's that you might not get much from them about their particular topic of interest until you hit on the right topic. Then, it was like hitting the jackpot on a slot machine and all of this information came pouring out. Their demeanor changed; they became animated and even excited. I hadn't seen that side of Sam yet. He had followed his parents' rule and had not "come out" to me about his interest in pirates. So I asked Max if I could see him again, and she agreed. This time, she said, she would have his father bring him. "You gotta meet Frank. He's a piece of work."

A week later, Frank – or Poppy, as his family called him – and Sam rushed into the waiting room, late for an appointment that was actually scheduled for the next day. I could hear Frank from down the hall talking to the receptionist and laughing about the confusion about the date. She called me from the desk, and I agreed to see them. Frank was a big, energetic man with thinning dark curly hair and thick eyebrows, who looked like he was slightly uncomfortable being indoors. He was wearing work clothes, and his face was deeply tanned up to the forehead, where there was a tan line from wearing a baseball cap in the sun. His forearms were tattooed, and his hands were calloused and scarred from years of welding and working with jagged steel. He didn't make eye contact when I came out, but turned to Sam and swatted him on the back, just about knocking him off the couch, "Okay, son, the doctor's here, get going." Sam got up, and I put out my hand to Frank who shook it, without looking up.

Sam and I met in the playroom, and he wandered around at first, looking at the toys and creative materials. "What are we going to do today, Dr. Dan?" He picked up a dragon puppet and turned towards me with it. "Roar!" he said, opening the puppet's mouth wide and bringing it close to my face. Then he picked up a parrot puppet and the dragon and parrot carried on a Punch and Judy style interaction. He moved closer to the bookshelf and looked at some of the LEGO® creations there, and then noticed a small catamaran which was from the Islanders series, a subset of the Pirates collection. He dropped the puppets, and took the catamaran down and put it on the table. "Cool," he said. He looked back up at the shelf, and then at some of the bins of LEGO bricks nearby. "Do you play with LEGO, Dr. Dan?"

I sat down next to Sam at the table. I explained that the LEGO was there, like the puppets and the painting easel, the sand-tray, costumes, and the other toys, so that kids could express themselves. "Ah," he said, "like therapy. I thought this was just a cool room you liked to hang out in and play." I looked at him closely; he didn't seem to be being sarcastic.

"No, Sam," I said. "I don't really play with toys anymore, except here, with the kids I see."

"Oh, okay," Sam said. "So I can mess with this stuff? It's not your personal collection or anything?" I was a bit puzzled until he explained that his father had a collection of model ships, with sailing and pirate figures, and some antique toy sailors and pirates that Sam had tried to play with. Sam said that Poppy had a collection of toys like this in his office at home and another one at work, model ships that he had built and that Sam wasn't allowed to touch.

We talked a bit about his father's collection, and Sam seemed uncomfortable. I told him it was alright, we could talk about anything here. That was enough of a cue for Sam, and he started telling me about wrecks and salvaging, the types of materials that were recovered, and then about ancient wrecks, treasure-seekers, and the process for looking for wrecks based on historical documents, old ships' manifests, etc. He talked about specific wrecks, and about shipping routes in the Pacific and the Caribbean. Then he talked about modern-day equipment used to locate sunken ships, dating of materials and detecting fake, replica coins or brass pieces. He talked breathlessly, like someone hurrying through a lecture, and he paced back and forth in the room, occasionally picking up toys or LEGO® from the shelves, looking at them, and then pacing, waving his hands in the air. He didn't look at me for the most part, but if I didn't seem to be paying attention, he noticed right away and would grab me by the shoulder, "Dr. Dan, listen, Dr. Dan," and then go on with his rapid monologue.

I was thinking the school staff might be correct about Sam having Asperger's, but he had characteristics that just didn't quite fit my conception of this condition. He was more creative, animated and expressive, as well as just generally more sociable, and used more idioms and gestures, than I expected to see from someone with a pervasive developmental disorder. He clearly had some social difficulties, and an excessive, circumscribed interest, but without seeing him in interaction with peers, I felt I couldn't really be sure. I was thinking about that when we walked out to the waiting room. Frank wasn't there. I asked the receptionist if he was around somewhere, and she said he had answered a phone call, and then walked out, so Sam and I waited.

I thought this would be a good chance for me to ask more about Sam's interactions with his peers. I asked him about friends at school, and playdates. Sam took a Gameboy® out of his book bag and turned it on. "What's that, Dr. Dan?" By his mother's report, he was clearly having difficulties developing peer relationships, but this might have been due to his impulsivity and distractibility. What I didn't know about was how Sam interacted with his peers. I asked him again if he ever had friends over to his house. He was concentrating on his game, and made a pained expression. "Aren't we done, Dr. Dan?" I agreed the session was over. It was then that Aaron and his mother came in for Aaron's appointment. I started walking back to my office to make some notes on Sam – I was planning to ask his school if they would allow me to observe him there. Aaron came and stood by Sam, watching him play the Gameboy®. Aaron said something to Sam and Sam replied, without looking up. They were both focused on the game, and seemed perfectly at ease with each other, even though they were strangers, and Aaron was standing inches from Sam, hovering over his shoulder.

That image stayed with me. It seemed clear that there was an obvious solution to the difficulty of not having direct access to peer-to-peer interaction in the clinic setting. It also seemed that there was a likelihood that children with Asperger's might feel more comfortable with each other than they did with typically developing children. It was another week before I got to see Aaron and Sam in the waiting room together, and, by then, it was clear to me that I should be seeing them together.

## LEARNING THROUGH LEGO®

Frank never did come back to pick up Sam. He had gotten a call about work, and had been so distracted by it that he walked out and forgot about Sam. My receptionist eventually called Max, who came to pick him up. Neither Max nor Sam seemed to think this was all that unusual. Later, this happened again with Frank, and with some other parents as well. One of the drawbacks, I learned, of working with children with Asperger's and autism was that many of their parents clearly had autistic features. A few times, I wound up having to watch kids all day, and even drive them home after their parents dropped them off at a group or individual session, and then forgot about them. The next week, Max brought Sam, and she was apologizing to the receptionist on behalf of Frank when I came out to the waiting room. She was explaining that Frank had a habit of wandering off like that, and had left Sam in all sorts of places.

Sam and I went to the LEGO room, and coming into the room seemed like a cue to Sam that he was now allowed to talk about pirates, lost treasure and marine salvage. It was more noticeable to me then that he was not drawn to the romantic versions of pirates portrayed in books and films. He was more interested in the history, and the factual aspects of the shipping routes, dangerous conditions and the existence of unfound wrecks, the activities of private ocean-going militias, and why there were pirates to begin with. He explained about the exploration for new trading routes, and the competition and disputes between the empire builders at the time, including Spain, Portugal, France and the British Empire. I could understand his interest in this piece of history, especially since some valuable evidence of it lingered on today, and there were individuals, including his father, who saw the search for lost ships as a reasonable way to make a living. I could also understand why most other eight-year-old boys who just wanted to play pirates would lose interest in the topic, and in Sam.

Part of the problem, I could see, was that Sam did not have conversations about these interests. He talked, and he expected me to listen. I was just his audience. Whenever I tried to interject something, or ask a question, Sam became impatient. There was no back-and-forth involved in the communication. Luckily, Sam was showing an interest in the play materials, which allowed me to get more actively involved. We did a puppet show together, and when he offered to draw some treasure maps, I got involved, helping him, so there was interaction and reciprocity. He also showed an interest in the LEGO® and related materials. He saw in one of the catalogues that there were a number of LEGO pirate ship sets; in fact, at the time, they were a featured theme. The LEGO Pirate theme had expanded recently into a series, the Imperial Armada.

I expected Sam to be very interested in the Pirates and Imperial Armada series, but he was actually more interested in the Divers collection. I started to understand Sam better. He wasn't interested at all in what most kids found fascinating about pirates, the swashbuckling and swordplay. He was interested in the literal facts of historical piracy, sunken ships and marine salvage recovery operations. What the pirates were like as people – how they dressed, or talked, or behaved – was completely irrelevant to him. To his point of view, SCUBA diving and marine salvage vessels were much more relevant and interesting than tall ships, peg-legs, eye patches and parrots, although these were somewhat interesting related artifacts.

Once I had a better feel for Sam's interest, I wanted to see if he would show a similar positive reaction to related themes, and then engage with me on those topics. My goal was to see whether he could broaden or diversify his range of interests so that he would have a greater range of opportunity for engaging with peers, and to practice more of a reciprocal, back-and-forth communication with me on these interests. I had a feeling that what Sam was really interested in was the technology of exploration and discovery. With LEGO, this hunch was easy to test, since there were a number of exploration-based series, including Space Exploration, Divers,

Arctic Explorers, Outback, Rock Raiders, etc. I had started ordering LEGO® sets, and typically got input from my clients about what would be good additions for the LEGO collection, so I asked Sam about it. He had been looking at the catalogues and said he was interested in the Divers series, which was predictable, so I probed a bit more, and he surprised me a bit by showing an interest in the UFO series, especially the Warp Wing Fighter.

I agreed to add the UFO Warp Wing to our collection, and told Sam that he could build it. We talked about it, though, and Sam told me more about his interest in UFOs. To him, they were basically alien, interplanetary pirates. They had the freedom to explore space, where there were no civilizations or laws, and they could just take whatever treasures they could find. There was also the same sort of mystique about UFO sightings and findings, and the same combination of science and myth, that there was about lost treasure and pirates. He was very excited about the idea that I would order a LEGO set just for him, and I made sure he understood he wouldn't be going home with it. He was fine with just building it, and he even agreed to let me help him.

When the UFO Warp Wing set arrived, Sam was very excited, and I had to remind him that it wasn't a gift for him, but that it would be part of the clinic's collection, and he had the honor of building it. It was difficult at first to get him to allow me to participate – he was easily capable of putting it together without me – but I inserted myself in the process, taking over control of the pieces of the set. We kept dropping pieces from the table and they scattered on the floor, so I put the pieces in a shallow cardboard box (later, we started using plastic cafeteria trays for this purpose), and got Sam to tell me which pieces he needed. I also got him talking about the building process with me, being obtuse on purpose so that he had to be clear with me, and wouldn't just assume that I knew what he meant. We also got a chance to work on his voice volume, which was too loud for the context, and interpersonal distance.

Sam struggled to stay seated, which wasn't a problem: I let him stand or sit on the floor, or kneel on the chair. When he impulsively took over the building process, I re-asserted myself: "Hey, I bought this thing. Let me at least help build it!" Sam would sometimes intrude into my personal space, or even lean on me or push my head or arm out of the way as though I were something inanimate and in the way of his building, or blocking the light. He was less likely to drift off into the "solo zone," as we called it, when we were talking about what we were doing, and especially when I asked him to look at me when he said something to me or asked a question. I wasn't insistent on this contact every time, but every so often, when it seemed appropriate, I would just cue him to look at me or use my name so he wouldn't forget that I was there, or that he was talking to and interacting with another person, not just a mechanical presence.

So, we talked about the set itself, which had some new minifigures and a very jazzy pilot helmet, some unusual, large molded pieces which created the curved and sleek surfaces of the spacecraft, and a number of specialized neon-colored transparent pieces and stickers. We also talked about the implied technology, such as the robotic droid, some kind of laser propulsion system (the UFO had an engine compartment with a removable engine), lasers on the wingtips, etc. We talked about what the UFO could be looking for, what the droid did, where the UFO came from, and why it might need lasers. (For light? As weapons? Tools for breaking up rocks? Guiding itself through asteroid belts?) I also tried to introduce some human social and emotional questions: How long was the UFO on a mission and away from home? Did the alien have a family? Did the alien ever get lonely? Was the droid his friend? Was the alien on a private mission, or was this a military-style obligation? There was a lot to talk about.

Sam and I also kept his parents updated about what we were working on together, both in terms of the LEGO® sets we built, and the conversations we had about the "Y incident." We usually met with Max and Frank before and after our sessions together. I made sure they both understood that the LEGO activity with Sam served multiple functions for us clinically: first, it provided a positive, collaborative context for Sam and I to build a relationship and have something to do while we talked, which made it easier and less anxiety-provoking for Sam; second, it helped expand Sam's range of interests, allowing him to branch out from his "island of self-efficacy," which was pirates, treasure and marine salvage, to thematically related but distinct areas, such as UFOs and space exploration; and third, it created an accessible topic area which could be adapted to peer communication and interactions. Other kids Sam's age could be engaged about the history of piracy and the technology of marine salvage operations for only so long, whereas many or most of them would be willing to talk about LEGO®, at any level.

Expanding a narrow interest by incorporating other related topics was a strategy that I found effective with many other clients who presented as Sam did with a very narrow, deep interest in one topic. So pirates led to deep sea exploration, and then polar expeditions, the outback, and the rocket launch series, which led to UFOs, etc. All of these themes were reflected in available sets which provided a growing mini-universe of exploration-based interests, but with a common theme, LEGO. Often, the LEGO theme led to the growth of an interest in the broader topic, as it did with Sam's interest in space exploration and rockets. He started following the NASA shuttle missions for the space lab and international space station, which was carefully covered by the media at that time (mid- to late 1990s), and there were lots of details about technical innovations to keep him fascinated. Of course, we also tied his interests back in to the therapy, which included picking out another new set for the growing LEGO collection.

This time it was a space shuttle mission control set which included a shuttle rocket, which lit up and made rocket and other sounds, a launch pad, etc. A very elaborate set. Sam and I had agreed that we would need help assembling a set of this size, and Sam was enthusiastic about inviting our young waiting room friend, Aaron, to join us. Of course, I had already discussed this with Aaron, and both Louise and Max, and we were all in agreement about getting the boys together for a joint session. For them, this was not therapy, though. It was much more serious than that. It was a chance to build the biggest LEGO set that any of us had ever seen.

## JOINING OTHERS

It didn't take much to convince everyone involved that meeting with Aaron and Sam together to work on their social and communication skills was a good idea. From having worked with individual clients for a while using LEGO, I knew there were some aspects of this particular play material that would be advantageous right from the start. First, there was the mutual interest and motivation: this was a very rewarding activity for both Sam and Aaron, as well as a growing group of children who were like them in terms of their clinical issues, but also because of this interest. Second, the variety of the materials involved in terms of themes or topics that were already available from LEGO® at the time (the range and variety of themes continued to grow exponentially) was another bonus, since this allowed me to tailor the sets, as well as the freestyle projects, to the particular interests of the children, which were often narrow, rigid and idiosyncratic. Third, the building process was complex and challenging enough that there would be a need for this high level of motivation, and that it would lead to a sense of accomplishment – and, I was hoping, a sense of joint accomplishment. Fourth, I knew that the LEGO building process involved many detail-oriented steps. There were dozens or, in some cases, hundreds of pieces to each set, and each piece, each step, provided opportunities for functional, reciprocal communication, with a natural positive or negative outcome. The task provided its own feedback, and required clear, accurate communication if more than one individual was involved in the process.

The first two advantages of using LEGO as a therapy tool were immediately apparent when I came out to the waiting room to get Aaron and Sam for their first joint session. Not only had they each brought LEGO creations from home to share, but they had initiated a joint, reciprocal conversation in the waiting room about LEGO sets, their own freestyle projects, and their future projects. Space exploration, the shuttle missions and the Hubble telescope were being covered in rapid, technical exchanges. Their mothers were also engaged in a less enthusiastic conversation about LEGO and where to buy it cheaply, but also about their sons who both had long histories of failing to develop peer relationships.

The boys were so engaged in conversation with each other, they barely looked up at me when I invited them to come to the playroom. In the playroom, there seemed to be an immediate pressure on them both to show that they belonged there – they went right to the LEGO shelves and showed each other their creations and previous set-building projects. Aaron had the advantage since he had been coming longer than Sam, but then Sam turned the tables on him since he already knew about the set we would be building today (I had purchased it that week), and that it was his idea to select it.

When I took the box out, they both wanted to rip into it right away and start building, but I paused for a minute to set up some limits and the structure. I didn't have the titles of "engineer," "builder" and "parts supplier" clearly established in my own head yet, but I knew there would need to be an interdependent division of labor, and that we would need to change whatever roles we were in during the project so that it was clearly a collaborative effort, and no one could claim sole ownership of the project or even part of it. I wanted to emphasize that this was "us," and "we," with no clear sense of "I did this," or "My part in this was..." I let them get the box open and pull out the parts, some in bags, and the instructions, etc. This was a very elaborate set, so there were boxes within the bigger box, and multiple sets of directions for sub-components. Sam and Aaron started dumping LEGO® pieces onto the table, and they rolled and bounced all over the place and then onto the floor. "Woah," I said. "We're going to lose pieces!" Aaron got up right away and collected up the pieces from the floor. Sam started opening up bags of pieces and carefully putting them in the cardboard box, but there were still so many pieces all over the table.

Aaron and Sam kept emptying things out, including the direction booklets, which they splayed out on top of the pieces. We were running out of table space, and things definitely looked chaotic. Sam said, "We need a couple of those trays, Dr. Dan," so I didn't need to suggest it. I did say, "This is our first attempt at something this big and complicated. I guess when sets get to be this size, we have to be more organized about it." Both of them stepped back from the table and looked at the pieces all over the place, some in the box, some in trays and some on the table, with the direction booklets laid out, and they agreed this wasn't going to work. Sam said, "I don't even know where to start, Dr. Dan."

I knew if I was going to structure the building process to emphasize communication and collaboration, I would have to jump into the center of it. So I came back with a couple of plastic cafeteria trays (purchased at the local dollar store), and started sorting out the pieces into the trays. I gave the first direction booklet to Aaron, and asked him to describe the project. Sam started to tell him, since he knew already, but I held up a hand and asked him to let Aaron answer the question. Aaron responded, "It's a space shuttle, with a launch tower, a mission control station, a crawler transport, and a small buggy carrying an asteroid." He picked up one of the direction packets. "Okay, this is the little ground vehicle. You want to start with that?" Sam wanted to start with the main shuttle rocket. "This is so cool! It's got sounds and lights. We need some batteries, Dr. Dan." I asked Sam about Aaron's idea of starting with the small ground vehicle. "What?" he said. "We can do that after. We gotta get going on the rocket." Aaron disagreed: "Look, this is going to take a while. Let's get the little stuff out of the way first." They went on like this for a while, back and forth. I told them, "Look, you can spend your whole time here today arguing, or you can settle this and get on to building."

Sam was exasperated and was starting to get loud. I had an impulse to try to rescue them, but I knew it was important for them to sort this out with as little input from me as possible. They did seem stuck, though, and I didn't want to side with either party, so I suggested a third option: since everything was going to wind up going on the platform for the launch tower, I suggested we start with that. Aaron agreed right away, but Sam was still looking at the directions for the main rocket. Finally he agreed though: "Yeah, okay, we'll do the tower, but I get to build the rocket." I had to set a limit with that, since that was expressly not what I wanted to happen, taking solo credit for individual achievements: "Sam, we're going to build the whole thing together. At least we agreed about where to start, so let's get going and get something done today."

Sam put the directions for the rocket aside, and picked up the packet for the launch tower and opened it. "Whew, this is big!" Aaron started sifting through the parts in the tray. I wanted to make sure I could regulate the process and so I asked Aaron for the tray so I could help him start building. Sam wanted to start building, so he put the directions down and grabbed for the first parts. I held the tray up over my head. "Hold on. Really, you two, back up. Sit down. Sit. Okay, Aaron, you tell me what I'm looking for, and I'll give the pieces to Sam who will put them together." I brought the tray back down, and pulled out the pieces for the astronaut and ground crew minifigs and gave them to Sam. Aaron watched him intently and looked at the directions.

"Nah," he said. "You got the bodies wrong. Put that head on this body," he said, pointing. "See?" he continued. They both liked the minifigs, especially the astronaut's helmet which had a golden face shield. Once we got the minifigs sorted and together, we started on the launch pad and tower, which was quite complex, and had a number of large, unfamiliarly shaped pieces which were not easy to assemble. Sam and Aaron were very focused and eager, but once they accepted that they had specific roles, they were pretty good about keeping their activities within those bounds, and there was a natural pressure on them to communicate more, both verbally and nonverbally, as a result. Aaron struggled not to reach out to take pieces from the tray and to let me do it, and he also refrained from giving Sam a hand with the building and just coached him through it. "Nope, that's the wrong side, Sam. You gotta put that part...yes, over there. Now, Dr. Dan, we need the one for the other side, a blue support. Sam, it goes on the other side, just like that..."

After about 20 minutes, I suggested swapping roles, so I took the directions from Aaron, and gave the pieces to Sam, so Sam was now giving pieces to Aaron, who took over the hands-on building. I modeled for them both how to give the directions to both the parts supplier and the builder. This took some careful wording – describing each of the pieces and where and how they are put together was not easy. It also required considerable timing and there was pressure on me from both of them to keep up. I had to tell Sam what pieces Aaron would need for the next step, so he could start looking, while I was coaching Aaron about the current step. It was a quiet, serious, focused business for a while. After about another 20 minutes, I suggested we switch roles again. Both Sam and Aaron complained a bit, as they were eager to get the launch tower completed and they could sense we were getting short on time. I looked at the clock. "Alright, don't worry, we'll get it done." I took over as builder, Sam took the directions and Aaron started sorting through the remaining pieces.

This last phase was difficult for Sam since he no longer had hands-on contact, and he was impatient with both of us. He talked rapidly and loudly, and Aaron winced and held his ears. "Sam! I'm sitting right here, not across the room, you don't have to yell." Sam apologized, and said, "Okay, I know I have a loud voice." I told Sam that Aaron was right, he was louder than he needed to be, and that we would both be able to work better if he could at least make an effort to speak more softly. Sam whispered the next directions, and then laughed: "Like that?" Aaron smiled and nodded: "You don't have to whisper, but yes, like that." Sam tried, but then he looked at the clock again. "Eww! We're going to run out of time." Aaron stayed focused on the parts. "Never mind, Sam. What's next? What step are we on?" Sam checked the directions, then flipped to the back of the directions: "We've got six more steps."

"Alright!" I said. "We're almost done. Sam, where does this go?" Sam talked quickly, but less loudly, and pointed at both the directions and the launch tower, holding the picture up where I could see it. Aaron lined up the pieces, looking across at the directions. He pushed Sam's arm out of the way. "Hey!" Sam called out. "Sorry," Aaron said, "I just can't see what's next."

Sam: "Don't rush me. I'll tell you."

Aaron: "You're the one that's in such a hurry."

Sam: "Alright, alright. Here, look. We're going to need those two gray arm things."

Aaron: "Got it. Okay, here you go, Dr. Dan, these go on the top."

Sam: "They go between here and here, Dr. Dan. Just put them...yeah!"

Aaron: "What's next? What's next? The yellow fuel hoses, we gotta do the fuel hoses."

We continued like that for the next while, then I held up the set, and had them both inspect it. I asked Sam to look it over with the directions. There were a few little pieces left over, and Sam and Aaron looked carefully over the set and then the final page of the directions and they agreed these were just "left over." "Nothing's missing," Sam said. "It's done!" Aaron held up the UFO set, and swooped it through the air, then set it back on the table. Sam reached over and patted him on the shoulder, then Aaron put up his hand and Sam returned a "high five." "Good job, guys. We just made it in time!"

Sam and Aaron smiled at me, and at each other. "We did it!" Sam said. "Yep," Aaron said, getting up, and looking at the launch tower from various angles. "It's very cool, and we made it." They carefully put the tower into the box and put the rest of the parts and directions in around it. Then they looked for a suitable spot to stash it so it wouldn't be disturbed until they came back next week. Sam put it on a side table. "No one's going to touch this, right Dr. Dan?" Then they both ran off to the waiting room to tell their mothers about their accomplishment. They came back to the room a minute later with mothers in tow, pointing and explaining about the set. Then they stood next to each other in front of the table, smiling as if they were getting a photo taken.

During the next few days, I got to speak to both Sam and Aaron, and their parents, about their experience, and they all agreed that it was positive, and seemed like a very natural transition from seeing me alone to sharing a session with another client. All of them also agreed that there was a strong motivation now for the two boys to get together for "LEGO® dates," outside of the clinic, but I asked them to hold off on that. I wanted to make sure we had more of an established working relationship here, and that their experience on their own would not get derailed by the usual sorts of conflicts that tended to intrude with other peers. I felt we were making good progress when I asked Aaron to suggest another set for the collection, and he suggested one of the new pirate ships because he knew that Sam would like it.

At the next group session with the two of them, we talked about working on a freestyle together. Aaron had an idea about building an underwater scene, with some of the boats mounted above the scene on coral and rock, and then sea creatures and divers underneath. Sam agreed to this concept, and wanted to have some treasure chests, and maybe a sunken ship. They both thought a sunken ship with divers and a salvage crew would be a great idea, and Sam suggested using some of the painting materials in the room to create a backdrop, with an island above, and then water and reef below. The painting took us a couple of sessions to complete, but they collaborated nicely, shared ideas about the layout and colors, and even brought in some images from magazines and books from home.

The scene that the two of them created together was certainly noticed by the other clients who were visiting my playroom. Unfortunately, as popular as it was, such a big, fragile display couldn't last forever, so we took photographs, including one with both of the artists. This initial scene work quickly caught on with other LEGO fans, and we soon had a number of other participants and their friends collaborating on creative LEGO scenes with painted backdrops. The photos of these scenes were eventually included on a large corkboard of photos and drawings that the members created, and which subsequently inspired other members, but the oceanic scene created by Aaron and Sam was the first.

Over the next few weeks, I met with both Aaron and Sam individually and as a pair, as well as having ongoing contact with their parents and siblings. In the individual sessions, we focused on particular issues or conflicts that were facing them in their own lives and families. For Sam, the issues revolved around his reaction to the unwanted sexual exposure that occurred at the Y, and then some emerging family conflicts as well. Aaron was becoming more aware of and bothered by the issues between his parents (described in Aaron's story earlier in the book), which had become increasingly painful and even overwhelming at times. He was frustrated and anxious when the time with his father, already limited, was cut short, rescheduled or cancelled due to his parents' conflicts, his father's travel or his mother's or sister's other commitments.

Sam's parents had started disagreeing about how to help Sam with his excessive preoccupation with pirates and treasure hunting. Max's mother had come to the conclusion that her husband, Frank, had Asperger's Disorder, and that his own excessive focus on marine salvage, even though it was at the core of a successful family business, was not to be shared with Sam. Max had accepted my argument about allowing Sam to pursue his interests here in the clinic as a means of capturing his motivation to participate in therapy, but she did not want this "obsession" spilling over into his home life, or at school. Unfortunately for Frank, this meant that spending time with his son had to include a focus on something other than his work, which seemed inconsistent with his goal of someday bringing Sam into the marine salvage business with him.

A key aspect of the eventual growth and success of the LEGO® Club groups was the spontaneous connection that emerged over time between the parents, and it was not just the mothers. Frank and Jim met in the waiting room eventually, and just as Sam and Aaron had recognized something about each other and sensed a common bond, so did their fathers. They were from completely different social and cultural backgrounds, but they shared this passion for aquatic technology and exploration. Jim noticed Frank's ball cap, with the logo for his marine salvage and welding company, and asked him about it. The marine research station that Jim ran for the University of Hawaii (UH) needed some repairs to the steel supports for some of their holding tanks. Pulling the tanks and replacing the steel girders was going to be very expensive, but Frank thought they could be repaired in place.

At that point, although the repair job on the holding tank footings was the focus of their connection, the social support and empathy they shared about their sons' struggles, the educational system and the family pressures from their wives and other children sort of leaked out in between the talk of structural steel and erosion.

I found later that this was a common form of communication and support between the fathers of the children I was seeing in therapy. They talked easily about their work or hobbies, but in a less direct but important way connected with each other emotionally because of the shared experiences, anxieties and frustrations that were closer to home, and much harder to put into words. Frank wound up getting this job and then a number of other contracts through the marine biology department at the university. Jim learned a lot from Frank about the local waters, wreck locations and fishing spots around the islands. They also learned that their sons needed to improve their social and communication abilities, and they understood that they could help. They agreed to help find some interests that the boys could share with their peers, other than their fathers' occupations. They settled on fishing and diving. Frank had his own boat, both had scuba gear, spears, rods and nets, and they both knew the waters. The boys were not hard to convince.

Of course, while the social support between Jim and Frank was developing slowly, the relationship between Louise and Max had blossomed overnight. The first time Max caught sight of Louise melting into tears in the waiting room after an argument on the phone with Jim, she was on a mission. Stories, tears and phone numbers were exchanged, and Louise and Max were allies. They shared their struggles and worries together in the waiting room, and often took the boys out for shave ice after the sessions. Max became an advocate for Louise at her IEP meetings, and picked up the phone to call any number of local connections she had at the health insurance company or the school district. There weren't too many sites on the islands where Max didn't have a "cousin." Louise was shocked to learn about Sam's abuse experience at the Y, and she provided emotional support, as well as helping Max with some of the legal issues that emerged later. Louise also arranged playdates for the boys once I was confident good collaborative patterns had been established between them, and while they played together, Kea and Lani learned quilting and cooking with their mothers. Over time, other mothers were adopted into their support circle, but the connection between Louise and Max remained strong and, in many ways, was at the core of what eventually became a large support network of families with autistic children.

# EVAN

## INITIAL CONTACT

Evan, a six-year-old boy from Beijing, China, was referred to my practice by the University of Hawaii's counseling services, where his mother, Sue, had taken him for an assessment. Evan had recently arrived from Beijing to join his mother after they had been separated for four years, much longer than had been planned when Sue came to the university's East-West Center to do a doctorate in anthropology. Sue had heard from Evan's father that he had not been able to take care of Evan on his own, and over time, he became less and less willing to raise him. After a couple of years, when Evan was four years old, his father had placed him in an orphanage. He was in the state-run orphanage for two years before his mother was able to arrange to have him brought to the US to join her. Sue had heard from other family and friends in China that his father had neglected him, and that the care he was receiving in the orphanage was not much of an improvement.

The psychologist at the university who had seen Evan told me he was "a mess. He needs a lot more than counseling." She wasn't sure how much of his current functioning might be due to pre-existing developmental delays, or possibly the effects of neglect at the hands of his father or the orphanage. In either case, he was malnourished, physically and mentally under-developed, and very weak physically. He was fairly tall for a six-year-old – his mother was also very tall – but far below normal weight, with low muscle tone, and very limited language abilities. The university psychologist also described him as having institutional autism, a condition associated with prolonged experiences of neglect and diminished social interaction typically associated with children who were adopted from foreign orphanages.

I met Sue in the hallway outside the waiting area where she was pacing vigorously, holding a bundle of papers which she had apparently been reading. She greeted me with a salute, and then a handshake, seeming distracted and anxious. When I asked her about her son, she handed me the assessment report from the university counseling center, saying that she barely recognized her son now: "He's not the child I remember. Not the boy I left in China." She seemed exasperated, and nodded towards the waiting room. "Come see."

Evan was in the waiting area playroom, slumped on the floor near a collection of toys, but not playing with anything. He did not respond to my greeting, or even look up. His eyes were focused on his hand, which was splayed out on the floor like a spider. He was wearing a pair of shorts, with a pull-up underneath, and a t-shirt. The shorts were on backwards. He had short-cropped black hair, with delicate facial features, and wide-set eyes. There was food crusted around his mouth, and stains on his t-shirt. I got down on the floor and tried to get him to look at me. "Hey, Evan!" I smiled, "I'm Dr. Dan." He looked at me, made eye contact, but didn't smile or respond otherwise. I thought the fleeting eye contact was a good sign, but he did not repeat it much. He often looked at me, but seemed to be looking at my chest or over my head, not at my face. He also seemed exhausted, too tired to move. His mother explained that they had had to run from the bus-stop to get here on time: "Evan doesn't run very well."

I couldn't picture Evan standing up, let alone running. His mother, on the other hand, didn't, or couldn't, sit down. She had some more papers she wanted me to look at. I took them and glanced at the titles – journal articles from the medical library on institutional autism. "You are familiar with this, no? There is a good prognosis. He will be getting better quickly." At that point, I was more worried about his physical health and his nutritional status. "He eats! Yes, he is picky, but he has been eating. He doesn't know how to feed himself, though. Or chew." I looked at her, standing over him, with her arms crossed, bouncing on her toes. "He can't chew?"

"At the orphanage, they didn't feed him solid food. They are not supposed to have older children there, just infants, babies. They didn't have solid food. They fed him formula and soft rice." She turned angry and loud. "My husband was supposed to take care of him, but he was too busy with his work. He took him to a daycare for a while, but he couldn't afford it. He wanted me to pay for it, but I was a foreign grad student, I don't have money for daycare. He said he would take care of it. I thought he meant a relative, his mother or his sister. But it was an orphanage. He said he would come back for him, but he didn't. Not for two years. No one visited him. And now," she pointed at him on the floor, "he's like this."

I suggested we go to my office to talk, and Sue pulled Evan up by one arm, and he somehow balanced on his feet and shuffled down the hall, with his mother holding his arm. In the room, she set him in an armchair and I sat across from him, while Sue stood there, until I suggested she might want to sit. In a rush of words she explained more about the situation with her graduate training, the opportunity at the UH and her need to leave Evan behind. She had thought it would only be for a few months, but it turned into four years. After she learned that Evan's father had put him in an orphanage, she started the process of getting a visa for him to come stay with her. "What was he thinking? That man is useless." It took her a year and a half to acquire the visa, and by then she was no longer a graduate student, but a lecturer. She was now teaching lab work at the university, and had had to apply for a different visa herself. "It's paperwork, endless paperwork."

After turning our attention to Evan, I learned from his mother that he could speak, mostly Mandarin dialect, or pinyin, but Sue was also encouraging him to use English. He could follow simple commands, and appeared to understand what was going on around him, although he did not always respond. She had enrolled him at her local public school, and the school staff insisted that he needed to be evaluated for placement in special education. "He can't understand much, and he can't sit up in a chair." The special education staff had recommended a placement in a special needs Kindergarten class, for students with a range of disabilities, even though he was already six years old, and Sue had resisted. "He's not like them, he's not retarded. He will get better quickly."

At that time, I was not doing direct work with the school district, but I assumed that they would have him in the classroom setting that best met his needs, even though there were probably limited options for a student as unusual as Evan. In the end, he was placed in an "MD" (multiply disabled) Kindergarten classroom, with English as a second language, and speech-language, occupational and physical therapy provided weekly. I made contact with Evan's classroom teacher, Mr. H, who was certified in special education, and, as I found out, was studying law in evening classes. He seemed like a very bright and capable teacher, and was interested in helping Evan, although he was not always sure what to do with him. He had discovered that Evan seemed to have an ability with numbers, and was much more motivated to do math work than any other subjects.

Evan and his mother came to my office on a weekly basis, and sometimes I met with them both, and sometimes with just Evan. His mother reported that he was making good progress at home and at school, and was quickly gaining back his strength, although he was still very awkward and clumsy. They traveled on foot, or by bus, and Sue was trying to teach Evan to ride a bicycle. This seemed premature to me at the time, given that Evan was still shambling when he walked and could not sit up in a chair for more than a couple of minutes without sliding out and slumping to the floor, but she was very determined. Sue was very energetic and assertive with Evan, and with me. When she arrived for appointments with Evan, she would come straight into my office to announce herself, bypassing the waiting room. If I was still with another client or family, she walked in and stood in the doorway, breathless and perspiring from running from the bus-stop, not seeming to understand that she should go to the waiting room first. It was many weeks before she complied with my request to just wait there until I came for her.

Evan and I worked on basic communication and interaction, and I tried to get him to express himself using a variety of materials including modeling clay, paints, a sand-tray with small figures and objects, and puppets. He had started using short sentences, and his speech was clear, but with a stilted, robotic manner of speech – his voice prosody was flat, and his voice quality was off somehow, as if congested. He sounded like a robot with a bad cold. His fine motor skills were very limited, and even though his ability to hold utensils improved over time, he seemed to have no idea about how to be creative. Unless he was asked to copy something, a drawing or words or a figure, he did not seem to know what to do with a pencil, clay, paints or figures. He tried painting a few times, but painted only letters and numbers, and he read them aloud to me, as though he were teaching me. He also made numbers or letters out of clay, or he made small balls of clay and arranged them in rows. He lined up figures in the sand-tray, or made long lines of them, and then counted them. If I tried to interject some question about the figures, why he chose certain ones, or if they had some relationship with each other, he got angry.

When Evan was angry or frustrated, he huffed his breath and growled deep in his throat. He would say "No!" very loudly, and sometimes made threatening gestures, raising his hand as if to slap me. He puffed his breath hard and saliva flew from his mouth. Sometimes he spat, or threw the materials we were using, either across the room or at me. This happened if I tried to move objects on the table, or tried to join him. He didn't want me to paint or model with clay, or position figures in the sand; he preferred it if I just sat still and listened.

Evan understood that I did not speak Mandarin, and he used Mandarin only with his mother. She had started discouraging him from this, and asked him to speak only in English, but I told her this would not be a good long-range strategy. He should be encouraged to communicate in any way he felt comfortable, but she was suspicious about this: "He needs to learn English. We live here now!" Evan's teacher and speech-language therapist were encouraged with his steady improvement, but his occupational and physical therapists were more stymied. He continued to have very poor fine and gross motor skills, with hypotonia (low muscle tone) and hyperflexion (loose joints). He also didn't like to be touched – even when the therapists were trying to guide his movements – and he would get angry quickly and huff and spit when they used hand-over-hand or otherwise guided him. He had hit both of them, and his mother complained that he would slap her sometimes, even if she were just wiping his mouth (he was still clumsy at feeding himself) or bathing him. He would also get angry when others misunderstood him. His voice would quickly get high-pitched and loud, often when he felt that something was terribly important, and others (including me) didn't understand.

Evan and his mother did everything together when he was not in school. They went grocery shopping, or on trips around the island. Sue did not have a car and did not have much income, and could not afford to have someone watch Evan, and she was also mistrustful. She thought that someone other than her would not understand

Evan and might mistreat him. Evan seemed to enjoy their trips together, usually by bus, and he was soon very interested in the bus routes and schedules. He was able to tell his mother – or anyone else who would listen – how to get from any place on the island to any other by bus, with transfers, etc. He told me about going to the zoo by bus, and to a temple in Manoa valley. I asked about the temple, and he said he hadn't been there yet, but he and his mother were planning to go. He also told me how to get to the Kahala Mandarin Hotel where there were dolphins in a pond. He had not been there, either. I asked his mother about this, and she confirmed that he had memorized most of the bus routes for the entire island of Oahu, and for some of the other islands as well, by studying the bus schedules. She said he was also learning to read and write Mandarin, which she was teaching him at home. Evan was learning very quickly, and had already mastered many characters for common words.

Evan's teacher also reported that he was making incredible progress with reading and spelling in English, and that he was already past his grade level in math, although there was a problem – he refused to follow the instructions. He completed the homework and worksheets in school, but often without following the directions, and he refused to show his work in math. He was already past basic arithmetic after being in second grade for only a few months, and was doing multiplication and division, but without following any procedures, and without showing his work. He did all the questions in his head. Evan's teacher was following the core curriculum standards and was using the textbooks provided by the school district, but Evan seemed to be learning to read, write and do math on his own.

Evan was often incapable of giving me a narrative about his daily experience, unless it was about something that had just happened and that was particularly exciting or bothersome. If something happened on the way to the session he could tell me about that, but that was about it. I asked him to write a story for me – I was assessing whether he might be able to use a journal for keeping track of his experiences, and so we would have more content for our sessions together. He couldn't write a story, he said. He took the pencil and paper a few times, moved to write something and then stopped. "I don't know what to write!" I told him to just write about anything that interested him. Then he started writing. I sat back so he wouldn't feel self-conscious, and he wrote for a while. When he had written almost a page's worth, I looked it over. It was a series of numbers and letters, separated by dashes.

"Evan, you're writing numbers and letters, not words," I said. Evan looked at me with a twisted sort of smile; he explained that these were license plate numbers. He pointed to the last one on the page: "This is yours." He had written down all the license plate numbers that he had seen for the past week, in order. "They tell a story," he said. Each license plate was a vehicle, a place and time that he had experienced, and an event that he could describe, but he felt overwhelmed to be able to write about the streets, the traffic, the time of day, the directions the vehicles were moving, where he was going and why, and the makes, models and colors of the cars. He would have had to write in words what was actually a long sequence of visual events much more easily captured by simply writing down the license plate numbers. I asked him if there were any other stories he could write about. "Oh yes!" he said. Evan took another sheet of paper and quickly wrote another sequence of numbers and letters, this time with some symbols including arrows, circles and lines, as well as the names of locations on the island. It was a list of the buses he had seen, their bus numbers and license plates, followed by their locations at the time, and their destinations. He used symbols to indicate directions, north, south, east and west, whether the bus was an express or local, and whether it accepted bicycles or not.

At the same time, Evan was still struggling to sit in a chair for more than a minute, and his teacher had to give him frequent breaks, during which he lay in a beanbag chair or on the floor. He was still struggling to use utensils to eat with, and preferred to eat with his hands. He could not use buttons or zippers on his clothes, or tie shoelaces, but luckily, it was Hawaii, and he was routinely dressed in shorts, t-shirt and flip-flops ("slippahs"). He carried a backpack, but it was often dangling off of him, with the zipper open and his books and materials falling out. If his mother put a hat on him to keep the sun off, he lost it. He also lost his slippahs more often than Sue could count, or stand, and he was often wearing mis-matched pairs, which she now got from the Goodwill stores because she couldn't afford to keep replacing them. These issues often led to conflicts between Evan and his mother. She would scold him for losing a hat, slippahs, books or pencil, or putting his clothes on backwards, etc.

Evan would argue with her, in a pedantic, whiny voice, "It's not my fault! I have too many things to carry." If she persisted in holding him responsible, he would huff, throw things, and spit at her or try to slap her. The school heard from other parents about the two of them arguing and hitting each other like siblings, and they asked me to address this with them. They arrived at my office the next day, both out of breath, red in the face and sweating. Evan had bleeding scrapes on his knees, elbows and the palms of his hands – he had fallen on his bicycle on the way here. He was furious and blamed his mother for making him go too quickly.

Sue defended herself, and scolded him for being clumsy. "You are a big boy now, you should know how to ride a bicycle without falling down." Evan spat and huffed, "And you are an idiot and a useless mother. I hate you." I had to laugh, and interjected that Evan should be more respectful, but I also needed to schedule some time with Sue to talk about parenting skills. We talked later about not giving Evan the opportunity to argue with her, and about being more protective of him while also making sure that Evan understood their respective roles in their little family. I also asked about her being nurturing with him – I had never seen her be affectionate or even protective towards him. She was not very open to this idea: "I protect him too much. He needs to start growing up. I can't keep dragging him around with me everywhere. He has to learn to take care of himself."

## LEARNING THROUGH LEGO®

Evan and I had become fairly comfortable with each other over the period of about a year, during which time his language had improved significantly, and he was showing unusual rates of learning for academic material. He still did not like to be touched in any way, and had a very distant, matter-of-fact manner with me and other people, including his mother. He was more quickly angry with her, but otherwise showed little emotional attachment to her. He had also started showing some signs of imitating the speech and mannerisms of his peers, but he used their language, and cursing, sporadically and often in very inappropriate ways – cursing at his mother, clumsily and with his usual robotic speech patterns, or at me. Evan was confused when I laughed at him for cursing at me or

66

threatening me, and he would then pick up something from my shelf and threaten to throw it or break it.

One day he arrived seeming flustered and harried. His mother ushered him into the room and then left. He took off his backpack, opened it and dumped the contents on the floor; then he kicked at the books, papers and writing instruments, and stamped on them. He picked up a book and threw it. "I'm supposed to show you my schoolwork, so I am showing you." He picked up a notebook and tried to tear it in half, but he couldn't. He stuffed it into the wastebasket, and then picked up a picture frame from my desk and got ready to throw it. "Dr. Dan, you love your children more than me. I hate them," and tears came into his eyes, and he didn't know what to do. He put the picture down and tried to leave the room. I went over and took the notebook from the wastebasket and opened it. It was his Chinese character exercises. "This is very good, Evan. Wow, look at all this! Did you do this yourself?" He slumped down at the door. "Yes, my mother makes me do it, after school, every day for two hours." Then he brightened up. "You're reading it backwards, Dr. Dan. My teacher does that, too. Let me show you," and he came over and explained the characters to me. The notebook showed remarkable progress. "You've gotten very good at this, very quickly. You're a smart kid, Evan." He looked at the pile of papers and books on the floor, looked at me, and picked up his backpack and sighed. "I know," he said, "but I am not good." We picked up the books and papers, and I helped him organize them and put them back in his backpack.

One day, he came in angry at his mother about their missing the bus he wanted to take, and I supported Sue to tell him he was not allowed to yell at her. In a way it was somewhat humorous, because Evan was complying with our request not to curse at his mother, so he called his mother object names. "You're a shoe! A door! You're as stupid as a lamp." I couldn't help smiling, and Evan noticed this. At first, he started to giggle a bit, calling his mother a "dumb fish," then he caught himself, and tried a growl, which was not very convincing. His mother just sighed and slumped in a chair in the corner. I went back over my lecture to Evan about it being important to be respectful towards adults, especially his mother. Evan walked over to the shelf of toys and picked up a LEGO® creation that one of my other clients had made, and he arched his arm back to throw it.

"Woh, woh, woh!" I said. "Someone made that, and they're going to be very upset if you break it."

"Oh? Who? Who made it?"

"Another child. A boy. He spent a lot of time making it, so please be careful with it."

Evan looked at the LEGO® creation, a space ship with wheels and many small weapons attached precariously to it. "I could do better than this. What is it? A space ship? I could do much better." Then he dropped the LEGO to the floor where it broke into pieces.

"Oh, Evan! I asked you not to break it!"

"No you didn't. You said they would be upset and I should be careful. I was careful. I didn't drop it by accident. And if they are upset, good! I don't care about them."

He turned his back on the broken space ship and went over to the LEGO materials in the corner. "That was very bad of me, wasn't it? I am trying to be bad so you will hate me. Do you hate me, Dr. Dan? Now I am going to build a better ship, so you will display it on the shelf; the other child will see it and be jealous, and you will hate him."

Sue was exasperated. "He's been like this lately. Everything is about hating him, and being bad, or evil. He wants me to put him back in an orphanage." Evan was sitting with a bin of LEGO at this point, and raking loudly through it. "Yes! You hate me and I should be put in an orphanage again, and starved, and fed nothing but dirt and poo." Despite his agitation, Evan seemed very intent on building something from the LEGO. He searched noisily for pieces while his mother and I talked. I noticed that he struggled to put pieces together – he didn't have the strength or the fine motor coordination to press the blocks together, and the pieces fell apart again as soon as he had a few together.

After a while I joined him, and for the first time, he let me help him. I showed him how to squeeze the pieces together so they wouldn't fall apart, and he grabbed the small creation back from me. "Let me do it! I can do it." I took some bricks and put them firmly together, not saying anything. He picked up my LEGO creation, looked at it briefly, and then threw it across the room, with it bouncing off the far wall but the bricks staying together. This surprised and delighted him and he lost track of his initial destructive impulse. "Hey, look at that! They stuck!" Evan looked at me, and held up his own loosely jointed structure: "Would you help me, Dr. Dan?"

I told Evan I would help him build whatever he wanted, after we fixed the space ship that he had dropped on the floor. "Oh yes, of course. We should do that first." He picked up the pieces and handed them back to me, and told me how they went back together. "I remember it was like this, this piece was here, and the wings were just here." He pointed and I put it together. I noticed he was looking at my face, watching my eyes and checking to see if I was looking where he was pointing. He watched my hands carefully, and a couple of times, he reached out and moved my hands and fingers to the right position, directing my hands as though they were tools.

I tried making mistakes, putting pieces in the wrong place, and he reacted immediately – "No! Not there" – and he gently patted my hand and moved it slightly: "Here." Our heads were almost touching, and when we were done, he reached up and patted me on the shoulder: "Good job, Dr. Dan." He held up the repaired space ship and turned it. "Yep, this looks right, phew! We did it." Then we sat down with the LEGO® bin, and he picked out pieces for his space ship, and he asked me to help put them together for him. "Okay, that's good there, but now I want this here. There has to be room for a pilot – the guy sits here, under this canopy, put it there." We ran into design snags and couldn't find certain parts, but we worked at it closely and cooperatively for some time. Sue got impatient, dug out some papers from her backpack, and then got up and left the room after a while.

Eventually, Evan's own space ship was looking the way he wanted it. He took it from my hands and wanted to add just a couple more small pieces, an antenna, and something more, another weapon. "I need one of those, you know, like this," holding up a piece, "but with the bumps on the bottom." I thought I knew what he wanted, but I offered him another piece that was similar, not quite what he wanted. "No," he said impatiently, "you know, the one that fits on top," and he started digging around in the bin with one hand, holding up the space ship in the other. "You're not a very good helper, Dr. Dan, I will find it myself." I saw the piece he wanted in the bin, and said, "Is that it?" He looked up, a little frantic, as he was almost done, but not quite satisfied; he wanted that last piece, and looked at me closely, again tracking my eye gaze, then looking down at the bin where I was looking: "Yes!" He grabbed the piece, and then tried to place it on the top of his craft, the jewel in the crown, but the pressure collapsed the top of the space ship and the wings fell off. "Errr!" he growled, and he tensed up.

Then Evan reached out for my hand and placed the broken ship there, with tears in his eyes. He didn't say anything, just looked at the broken ship, and then at me, waiting. I pressed the broken ship back together, and he held up the final piece. He offered it to me, and I said, "No, Evan, it's your ship, you do it." I held the ship out, supporting it so it wouldn't break again, and he carefully put the final piece on, then he took the ship, held it up between us and smiled, looking back and forth from me to the ship, to make sure I was looking, and I smiled, too. "It's very good Evan. That last piece looks really cool." He took it and carefully put it on the shelf with the other creations. "Don't let any of the other children break it," he said. "They will be so jealous!"

## JOINING OTHERS

After that initial building session, Evan would come in to the playroom and immediately look over at the shelf in the LEGO® corner to see what the other clients had been working on. At first, there were mostly small freestyle creations, but we were also working on LEGO sets, including some larger, fairly elaborate ones with structures and vehicles – a NASA launch pad, aliens, pirates, Robin Hood, knights and castles, wild-west, boats and divers, police and firemen. Evan was fascinated by the skill, creativity and diligence shown by these creations: "Did the children do these themselves? How old are they?" He wanted to know their names, and where they went to school. "When do they come here?"

At first, I thought it was just his jealousy – that his attachment to me was emerging and he was feeling threatened by them – but it was more than that. He felt challenged by the process, and he was fascinated by the systematic quality of it, often counting, then multiplying and dividing, the pieces and plates. He was fascinated by squaring and cubing numbers, or finding the roots of them, and he did this with LEGO. We didn't have access to an official description or naming system, but Evan quickly learned that there was a system involved, and that the pieces were designed and fitted together with a predictable set of variables and relationships that he enjoyed pointing out to me. "Did you know three flats equaled a brick, Dr. Dan? And flats can fit sideways." At the same time, he was also showing some interest in the builders, the other children. Even if some of his reaction was jealousy, underlying that I felt that there was also a positive interest, a sense of wanting to be part of something exciting, and not be left out. Evan and I settled on some LEGO® projects of our own. I gave him the lead, but his fine motor skills were still frustrating him. He wanted to show off for the other children whom he had not met, and even for their parents. He was very excited to do some elaborate LEGO sets here and at home. Sue tried, but she could not afford the sets Evan wanted to buy. She came home with knock-off imitation LEGO, which Evan railed against, and refused to build. Sue insisted that they were the same, and Evan yelled at her, "Does this say LEGO on the box? No! It's not LEGO!" We had started to use the LEGO catalogues and the LEGO fan magazines for finding new sets or ideas for freestyle creations. Evan was becoming a LEGO fan, and each week asked about the catalogues and magazines, asked if there were any new sets, or if anyone was working on something new, which he always wanted to inspect. Now, though, he was very careful and respectful about other clients' creations and set building. He would even caution me not to touch a set or a freestyle. He warned his mother to stay away from them, too. "Don't touch these. The children will be very angry if you break them. They are LEGO maniacs like me." (The official LEGO fan magazine at the time, which came with the monthly catalogue, was called *LEGO Mania Magazine*.)

I told Sue and Evan about Sam and Aaron. I explained there were two other boys who had met each other in the waiting room and were meeting with me together, after their parents had noticed the shared interest and the motivation to communicate with each other. I told them about the system we had worked out for collaborating with each other which helped structure the interaction so that there were not so many conflicts or unilateral building. She and Evan were aware that some children were working on elaborate sets, hundreds of pieces and dozens of steps, and I explained how we shared the project by taking interdependent roles: The engineer viewed and interpreted the visual directions, while the parts supplier organized and located the pieces, and the builder put the pieces together that were given to him by the parts supplier, and in the order and locations as directed by the engineer.

Evan was excited about joining them: "I will be the engineer!"

"No," Sue said. "You will share like the others, and listen to Dr. Dan. You will not be in charge." Later, Sue admitted that this sounded like a good next step for Evan: "He needs to learn to work with others, and to have some friends. He spends too much time with me. We are always together, and he doesn't make friends at school." I had to agree that this was a good option for Evan, but I wasn't entirely sure how it would affect Aaron and Sam. They had developed a bond fairly quickly, and although I had to prompt Sam at times not to be overbearing, and to support Aaron to stick up for himself and be assertive, they genuinely liked and cared about each other. By this point, they had also started seeing each other outside of the joint sessions, and there was a growing bond between their parents. I wasn't sure what any of them would make of Sue, although I was hopeful she would get along with Aaron's father, Jim, since they both taught at UH. I was hoping it would be agreeable to both sets of parents, and we had discussed the idea of turning the small unit of Sam and Aaron into a group, which would allow for more social challenges, and more social growth.

Luckily, I was just in the process of changing offices at the time, joining another group practice in an office building downtown, so there was a natural break which created an opportunity for change. I had planned to add Evan and then another couple of boys (Jonathan and Keith). In the new offices, I had a smaller playroom, but it was to be exclusively for LEGO® activities, no longer a mix of different play and expressive materials (although I kept drawing and painting materials, as these were being used to enhance scenes). I set the room up with lots of shelf space for display, but the shelves were up high, above the reach of younger children, so there was less risk of dismantling incidents. There was plenty of table top space for construction projects, small classroom chairs, and lots of plastic bins with see-through drawers for varieties of spare parts. I decorated the room with LEGO posters, and included a large cork board with the photos and drawings from the freestyle creations and scenes the kids had been working on.

The LEGO sets that had been built at the previous office had been taken apart and were packed in Ziploc baggies, with the instructions, so that they could be re-constructed at the new site. This gave the LEGO kids and me a lot of work to do right from the start. We also had acquired a considerable amount of unassigned freestyle LEGO, which some colleagues and parents had donated, and which needed to be sorted through and organized into bins:

assorted bricks of all shapes and colors, flats, road plates, hinges and other connectors, architectural features, minifigs, weapons and tools, animals and other creatures, wheels, tires and axles, motor vehicle parts, marine pieces, etc. There were also a lot of plastic cafeteria trays used for sorting and storing ongoing projects, stacks of LEGO® magazines and catalogues, and piles of photos from home-based projects.

For the first joint session with the three of them, Evan arrived late. Sam, Aaron and I were settling down to work on restoring a favorite Robin Hood set. We were just a few steps into the process when Evan arrived, out of breath, carrying a snack and a backpack that was open and had papers falling out of it, as usual. "So this is the new LEGO room!" he said, in his pedantic style, with a stuffed, nasal voice – he seemed to have been crying, but was making an effort to put whatever had been upsetting him to the side. I had told Aaron and Sam that we were expecting a new member to our little group, and they both welcomed Evan appropriately, although the whole scene seemed a bit stilted and formal at first. Sam stood up and offered his hand to Evan. "Welcome to the new LEGO Club, Evan!" he said, in his usual loud, raspy voice. Evan looked him up and down and said, "I would shake your hand, but my hands are busy holding this!" He held up the backpack and a large home-made futomaki (basically, a rice, vegetable and seaweed burrito). He made a smile – I would say he smiled, but that's not quite what Evan was able to do at the time: he imitated a smiling face. There was rice and seaweed in his teeth. He dropped the backpack on the floor and shuffled over to the table, losing a flip-flop and taking a bite of futomaki on the way. Sam took back his hand, and went over to join him. Aaron turned halfway around, and opened his hands in a magician's "Ta da!" gesture, but didn't look up.

Evan stood over the project, which was just a large green plate with a few bricks placed, two trays of parts, and the instruction booklet at this point. "Iss Rof'n Hoob," he said through a mouthful of futomaki. Sam stood close to him. "Roffin Hoop? Is that what you said?" Evan laughed, tried to swallow, choked, and then coughed futomaki and snot all over himself, the table, and Aaron. "Robin Hood," he gasped. Sam jumped back: "Oh, gross!" Aaron hardly noticed. He was focused on looking for a piece for the set, but picked out a few bits of rice and vegetable from the tray and flicked them to the floor. Evan was still laughing and coughing a bit, and snot bubbles were bursting from his nose. Sam got a box of tissues and handed a couple of them to Evan, and then to Aaron. "Aaron, I hate to tell you this…"

"Yeah, I know. I got rice on me, from this guy," he said in a mock tough-guy voice, pointing his thumb over his shoulder at Evan.

Sam dabbed at Aaron's shoulder with tissues. "Uh, it's more than just rice."

Aaron finally looked up at Sam. "What?"

Sam said, "It's phlegm. You know, boogers. Snot."

Aaron cringed. "Eww." He looked at Evan, who was ignoring them and looking around the room, chewing futomaki, pulling open drawers and looking at the sorted LEGO® parts. Rice, vegetables and seaweed were falling from his hands and mouth onto and into the LEGO bins. He stuffed the last of the seaweed into his mouth, shook some rice from his hands, and sat down next to Aaron. Aaron and Sam were just staring at him. Evan nudged into Aaron as he reached across him for the parts tray and the directions, his hands still stubbly with rice. "Alright, hold on," Aaron finally said, reaching for the tray. Sam hovered over them, then reached in to take the directions back from Evan. Evan looked up at me and then at Sam, still struggling to swallow, and having difficulty breathing through his clogged nose. His cheeks and ears were noticeably pink. I realized it wasn't from rushing to get here. Something had happened to make them late, and he was upset.

I understood. It was his first group and he had arrived late. His mother had probably insisted that he eat his after-school snack after arriving, since they probably rode bicycles here from the school. He had probably argued with her and gotten tearful, and was now trying to choke down a large futomaki roll, communicate and get involved all at the same time. Sam and Aaron were clearly not impressed, and this was all starting off on the wrong foot for everyone. I was also feeling a little tense, since this was a new venture for me, and now the kids were getting to know each other in a negative light, there was rice and vegetable all over the room, and snot and rice in Aaron's hair which I had not dealt with yet. I took a deep breath. "Evan," I said, "I think we're going to have to have a rule about food in the LEGO room."

Evan held up his hands and opened his mouth wide. He had rice and seaweed all over him. "It's gone, Dr. Dan. I ate it already." I sighed.

Sam pushed in between me and Evan. "I don't want to butt in here, but I will. Evan, you made a mess already, and you barely just joined LEGO® Club." Evan ignored him, but said to me, "This is the new LEGO Club! I like the room very much, Dr. Dan." Aaron groaned and put his head down on the table. "Can we get back to building?" He pulled the tray out from under Evan's elbows, and took the directions back. Evan looked at me, alarmed and confused, but seeming to want some direction. "It's okay, Evan. We're going to re-build the Robin Hood set together, right Aaron? Sam?"

Aaron grunted and pushed a tray of parts over towards Evan. "Yep. Evan, you can start by helping me find some parts." Sam brought some more tissues over and handed them to Evan. "You might want to wipe your hands first." Then he dabbed and plucked maternally at Aaron's hair. Evan took the tissues and crumpled them into a ball. He stiffened, and I called out "Evan!" just as he knocked the tray of parts flying into the air. "No!" he yelled. He pushed Aaron out of his chair and stood up to face Sam, with his arms wide and his hands in fists, grimacing. Sam took a step back, but didn't seem worried. He had been in his share of scraps and could tell Evan wasn't much of a threat. "You're not having a very good day, are you, Evan?"

Aaron was picking himself up off the floor, and Evan was growling and hissing at Sam who was standing in front of him with his arms crossed. I put my hands on Evan's shoulders and told him to take a deep breath. Very slowly and calmly I told him we should go to my office across the hall and talk for a bit. Evan kicked at a chair, then picked up his slippah from the floor and threw it at Sam. "Great!" I said. "Sorry, guys. Evan and I are going to talk. We'll be right back. Come on, Evan." I opened the door and Evan followed me, head down, out of the room and across the hall. He was breathing heavily, and when he sat down, started sobbing and huffing. "Evan, it's okay. We're going to be going right back in there. You just need to re-group, and start over. Got it? Take slow breaths, slow." He started to calm down, and wanted to explain, but he was still gulping. I told him just to sit quietly for a minute. I left him there in my office and went to the waiting room to get the back-story from Sue.

She explained that Evan had been excited about coming here today, to the new office and with the other boys, and had been talking about it non-stop for two days, even at school. He had been waiting for her after school, with his bicycle, but Sue had been late getting there from the university, and when they got going, they went in the wrong direction, towards the old office. When they realized they were going in the wrong direction, they had to backtrack, through downtown rush hour traffic. Then they got here, and Evan wanted to rush up the stairs, but it was the sixth floor and Sue had insisted they take the elevator, and asked Evan to eat his snack on the way in. Evan didn't want to eat, but she had insisted: it was the order of things – school, then snack, then Dr. Dan.

So, my assessment of the situation had been pretty accurate, and once Evan had calmed down enough, we could re-join the others and make the best of it. I went back to check on Aaron and Sam, and they were busy picking up the pieces of the Robin Hood set from the floor. Then I checked in on Evan. He was sitting at my desk, holding a ballpoint pen. He had scribbled all over his face and neck. He grimaced at me, and was huffing his breath. "I'm bad, Dr. Dan. I am in time out because I was bad and so I am punishing myself with this," and he started drawing on his face again, pressing hard. I reached over and took the pen from his hand. "Oh, Evan!" I said. "You're not bad, and you're not being punished! I just..." Evan shook his head and started crying. "I am in time out. I go to time out when I am bad." I got him some tissues, and started looking for something to wipe the ink off his face with. "No Evan. You were just upset. Frustrated and upset, and I wanted you to have a quiet place to calm down a bit. I totally understand why you were upset. I'd be upset, too. But now, oh boy. You've got ink all over your face." Evan grimaced at me. I couldn't tell if he was smiling or trying to make a scary face. "Do I look like a Maori warrior?"

Evan had calmed down enough to let me wipe his face, and luckily, I was able to get most of the ink off using disinfecting sheets from a first aid kit and baby wipes. While I scrubbed at his face, we talked about the events leading up to coming here, and he expressed a lot of anger towards his mother. Daily frustrations in their relationship were fairly unavoidable, due to her being a working single parent without a car, but his rage at her seemed excessive at times, and he seemed to want to interfere with her – basically, he initiated or exacerbated situations in which he could get angry at her for being incompetent or neglectful. In these situations, she sometimes resorted to telling him that she was going to send him back to the orphanage in China. I had heard her saying something like this in the waiting room at times. "I can't do all of this on my own, Evan. You have to grow up and take care of yourself more, otherwise, I can't keep doing this. I can't take care of you, and you will have to go live somewhere else."

We didn't have the time to process all of this, and clearly, it was a much bigger, long-term goal to address the abandonment and reactive attachment issues which were complicating Evan's autistic condition. I had considered the possibility that Evan may not even have an autistic condition, and that his issues could all be accounted for by the institutionalization, but institutional autism or hospitalism usually clears up quite quickly once the child is in a supportive, stable environment. He continued to exhibit quite severe problems with both social development difficulties as well as rigid, repetitive behaviors and insistence on certain routines, as well as idiosyncratic interests and unusual splinter skills (math, maps, bus routes, etc.), none of which was accounted for by his orphanage experience. Reactive Attachment Disorder (RAD), on the other hand, was much more likely to be an ongoing contributing factor or co-morbid diagnosis, and this rather dramatic display of anger and self-mutilation, sparked by an experience of rejection and disappointment, was something that would continue to affect Evan for years, especially in his relationship with his mother.

Before going back to the LEGO® room, I made sure Evan was calm again – it wasn't always easy to tell with him – so I took his wrist.

---

I had started a habit, with Evan and some other kids, of gently holding them by the wrist when I wasn't sure how upset they were, just long enough to get a feel for their pulse rate. Initially, I would try to count beats and surreptitiously look at my watch for 15 or 20 seconds, to estimate their heart rate (I used a rough guideline cut-off of 100 beats per minute – over that, and we needed to spend some more time talking and breathing slowly, away from any stimulation). Later, once I had done this enough times, I was able to estimate heart rates to within a few beats per minute with just a few seconds of sampling, and I didn't need to count beats anymore.

---

Evan's heart rate was down, and he had stopped crying and sniffling. I reminded him that the other boys, Aaron and Sam, had been meeting for a while together, but they were looking forward to having Evan join them, so they would be happy to help him, but he shouldn't try to be in charge, at least not right away. In fact, the first thing he needed to do was apologize to them for flipping the tray, and to Aaron for pushing him out of his chair.

This upset Evan a bit, and he had a brief tirade at me about liking the other boys better and thinking they were better or smarter than him, etc. I reassured him that he was just as important to me as anyone else, and that I wouldn't be inviting him to join this group if I didn't have confidence in him. I also reminded him again that he would need to apologize to Sam and Aaron, and he enthusiastically agreed – that was something particular about Evan, he always seemed to make the most of apologizing. He really seemed to have a sincere belief that this would restore him to his mother's or teacher's, or my, good graces, and at times he seemed to be offensive or disruptive on purpose, just so that he could apologize, sometimes doing the same thing over and over, on different days, or even sometimes the same day. This seemed to me to be such a clear characteristic of both Evan's RAD and his Asperger's: testing people's attachment, and doing so in a highly repetitive, routinized way. So on the way to the room, I also reminded him: "Evan, you're going to apologize, and that's going to be it, right? We're going to join the boys and move on – forget about this. You won't need to apologize twice."

"Right, Dr. Dan," Evan said. "I will join them and be a useful member of LEGO® Club."

We went back in to the LEGO room. Sam and Aaron had collected up the Robin Hood set pieces, and had gotten a few more steps ahead on the assembly. I made sure I got Evan off to a good start right away by assigning roles. Sam had the LEGO pieces and Aaron was doing the building; they were sharing the directions, so I asked Sam to take over as engineer, and I had him turn the pieces over to Evan: they were on two lunch trays. Then I prompted Sam to get things going: "Sam, what step are we on?"

Sam: "Step ten, Dr. Dan."

Dr. Dan: "Evan, are you okay with that? Do we need to back up, or can we keep going?"

Evan: "We can keep going, Dr. Dan." He looked at the trays, and then over to Sam. "What do we need next?"

We quickly got into the rhythm of building, focused on the set which all three of them knew quite well and had worked on before. Sam prompted both of them in his loud, pedantic voice. Aaron was very fast at building, and took the pieces from Evan without looking up, checking in with Sam about where each piece went. Occasionally, I prompted them to use each other's names, and to look at each other. I also prompted them to notice what each of the others was working on, and to think about what the others needed to know (or not know) in order to do their work more efficiently. After a while, I had them switch roles.

Dr. Dan: "Sam, you can take over building. Evan, let Aaron have the pieces, and you get the directions."

Evan: "I'll be the engineer!"

Sam: "Here you go."

Dr. Dan: "Sam. I think Evan needs to know what step we're on."

Sam: "Oh yeah, we're here, on this page. See?" He showed the directions to Evan, and pointed to the drawing.

Dr. Dan: "Evan, you see where we're at?"

Evan: "Yep. Okay, Aaron, Sam is going to need four more of these brown parts," pointing to the parts on the tray.

Aaron: "I got them. Here."

Dr. Dan: "Aaron, look up. 'Here, you go, Sam,' okay?"

Aaron: "Right, here Sam. One, two, three, four." He handed over the pieces to Sam one by one.

Evan: "Wait, we're missing something."

Sam: "What?"

Evan had looked ahead a page, and noticed that there was a piece in the directions, a piece of foliage, missing. "This here. We're missing one of these."

Aaron was scanning the tray, and then looked at Evan. "We have a bunch of those, look," he said, showing a pile of the foliage pieces.

Evan: "There are five of the big ones left there, but we need six."

Sam looked at Evan. "How did you know that?"

Evan: "I just looked. I looked ahead and there are six more, but there are only five on the tray."

Dr. Dan: "Good job, Evan. Are you sure it's not there?"

Aaron was already checking over the trays. "Yep, there's only five here."

Sam was already under the table, crawling around looking for the piece. Both Evan and Aaron looked under the table and around the room. I looked up and spotted the green foliage piece on the edge of one of the bookshelves.

Dr. Dan: "It's not down there."

Sam: "Hold on, Dr. Dan, I'm still looking. I thought we got all the pieces..."

Dr. Dan: "Sam, you did. The missing piece isn't down there."

Aaron followed my gaze to the shelf: "It's up there," he said, and got up to reach for it. He couldn't quite reach, and took one of the chairs to stand on it.

Dr. Dan: "Hold on Aaron, don't get on the chair. Guys, how did Aaron know the piece was up there?"

Evan: "He looked up there."

Dr. Dan: "How did he know to look up there?"

Sam: "Cause the pieces flew all over when Evan..."

Dr. Dan: "No, not quite. Aaron, how did you spot that piece?"

Aaron: "I saw you looking."

Dr. Dan: "Okay, good. Aaron saw where I was looking. Do you do that, Sam, Evan? Do you watch where people are looking?"

Evan to Aaron: "You watched his eyes."

Aaron: "Yeah, I just...I looked where he was looking."

Dr. Dan: "So Aaron saw what I was looking at, and I didn't have to tell him. I think we can use that a lot here. If we look where other people are looking, we know what they're seeing, and probably, what they're thinking about, if they're looking at something, right?"

Aaron pushed the chair over to the shelf and started to get on it.

Dr. Dan: "Probably not a good idea, Aaron."

Aaron had one foot on the chair. "What? How else am I going to get the..." He pointed up to the piece on the shelf.

Dr. Dan: "Sam, Evan? Should Aaron climb on the chair?"

Evan: "No, he will probably fall off and hurt himself."

Sam: "I don't care. Needing that piece is all I care about."

Dr. Dan: "Well, I'm going to say we shouldn't climb on the chairs, or the tables, just as a safety rule. Is that okay?"

Sam: "It's your club, Dr. Dan. Yeah, okay."

Aaron: "But what about the...?"

Dr. Dan: "Yeah, okay, but how are you going to get that down if you can't use the chair?"

Evan: "I can reach it." He got up and reached up to the shelf, and took the piece down, and gave it to Aaron.

Dr. Dan: "Thanks, Evan. It's a good thing you are so tall. Aaron, the next time you need to get something from a high shelf, you can ask Evan, or me, to reach it. Got that everybody? Can we make that a rule?"

Evan, Sam and Aaron: "Yes."

Dr. Dan: "We're running out of time here. Let's get this step done and then wrap up. Next week I think we should spend some time talking about rules. If we're going to have a LEGO® Club, we should probably have some rules, right?"

Sam: "Rules, okay! Like no knocking people down or throwing LEGO all over the place, like that?"

Aaron: "And indoor voices, Sam."

Evan: "No smoking. We should say no smoking and no pets."

Dr. Dan: "I don't think anyone here will have a problem with that. But let's say we think about some good rules for LEGO Club, and we'll write them all down next week. Deal?"

Aaron: "Okay, Dr. Dan. Let's get this step done."

After the group, I asked Evan to wait in my office again. He was calm and cheerful, so I wasn't worried about how he would react to that. I went out to the waiting room to give feedback to Louise and Max, who were happily chatting with each other, and then asked Sue to come in. "Was he bad? He was being difficult on the way here because we were going to be late. He said he didn't want to come if he was late, but I told him it was better to be late than not go at all."

I didn't get into that with her, but stopped her in the hallway outside of my office, and told her what had happened with Evan, the snack and the interaction with the other boys. She was immediately angry at Evan and wanted to go into my office. I told her that he had scribbled with a pen on his face, and suddenly, she was also angry at me. She was loud and stood with her face close to mine – she was almost my height – "You left him alone! You are supposed to be watching him while he's in here! He could have hurt himself. This is not acceptable, do you hear me! He's supposed to be supervised. You have to take responsibility and supervise him! You can't leave him alone like that!"

I told her I understood how she felt, and that I felt terrible about leaving him alone, and I apologized for allowing him to be alone and to write on his face like that. She seemed to want to keep shouting in the hallway, and since there were other providers working at the time, I suggested we go into my office. Evan was sitting in a chair by the door, crying.

Evan: "It's not Dr. Dan's fault. You made me late, and you made me eat snack when I didn't want to."

Sue: "It is Dr. Dan's job to watch you when you're here. Don't correct me. You are a child, and you should be doing as you're told, by me, it's that simple."

Evan: "You are not a good mother! I hate you! I won't listen to you, and I will call you Sue Lee, because you are not even my mother."

Sue turned away, red in the face, with her and Evan's backpacks in her lap. She was close to tears. Then she turned back, and looked carefully at Evan; she reached out and took his chin, turning his face to look carefully. "Did Dr. Dan clean you up?"

Evan was still crying and he reached up to swipe at his nose with his hand. Sue pulled some tissues from the box and gave them to Evan. "Blow your nose. At least Dr. Dan got most of the ink off your face. There's still some here," pointing to a spot below his ear, "and here." She pointed at the bridge of his nose, next to his eye. "Yeah," I said, "he had his face pretty much covered."

Evan said, "I was a Maori warrior. Someday I will have real tattoos on my face, and I will look like this," grimacing again.

I handed Sue the container of baby wipes I had used to get most of the ink off, and she took one and dabbed at the remaining marks on Evan's face. She held his hair back, and saw that the ink went up into his hair line. "Oh Evan! You got it all up here!"

"You can't see it up there," said Evan, and he pushed his mother's hand away. "Don't do that. I want everyone to see that I am punished for being bad." He reached for a pen on my desk, but I took it away first.

"No, Evan," I said. "You've punished yourself enough, and I told you before, you weren't bad. You were just upset, and I understand why. It was important to you to be here on time, and you were late, and then the boys didn't want to let you be the engineer."

Sue turned to Evan. "We talked about this. I told you, you were not going to be engineer today, but you won't listen..."

Evan, looked at me, and smiled. "But I was engineer. I was parts supplier, then I got to be engineer, right Dr. Dan?"

"Yes, Evan, you were the engineer, and you'll get another chance to be the engineer next week, too."

Evan: "I will be the best LEGO® engineer ever."

Sue: "Good. First, we have to go home and you need to work on your characters. Next week, we'll see if Dr. Dan will let you back in, and keep an eye on you."

I stood up, and went to the door. "Evan is very welcome to come back. But maybe he should try to get here in time to eat his snack before he comes in."

Sue looked up at me, still a little angry. "We will do our best."

Evan got up and gave me an awkward hug, knocking me back into the door. "I will get here on time, and be the best engineer, even if I have to come here by myself." In the next few months, Evan continued to attend the LEGO Club group on a weekly basis, and became an active participant and both a follower and a leader in this group with Aaron and Sam, and then a growing number of others who joined them. His progress was quite remarkable at first, especially as his gross and fine motor skills improved – he was getting both occupational and physical therapy at school. He also became less irritable, his mood improved overall, and even when he arrived seeming rushed or bothered by a conflict or an unexpected event, he seemed happy enough to be at the group that he was willing to let it go, and join in the fun.

Sue asked to speak to me a few months later. She explained that she felt Evan may not need the LEGO Club or therapy with me any longer. She felt that Evan had overcome the residual effects of his "institutional autism," and although he was still exhibiting some problems with learning at school, his social and emotional adjustment was complete. The question of when Evan, or any of the kids that I was treating at the time, was ready to transition out of therapy was one that I had been already been considering. Evan was one of a number of children referred for treatment of autism and other PDDs, including Asperger's Disorder, by the Hawaii Department of Education (DOE), as part of their IDEA-related services; that is, my individual and family therapy and the LEGO Club social skills group were considered related services, part of their Individualized Education Plans (IEPs). As such, it was not only a clinical necessity to have measurable outcomes, it was a legal necessity as well. Although I had written specific IEP goals, with measurable outcomes for the DOE referred clients, I also felt it was necessary to have a more comprehensive and standardized measure to justify continued services, and to guide future goal and objective setting. So it was around that time that I had started asking parents (and some teachers) to complete the Vineland Adaptive Behavior Scales (VABS, which is now the VABS-II). The VABS is a parent or teacher interview-based rating form which assesses a child's or adult's level of adaptive functioning in three domains, Communication, Socialization and Daily Living Skills, and compares their results to a norm (data on a large sample of individuals who represent the population base against which to compare an individual's scores). There is a fourth domain, Motor Skills (gross and fine), but it is used only up to age six years.

When Sue suggested that she thought Evan might be ready to graduate from the group, rather than pointing out that he was still struggling socially and with regard to his communication and daily living skills, I asked her to complete the Vineland interview with me. Sue was surprised to learn that Evan scored very low on all three of the domains, especially Socialization. She felt that he had made so much progress that he must be within the average range. Unfortunately, she did not have a very good sense of what was typical for other children Evan's age, so the Vineland norm-based ratings were helpful. At the time of the assessment, Evan was functioning about three years behind his age level in Communication and Daily Living Skills, and was still five to six years behind on the Socialization domain. The Vineland also helped us identify some goals for Evan that were just about six months to a year ahead of where he was functioning at the time, so both Evan and Sue had a clear sense of what we could be working on, and also what was reasonable to put into his IEP in these areas. Using the Vineland as an assessment and progress tracking tool like this, for Evan and many of the other LEGO® Club participants, also allowed me and my colleagues later to use this data to assess the longer-term outcome efficacy of the LEGO Club therapy approach.

# FACILITATING THE GROUPS

The week after this initial group session, Evan, Sam, Aaron and I spent some time at the outset working on an acceptable set of rules. I let them take the lead, although I did help by pointing out when rules were either redundant ("No yelling" and "Indoor voice," for example, were different ways of approaching the same rule, so we combined them) or unnecessary. Evan had initially insisted that we include "No smoking," since that was a common rule he saw posted in various public places, along with "No loitering," "Dogs must be on a leash," "No skateboarding," and "No shirt, no shoes, no service." As new group members joined this triad, we would typically introduce them to these proscriptive rules, and then invited them to suggest any additional rules that they thought the group might want to consider adding. We eventually came up with a set of eight rules, which became fairly standard across groups, and seemed to cover all of the foreseeable issues, although no set of rules could have predicted all of the ways that the growing group of participants might decide to challenge the situation (e.g. no spitting, no trumpet playing, don't dump the sand out of your shoes in the room, don't use pencils as a weapon, don't kick the walls, don't put gum on the LEGO®).

*LEGO Club Rules*

If you break it, you have to fix it.

If you can't fix it, ask for help.

If someone else is using it, don't take it, ask.

No yelling. Use indoor voices.

No climbing or jumping on furniture.

No teasing or name-calling.

No hitting or wrestling – keep hands and feet to yourself.

Clean up – put things back where they belong.

In addition to the LEGO® Club Rules, I found it necessary to impose a structure on the group process itself, not so much that it interfered with the sense of playfulness and fun, but enough so that the sessions didn't devolve into chaos, which did occasionally happen. In the evolution of the group structure, there were some times, and incidents, that involved a lot of yelling and even some peer-to-peer aggression. No one was ever hurt, but there were definitely some threats and intimidation, smashed LEGO creations, and pushing and pulling. It was playground-typical behavior for a group of boys, but not at all what I was aiming for in terms of social interaction opportunities. Over time, I found the best way to avoid having the group activity dissolve into a room full of individual agendas was to start the group with a "check-in" period. This involved a few minutes of having each group member share with the group some thoughts or feelings regarding recent events in their lives from earlier that day or the past week.

For many group members, it was a struggle to generate any sort of narrative account of their experiences, and this check-in ritual seemed painful and difficult for them. Luckily, for most of the group members, I was also seeing them and often their families for individual and group therapy, so I often had a very good idea about what positive and negative events were taking place in their lives at home and at school, and I was able to give them a little prompting or reminding, if necessary. We also often had siblings or other peers in the group early on, and they were good role models with regard to this social sharing component, so the other club members got the idea about what a check-in looked like from them. Later, I also had co-therapists (graduate students and other child-care professionals) who also participated in the check-in process and modeled this type of narrative self-disclosure. This five- or ten-minute phase at the beginning of the group helped set the tone for the rest of the group process: calm, reflective, mindful of others, and aware of them as individuals with complex lives and challenges. Without it, the group members often got quickly focused on a project, and completely forgot about the social aspects of the process.

The check-in also allowed for a nice transition into the next important phase of getting the group going in the right direction, which was having a discussion about the group's project or goals for the session. Again, without the group participating in a discussion about a joint goal or project, it was quite natural for them to all dissipate into individual pursuits right away. There was no doubt that they typically found it easier and more enjoyable to pursue their own activity, but, in the end, they clearly showed more benefit, and were often more animated and excited about group achievements. Over time, they also had all learned that they were more likely to be able to accomplish bigger, more elaborate and exciting projects if they worked together. It was a common early insight for new group members to realize how much more efficient the building process (or later, the stop-motion animation process) was when they did it with the others. This group discussion about joint projects, however, could become very problematic and involved a lot of negotiating.

In the early stages of getting the first groups together, I would sometimes try to avoid all the arguing by having a project prepared, or a new set ready to build. It seemed a sensible approach to be prepared for the groups with an activity for them to engage in. If I was honest with myself about the outcome, however, I realized that the participants were more likely to be more animated and energetic about a project if it was one that was of their own ideas. Of course, the best case was when a group member was able to convince the other group members that they had a good idea. Having the other group members working together under your direction on a project from your own imagination was a heady experience. There was also a very positive reaction, though, to participating in the creation of someone else's vision, whether it was a vaguely expressed freestyle ("a western town," "a skateboard park," "Pokemon"), a carefully described freestyle creation with drawings, or a new LEGO® set that someone had requested be added to the group's collection. It became important to group members that they were able to do favors for each other, and expect them in return. Part of the benefit of helping out with someone else's project, aside from the shared sense of delight in someone else's creativity and the joy of accomplishment as a group, was the anticipation of this experience being reciprocal.

Although the group members were often very willing and were even excited to work on a project of my choosing, the project didn't seem to add as much to the group's sense of cohesion, and the identification of group members with each other, as did projects that were developed by the group members themselves. I also found that we would be missing out on an important part of the process, which was the communication of ideas that resulted from having to come up with a project on their own. It was obvious that they were often very motivated to have the group acquire a favorite set (the group members often scoured the new magazines and catalogues, and later, the LEGO® website), or build a particular freestyle. This creative urge often gave them the motivation to improve their communication and social influence abilities, or to acquire new social skills – offering favors, trading points, salesmanship, even politics – building alliances with other members who might support their views and the projects they wanted to see included. I pre-empted all of that by offering a project of my own, and I realized, I was making it easier for me, but less valuable for them.

Sticking with the mandate that came from this insight was not always easy, however. Many times, the bulk of the group session time was used up with this discussion and arguing. This made things uncomfortable and frustrating for the group members. There were tears and occasional tantrums, especially with newer group members who had the idea that the others were there primarily to facilitate the realization of their creative impulses. It was sometimes shocking and difficult for members to accept that what they felt was a "genius" idea for a freestyle or a stop-motion film was either rejected or misunderstood by the others, or that they'd already done it before. Often, I had to intervene a bit, and help soften the blow when I could tell (or knew from individual and family therapy sessions) that a member had had to overcome considerable social and performance anxiety to present their idea, or had felt particularly inspired by an idea that was about to be rejected or ignored.

Having the additional contact with the group members outside of the groups was helpful since I was able to keep track of whose ideas were starting to dominate the group, or who was being ignored and marginalized, and could steer things a bit by putting in a good word or helping a member get the team's attention, etc. I also encouraged group members who had more limited verbal communication abilities to come prepared with drawings, or images cut out of magazines or downloaded from the internet. Pictures and images along with gestures often allowed group members who had very limited verbal communication abilities to experience a much greater sense of belonging and participation. This also modeled for other group members both the prosocial act of overcoming a limitation in order to share, as well as the personal effort and commitment it demonstrated. Group members with less verbal ability might otherwise become fairly marginalized, despite often having very good, even gifted, visual-spatial abilities and creativity. Some of the best freestyle creations and stop-motion films were made by group members who had little or no capacity for verbal communication. Since they were typically included in groups in which other group members had intact communication abilities, without some additional support from me it would have been very difficult for them to convey their ideas. Luckily, the other group members were often happy to accommodate them, and were pleasantly surprised by the quality of their unique contributions.

Of course, part of the difficulty with having prolonged group discussions was that it cut into the time available for building or animating. As parents and siblings got used to the group's process, they had developed the habit of wanting to see what the group had produced together. There was an inevitable sense of disappointment when the group ended and not much LEGO® building had been achieved. Many of the parents seemed to have the same expectation of LEGO Club that they had of school days: What did you learn at school today? Let's see what you brought home! When a group member's response to parents or siblings after a group was that we'd spent most of the time in LEGO® Club arguing about what to do, they naturally felt that this was not productive. Luckily, I was able to have some contact and was able to convince most of them that the discussion phase was not only beneficial, but may in the long run actually be more important than the building process itself. Of course, that didn't appease all parents.

There were some parents who were also fairly unilateral in their view of the group process, and who were very active advocates on their children's behalf in many settings, not just LEGO Club. This dynamic was much more of an issue later, once the groups had become well established, and when I had relocated to New Jersey, where there seemed to be a cultural difference in the extent to which parents would be willing to overtly advocate or even interfere with the educational system, and the LEGO Club system, in order to advance what they perceived as their child's needs. This form of social pressure – which was essentially aggressive and bullying in nature – cropped up occasionally in the groups, but also in the waiting room. Like parents on a soccer team who disagree with the coach not giving enough playing time or attention to their child, some LEGO parents were a little more challenging than others. Luckily for me, this was fairly rare, and the supportive, sharing and caring parents were by far the majority. Still, it didn't take more than one disgruntled parent to have a negative impact on a whole group. Typically, I would weigh the advantages and disadvantages to the individual and the group carefully – I did not want to be in the position of essentially punishing a child for their parent's behavior. Usually, a parent would come quickly to the realization that I was not willing to sacrifice the whole group's interests in order to meet their child's needs, and they would either ease off on the "advocacy," or just stop coming. Often, I felt sorry for the school staff, who didn't have this option.

Soon after the group had become established as a threesome, additional members were added, and additional complications followed. Adding group members drastically affected the dynamics and interactions in the room, but also had an impact in many peripheral areas as well. Scheduling the group, and then soon after, multiple groups, became a demanding, complicated task for my office assistant. I had run groups before, but these had been for adults, and most of them had been in inpatient settings, so transportation and adult supervision, siblings and other family commitments to schedule around were not an issue. Neither were interactions between the participants and their siblings and parents in the waiting room. At the new groups there were also toileting accidents, tantrums, lost or broken toys and electronics, forgotten backpacks and clothing, etc. to deal with. Some issues were fairly predictable, and we managed to accommodate them with some forethought, like parking, waiting room space, and bathroom accessibility.

Other problems were unanticipated, such as when one parent would drop off a child, having arranged for their spouse, or ex-spouse, or a grandparent, or neighbor, or parent of another group member, to pick them up, and then the plans fell through. My assistant and I had a number of complications to deal with such as this, and sometimes more than one at a time. Entertaining and feeding kids in the waiting room became a regular part of my assistant's job, which, although she was very good at it, admittedly was not in the description of the position for which I had hired her. Running the groups most often meant that there were parents and often siblings in the waiting room for a couple of hours at a time.

At the time, I was typically seeing most clients for one group session, which lasted about 90 minutes, and one individual session per week, plus at least one family session per month. For the first group members, it was convenient to schedule the individual session just before or just after the group, but that only allowed for two contiguous sessions per group, and there were at least six and up to about eight or nine group members. This meant that sometimes families could be in the waiting room through multiple hours, or on multiple occasions per week. Needless to say, they got to know my assistant as well as they knew me, if not better. There were also often more than one family in the waiting room at a time, and, during groups, as many as two dozen people could be milling around. Since the groups were usually run in the later afternoon, after school, and then there were typically two groups per day, and at least two on Saturdays, the waiting room got to be a very busy place.

I understood and accepted that the waiting room was going to get a lot of traffic and wear, and there would be some mess, especially since people were bringing siblings with them for hours at a time, and there was the necessity for entertaining and feeding them. I tried to incorporate some of these natural aspects of a social grouping into the groups themselves, for instance, by including some siblings or friends in the groups, and by sharing snacks. But I also knew that LEGO® activities were not naturally suited to sharing a meal. Anyone who has tried to combine LEGO building and eating will understand this conflict. After a few well-intended efforts to incorporate the pleasant social aspects of sharing snacks, we eventually had to settle on not having food in the room. This was a lot easier said than done, especially in Hawaii, where social gatherings just didn't happen in the absence of food under any conditions. Not only that, but although we could restrict food from the LEGO room itself, we certainly couldn't restrict it from the waiting room.

Unfortunately, there was no way around it: getting food, or even just residue, off LEGO without washing it was nearly impossible. I had learned that I could wash the LEGO in mesh bags (the ones you can use to wash fragile items in the laundry) in a dishwasher, but we were amassing more and more LEGO, and it was difficult enough to keep it all relatively well dusted when it was clean, let alone when it was being handled by greasy fingers a couple times per day. Keeping the LEGO grease-, dust- and germ-free could easily have turned into a full-time job. Eventually, we learned that de-greasing the kids in the waiting room before they came in was a lot easier than trying to de-grease the LEGO.

I had decided to limit snacks to crumb-less, grease-free, single-bite candies, like Skittles, m&m's, Jolly Ranchers and Hershey Kisses, but I soon learned that, in the right hands, even something as seemingly straightforward as eating a piece of candy can be an opportunity for remarkably unpredictable and messy behavior. None of the restrictions, however, were sufficient to withstand a carefully planned and well-attended birthday party. The best attempts to restrict birthday parties to the waiting room – even by my staff, who were considerably more assertive than I was – were completely overwhelmed by the combination of extended family support (the ohana), the inevitable photo opportunity, and the necessity for having the food (especially the LEGO®-shaped cake) in the picture. In the end, we resolved this issue by having the birthday and other celebrations (Easter, Hallowe'en, Thanksgiving, Christmas) restricted to a period of time after the LEGO activity.

Food or no food, though, there was also the mucus and saliva problem. Parents weren't as conscious or fussy about this issue back then when we first started. Coughs and colds didn't seem to be a big issue for the parents, but we did wind up having a few instances of inadvertent sharing of bodily fluids, with which anyone who works with children, disabled or not, I'm sure is familiar. Luckily, it was just about at this time (late 1990s) that bottled hand sanitizers came on to the market, so we were able to use this new invention, along with tissues, sani-wipes and peer pressure, to keep the sharing of bodily fluids to a minimum.

In addition to insistent younger (and older) siblings, cousins, neighbors, school chums and family pets who were troubled to learn that this was not an open venue, we also ran into difficulty convincing some parents that they were not an integral part of the process. Others took advantage of the opportunity for a respite break, and dropped off their child, along with friends and siblings, and then left to do errands. As mentioned previously, as was the case occasionally with Sam, some parents were late returning to pick up their children, or just forgot completely. In addition to asking parents to remain in the comfortably furnished waiting room to just wait, as opposed to leaving, we had to set limits with a number of things which we didn't anticipate. Many members arrived with instructions from their parents to get their homework done during LEGO Club, with the expectation of my assistance and that of the other group members. We also had a number of extended family members, teaching staff from the children's schools, and other curious mental health and social services providers asking if they could "just sit in and watch." We did eventually get a LEGO room with a one-way mirror along one wall, but that turned into a major distraction and we put blinds up over it. Some parents insisted on knowing what was going on with their children in the group, but it was clear that their being in the room interfered with the process, and completely spoiled the sense of it being a client-focused "Club."

This sense of being part of an exciting, creative and kid-focused group was also sometimes tarnished by parents, and other adults involved, who insisted on referring to it as a therapy group, or social skills group. The participants and I almost never referred to it as a therapy, but just as "the group," or "the Club." "Therapy," "treatment" and "social skills" all had the negative implication that we were there to fix something, something that was wrong with them, that they needed to get better in a way that their parents, teachers and doctors wanted, as opposed to being there because it was interesting to them, and they made friends, and had fun. At the outset, I didn't have any strong evidence that the LEGO® Club idea was going to bear fruit, that the participants would improve in ways relevant to their needs as children with autistic conditions, but as long as they were motivated to participate, and were willing to engage in interactive play with peers, to communicate, share ideas and solve problems as part of a group, there was a pretty good chance that it would yield meaningful results.

I had a hunch that just the label "therapy," or other similar labels, would have the same effect that I'd seen with "homework," "Get back to work!," "What are you working for?," and "Good job!" Inadvertently labeling learning activities as non-preferred by both the words ("work" and "job") or by actions (unnecessarily rewarding kids for engaging in learning activities, and then making the positive reinforcement overt and even emphasizing the contrast between the non-preferred activity and the reward) seemed to create resistance and to interfere with internal motivation; for example, a feeling of mastery, or simply to participate in an interesting activity for its own sake (I was thinking of the Lepper, Greene and Nisbett study on the over-justification effect from 1973). Using terms like therapy implied that the activity was being engaged in to meet the needs of the therapist, or the parents, or the teachers, and not the customers. Except in very exceptional circumstances, most of the LEGO Club participants came to the groups with the understanding that it was for them, and was intended to be fun, an intrinsically interesting and rewarding activity – not another "social skills group," or homework bunch, etc.

When they felt observed, and scrutinized, or judged – which tended to happen when the idea that this was therapy was introduced – this made them self-conscious about their behavior, or they felt that I was trying to manipulate them, and was reporting about their activities and interactions to their parents and teachers. Occasionally, a parent or teacher would inadvertently infect a participant with the idea that LEGO® Club was therapy by asking them about it or commenting in a way that implied there was some accountability. The group member might introduce this to the group for discussion, or to object to this idea – that LEGO Club was something adults had devised to have an influence on them – and this would have a negative effect on the mood of the group. They would lose the enthusiasm and spontaneity that seemed such a key part of the emerging group play process. The group became less playful, more conscious of the rules, and tended to focus on the routines of building, rather than the fun of creating. The freedom and playfulness seemed to need this bubble of privacy, and when it was burst, the fun evaporated.

My role in the group seemed to be less as an adult or therapist, but more like a facilitator, and the participants didn't seem to notice that I was an adult. I dressed casually and typically wore aloha shirts with shorts or jeans. I was surfing a lot so I was tanned and my hair was bleached by the ocean. To them, I think I must have seemed like a Peter Pan sort of person: an adult who never grew up. Why else would an adult have a big playroom full of LEGO? Not that they actually thought of me as a kid; most of them knew I had my own kids, but they seemed willing to forgo the formality of adult–child communication because I seemed willing to let it go. We worked things out together, and although I sometimes asked them for favors, most of the rule-following and behavior correction in the room came from their peers, not me. There was a tacit understanding that I was there to help with the fun, but the Club was theirs.

Sadly, there were also more serious incidents involving conflicts between parents who were divorced, separated or in the process of splitting up. The early years of LEGO® Club coincided with the rapid rise in the divorce rate, and the associated domestic issues. Domestic violence, restraining orders and custody disputes were probably not any more common in the group of parents we were seeing at LEGO Club than anywhere else, but I was aware that the incidence of divorce was generally higher among parents of children with disabilities, apparently at over 50 percent, which at the time seemed extremely high. Eventually, we had to institute some signing in and out procedures and be very careful about custody and visitation rules to avoid incidents (the police were called to our waiting room more than once over the years).

Although some siblings and typically developing peers were allowed in, and actually did quite well in the group as a source of peer support, and appropriate role modeling, others were not helpful at all. In fact, the first time we came across instances of graft (LEGO went missing, especially Star Wars minifigs, by far the most commonly pilfered item) it was during sibling or friend visits. The group members themselves seemed to understand and accept that the LEGO material stayed here in the Club and that the Club materials were sacrosanct. Not so much for visitors. This was such a clear and consistent distinction in how kids approached the group, that when we did find some group members helping themselves to the materials, I actually questioned their diagnosis. Children with autistic conditions have such difficulties with theory of mind and perspective taking that they rarely lie or steal, and when they try, they do so very badly. I found that if a participant was good at stealing, which necessarily involved a form of dishonesty, or lying, they were usually suffering from Oppositional Defiant Disorder, or general social maladjustment, not an autistic condition. We never did add "No stealing" to the LEGO Club rules.

Initially, I had included some behavioral strategies, other than just using the social pressure of the group itself. This seemed especially necessary early on when the groups were growing quickly, and a large number of children were being added with whom I often had had little opportunity to develop a rapport and treatment alliance. A couple of attempts were made to use a simple tangible reward – I always had Skittles,

Hershey Kisses, m&m's, Jolly Ranchers, Tootsie Pops or Starburst on hand – but these were complicated by both the fact that we started sharing these treats as part of the creation of a social milieu, and then by the inevitable mess. It was really quite impressive how much mess could be made with even a single m&m or Skittle and a healthy dose of saliva. We also had complaints from parents about the issue of dental decay, and sucrose-induced hyperactivity.

The groups were definitely a bit unruly at times, though, and, along with the incident with Evan and the pens, a few more negative experiences quickly taught me that "time out" cost more than it was worth. After a couple more attempts, no one was ever excluded from the group. Although exclusion might seem like a powerful tool for behavior change since time-out is noted to be an effective behavior change strategy during preferred activities (not so much if the activity is tedious to one or more of the participants), its use invariably created a rupture in the cohesion of the group, not to mention a problem with supervision, which both the parents and my receptionist were not very happy about.

For persistent rule violation, before I really got the hang of using a peer-mediated approach (there is definitely a learning curve for that skillset), we settled on a modified version of time-out, which was to have a chair set off to the side from the main activity, which was identified as the "break" chair. So, if a participant was consistently overwhelming his or her fellow group members, talking too loudly or being single-minded about their activities, i.e. participating, but not interacting appropriately, they would be asked to "take a break," maybe relax, get themselves together, take deep breaths, chill out. For some repeat offenders, I would work with them individually during 1:1 or family sessions during the week, and might have a cue or target word that we had identified to indicate when they were encroaching into forbidden territory, such as "chill," or "cool out," or "take a breather." After a break in the cushy "break chair" I would check in with them, and usually get a quick sense of their pulse or other autonomic indicators (redness, sweating, rapid breathing, excessive movement, etc.), and when they were ready, have the group invite them back over to re-join them.

Over time, as the LEGO® Club groups grew, the types of referrals increased as well. Initially, the groups were made up fairly exclusively of children with autistic conditions, and some who were thought to have mild autism, but ended up having social anxiety issues, or Obsessive Compulsive Disorder (OCD), or selective mutism. It was not uncommon for the children being referred to have already expressed an interest in LEGO, or to have a well-developed fascination with LEGO. This was often thought to be a pre-requisite by some who thought the groups were just for children who had an interest in LEGO – which is understandable, since we were calling it "The LEGO Club" – but many children who had previously shown little or no interest, or who even stated that they didn't like LEGO or weren't any good at building with LEGO, were much more interested once they were exposed to the range of creations and activities that were available. As we have seen with Aaron, Sam and Evan, their particular idiosyncratic interests fueled their fascination with LEGO, a creative process that allowed them to express these interests in an accessible way. They didn't have to have the skills or artistic talent necessary for painting or sculpting, and the materials themselves were very forgiving – they could correct mistakes invisibly many times over, and each creation could be recycled or improved upon without losing anything. So there was something attractive about this accessible and forgiving creative process, even to children who had never done much with it, and who otherwise had few expressive outlets.

There were not very many other play-based group therapies for children going on at the time, especially in Hawaii. The advent of IDEA (Individuals with Disabilities Education Act) in 1990 coincided with the early stages of what started to become known as an "autism epidemic" (growth in numbers of primarily mild and atypical forms of Pervasive Developmental Disorders). In the State of Hawaii at the time there was also local pressure from a state-federal government settlement to improve state-funded services for students with disabilities known as the "Felix Consent Decree" (see Chorpita and Donkervoet 1995). This had resulted from a class action lawsuit against the state's governor and the Department of Education for lack of provision of services to eligible children with disabilities.

In this context, it was not surprising that there was a sudden interest in an experimental therapy group that appeared to have some promise for improving social adjustment in children with autism and other mental health conditions: they had no choice.

Many of the children I was evaluating at the time, regardless of their diagnosis, had in common that they were not doing well socially with peers, and their social difficulties were often exacerbated by social avoidance, and then some negative social experiences with peers either at school or in the community. Getting teased, excluded or verbally or physically bullied was a very common experience for the types of kids that were being referred by parents and teachers. Although many of these kids were eligible for school-based mental health services, these services were simply not available at the time. Although there were a few school psychologists and school counselors, their availability was very limited relative to the growing identified needs. The state DOE had co-opted the Department of Health's Child and Adolescent Mental Health Division to help out, but even they were quickly overwhelmed, and the state decided to offer contracts to private mental health providers. Many of the children who participated in the first LEGO® Club groups were referred to my practice by their school districts in this context: IDEA and the Felix Consent Decree. Because of this, it was important for my practice to have more than the usual level of documentation and accountability. Although this was a bit onerous at the time, in the end it wound up being fortuitous since I was later able to use the detailed level of documentation and objective evaluation data to evaluate the benefits of this innovative approach, and publish the outcome studies (LeGoff 2004; LeGoff and Sherman 2006).

The broad net that was being cast in order to identify and provide services for children in the Hawaii school system also brought in many children who did not seem to fit in with the group that I was focused on clinically, i.e. PDDs and social anxiety. Quite quickly my practice was also inundated with children with a range of problems that included more "externalizing" conditions, such as ADHD, ODD and Conduct Disorder, as well as a mixed collection of congenital developmental disabilities, and children affected by fetal alcohol syndrome and other maternal substance abuse exposures, lead exposure, and acquired brain injuries. For these children, I was able to provide assessments, parent and family therapy, and individualized school-based behavioral interventions. Eventually, my colleagues and I also contracted with the state to provide after-school programs and in-school training and consultation services for children who did not appear to be good candidates for LEGO® Club.

Early on, I did not yet have a clear sense of what the limitations were with regard to the types of kids who might benefit from this approach. It didn't take more than a few experiments with children with externalizing issues to discover the drawbacks of over-inclusiveness. Children with ADHD and ODD often have social difficulties at school, and some are even suspected of having Asperger's or other mild ASDs, especially prior to the advent of wider awareness of ASDs and improved assessment techniques, and many of them were referred to LEGO Club in this context. Social problem? Try this social skills group. The children whose primary clinical issue was probably ADHD were somewhat difficult to manage, and they often were perplexed and irritated by their peers in the group, but they could often be coaxed to be accepting and to participate appropriately, with some benefit for them in terms of their frustration tolerance, and capacity for task focus and impulse control. Children who were more typically oppositional or antisocial, however, were much more inclined to be domineering, abusive and at times even aggressive towards the inhibited, socially awkward children with ASDs.

Even with increased awareness of the need to keep the groups safe from children who might bully the clients with ASDs, the children experienced teasing and physical intimidation from peers at school on a regular basis. Keep in mind that this was occurring well before there was anything like the level of sensitivity to bullying in schools that there is today. The children with ASDs often internalized and developed certain behavioral tendencies in reaction to this peer abuse, and these would sometimes appear in LEGO Club groups. Although I was immediately responsive to these intrusions of playground nastiness, LEGO Club was not initially designed to deal with this type of behavior systematically. As noted above, the use of time-out (exclusion from the room) did not seem to be an option – we could have sent them out to the waiting room to sit with their parents, and we did do this occasionally, but many of the parents would typically drop off their children for the group and then leave, or there were siblings and children of other providers in the group practice and their siblings out there who were just as vulnerable, so we needed some other way to address these issues.

The LEGO® Club rules were developed, and were posted, and the in-room time-out, or "take a break" procedure, was implemented. This seemed somewhat effective, but then some children, especially those with more externalizing tendencies, could spend much of their group time in the break chair. I eventually decided to attempt to implement a LEGO Club positive reinforcement token economy system. This approach continued to be implemented in various iterations as part of a number of LEGO Club groups for many years. The procedure initially involved me noticing and pointing out prosocial and helpful actions, which could be anything from finding a missing LEGO piece, to defusing a social conflict situation, and then assigning "LEGO points" as a way of acknowledging and rewarding these positive actions.

I had been using positive reinforcement and structured behavior plans in classrooms and homes for years, especially for kids who had problems with compliance and rule breaking (see the section on the "black hat," in Jonathan's story below). It was my experience, and also that of a growing group of my colleagues, that focusing on and rewarding positive behavior worked a lot better in the long run than identifying and responding to negative behaviors, which is exactly what I was doing with the in-room time-out procedure. So I chose to focus on increasing the salience and value of prosocial actions by using the LEGO points.

Of course, points in a token economy are secondary reinforcers and their value or power results from their relationship to primary reinforcers which have immediate hedonic value. As discussed above, I had given up on trying to use candy or other edible items for social context purposes or as rewards – there was always at least one kid in each group who would make a mess with whatever food was available, and at least one kid whose parents would object to the snack either because it had too much sugar, or gluten, or food dye, or all of the above. As I learned over time, the eating habits of children with autism is a very thorny issue of its own. So I decided to use LEGO® itself as the reward. I bought a number of LEGO sets of various sizes and themes, and assigned some points values to them, and offered them as prizes as you would at the county fair booths. This approach worked very well for a while, as the participants were very motivated to earn the points towards one of the prized LEGO sets, and I made it very clear what prosocial actions I was looking for and did succeed in getting the kids more motivated to engage in them. They would identify an item, note the number of points they needed to earn, and then very systematically decide on strategies to earn the points. It worked very well at first, and many group members collaborated and helped each other to move towards their individual goals.

Problems developed with this approach right away, though. The first issue was that most of the situations in which problem behaviors occurred were not in the typical course of a LEGO Club group process. In most instances something unusual happened, something unpredictable and upsetting that resulted in a strong emotional reaction, and in that moment, all interest and motivation for LEGO points and the associated prize sets went out the window. Arriving late for group, as Evan did for his first group, is a good example. Also, other events that preceded the group, like having a conflict with a sibling or parent on the car ride, or in the waiting room, resulted in us having to deal with a very angry and reactive group member who couldn't care less about LEGO points.

In these situations, a group member would get very excited – red in the face, animated, sweaty – and I would surreptitiously get a feel for their pulse, and it would be rapid. I learned over time that these were critical situations. If I handled it badly by being either too dominant or not assertive enough, things could get out of hand quickly, or if I didn't engage the group, a group member might run out of the room, bursting the sense of group cohesion and membership, and that group member would have a lot of difficulty re-joining. Sometimes, especially if their parents didn't respond well, for example by being angry with them or with me or the group (sometimes conflicts escalated to the point that parents got angry with each other about their children's behaviors), we might never see them again, or the group members might attend but be internally ostracized and left out of the play and the decision-making process.

But if we were able to resolve these crises in a way that maintained the group's cohesiveness, with no one excluded, and without having to involve parents, the group seemed to get stronger. The group members would spontaneously discuss the crisis later, and would incorporate what had happened into strategies for group communication. A good example happened when we had the first girl join the group – Marla. I had anticipated a bit of a reaction, and had told the all-male club members the week before that a new group member would be joining us, and that she was a girl. They argued a bit at first, especially Sam and Aaron, who both felt this was an encroachment into this boys' world, and that having a girl member might change the dynamic of the group. Of course, they were the original group members, and were still coping with the expansion of the group in general. But they felt that a girl might want them to play, communicate and interact differently. This was based on their experiences with girls at home and at school, who were often correcting them or scolding them for what they perceived as normal boy behavior (farting, cursing, playing with weapons, tinkering).

The boys also worried that a girl might not be as interested in LEGO®, or might not have the skill set necessary for participating in the process. As they soon discovered, Marla could hold her own with LEGO-based activities and had some very creative ideas about LEGO freestyle projects, but until they got to know her, they were quite resistant to the idea. In fact, they were frantic. They envisioned their kingdom of trucks, rockets and pirate ships invaded by the new Belville LEGO sets, with their pink and purple pieces, flowers and kittens. Aaron was especially upset about Marla joining the group, and he spent most of the session that week trying to talk me out of it.

The following week, Aaron was clearly on edge, and was standing in a corner of the waiting room with his arms crossed and tears in his eyes. Louise looked upset, and told me later that Aaron had been refusing to come that day: "Dr. Dan is going to ruin LEGO® Club. If he's going to let girls in, I'm quitting." Apparently, there had been some problems at home with Aaron and his sister Lani, and Aaron had been angry that things did not go his way. Lani had also been showing an interest in LEGO, doing some of her own building, and even asked if she might join LEGO Club. Aaron had told her that girls were not allowed in LEGO Club, and besides, LEGO was a boy thing, and she should leave his LEGO alone. I brought the boys in first so we could talk about it, and Aaron rushed in to the room. He handed me a note, and said he wanted a new rule added: "No girls in LEGO Club." I said I understood but… Aaron kicked a chair, then jumped on the table and yelled, "NO! Dr. Dan, this is a dumb mistake, and you don't understand." The other boys just looked at him, but when I asked them, they all agreed that they weren't sure LEGO Club was a place for girls.

Rather than focusing on Aaron's behavior at that moment – he was violating at least two LEGO Club rules – we agreed to talk about it. First, I agreed not to say "I understand, but…" which they all agreed was grown-up speak for "No." I said I would try to stay open to their concerns by saying, "Help me understand…" We also agreed that we had not really given Marla a chance, and that by rejecting all girls from LEGO Club we were making a prejudiced assumption that no girls could ever be good at LEGO or good Club members, and, conversely, that any boy could be a successful LEGO group member, which they all knew probably wasn't true. We discussed the idea of having a trial period, or initiation phase, for new group members, male or female, which would allow the prospective new member to check out the group, and to demonstrate their suitability. New group members had to be minimally competent at doing what they conceived of as beginner LEGO skills, such as finding the right LEGO pieces, putting bricks together, and following along accurately with set directions (parts supplier, builder, engineer). This discussion initiated the process that eventually led to the LEGO level system. For now, though, they agreed that if Marla had the basic skills and was not going to insist on the group acquiring a lot of "girl LEGO," they would give her a chance.

As it turned out, Marla was definitely from their planet, and she not only fitted in, but she added a lot to the group, and the boys knew it.

That situation could have gone much differently, though, if I'd been adamant about following the rules, rather than encouraging them to solve problems by talking about them and sharing their thoughts and feelings. Aaron was excited enough about it that he would have been rigid and unilateral, and probably would have progressed to a full-blown tantrum if I'd called him out for getting on the table and yelling, timing him out or otherwise disciplining him. In the end, he felt understood and supported by the other group members and me, and both the group members and the structure of the group itself grew as a result. Just sticking to a set of rules, even if they were rules that the group members had all agreed upon, and using a carefully designed positive reinforcement token economy system, would not have achieved this result; in fact, the group would have been stuck, and possibly weakened, by this unanticipated challenge, which in the end was a growth opportunity.

There was another problem with using LEGO® sets as the primary reinforcer for our LEGO point token economy: hedonic devaluation and inflation. Initially, many of the early LEGO Club participants didn't have much LEGO at home, and were well motivated to earn points so they could get more. But over time, the group members' personal LEGO collections grew, some more than others, and new group members coming in were more likely to already have more LEGO at home. The interesting result of this was not that the LEGO points system failed, but the participants just stopped asking to exchange their points for sets. The types of sets that they were interested in became more and more elaborate and more expensive, so it took longer for them to earn the points needed. In the meantime, though, there was a good chance that their parents or another relative might have gotten them that LEGO set as a birthday or Christmas present, or something new in the LEGO catalogue would come out, and they'd lose interest in the original set and move on to something else. They still seemed to want to collect the points though, and the real reward behind the point seemed to have changed from the LEGO sets to social approval or recognition. For the LEGO® Club members it seemed that social rewards, praise or high-fives, were somehow less valuable than the official, group-sanctioned recognition that came with the LEGO points.

Some group members did retain their interest in gaining access to the LEGO sets – those who were either less satisfied with their home LEGO collection, or who were less responsive to the social approval aspect of the points, or both. Evan was in this sub-group. His mother could not afford to buy him a lot of LEGO sets, and he tended to be less responsive to social approval and disapproval. Even though Evan was clearly aware of this, and had stated that he wanted to be well liked by his peers at LEGO Club, he didn't seem to be able to adjust his behavior to the subtle, or not-so-subtle, cues the other group members and I were giving him. Some more socially responsive group members quickly amassed a sizeable collection of LEGO Club tokens (the 1"x2" laminated pieces of paper with the LEGO logo). Since I had to keep printing, laminating and cutting out more tokens (our economy was experiencing a sort of controlled inflation), I eventually instituted a banking system. I kept a log of points that members turned in, and so was able to recycle the points that they weren't using for purchasing sets. The most interesting aspect of this, though, was that group members starting nominating each other for points, especially if I hadn't noticed it, or if they felt something that another group member had done had been especially difficult for them. In other words, they were expressing empathy and support for each other through the use of the points.

At first, just as I was encouraging the boys to regulate each other with regard to the LEGO Club rules, they started following my lead and commenting on each other's prosocial and positive coping efforts. Sam, for instance, noticed that Aaron had had a haircut, and he knew that Aaron hated haircuts at least as much as he did. "Dr. Dan, you should give Aaron two points for his haircut." I misunderstood at first: "Okay, nice haircut, Aaron. But Sam, you could just tell him you like his haircut." Sam clarified: "No, Dr. Dan. I don't care what his hair looks like. He had to get a haircut! He deserves some points for going through that." Aaron and the other group members agreed. Haircuts were miserable, and it was nice to be recognized by their friends for having suffered through something so traumatic. After a while, they stopped asking me to intervene with points exchanges, and they would just hand each other a point or two for being helpful or supportive. In addition to the "Good job," "Thanks," or high-fives, there were a lot of "Point for that," "Two points," etc.

We also learned to solve conflicts and dispel resentments using the points exchange system that was developing. Points were exchanged as a way of emphasizing "Thanks," but also "Sorry," or "Oops," or "Forgive me." I had previously emphasized to the group members that simply apologizing for hurting or offending someone, or worse, harming one of their creations, was not enough to resolve the issue. As I told them, saying "sorry" acknowledges responsibility for the action, but it doesn't amend it. Making amends to each other, truly resolving resentments and feeling good about each other and ourselves in the process, was a theme that we went back to over and over. The LEGO® points system was one way the members were quickly able to make amends. But the points, like currency in an inflated economy, became less and less valuable, and the greater value started to become the labor.

Aside from those few who were still interested in collecting points towards getting LEGO sets, and new members who were still learning the ropes and liked the structure of the points, the group members did not have much use for them other than these compensatory exchanges. Inevitably, group members started losing track of them – they forgot to cash them in, lost them, or they showed up in the laundry, stuffed into a pocket and then distributed in the washer or drier. So we started cashing in the points at the end of a group, and I kept account of the points earned each week in a log book. Naturally, the boys were interested in how many they each had to cash in at the end of group, as well as how many they had in their accounts. There was a social status associated with having a large number of points in the bank. Some of the members who had been members longer and had stopped cashing in points for sets had hundreds of points in their accounts. Others, like Evan, were chronically running low.

Sam was the first group member to start offering points as a way to recruit labor. I had initiated this earlier when I had needed help with some set repairs or extra clean up that resulted from the overflow from other groups. The room might be in a mess, or a set was missing pieces, and I'd just call out, "Alright, ten points for anyone who helps me put these pieces back in the bins," or, "I need help! Five points if you can find another wheel like this one." As the number of group members grew and we started having additional groups, there were more group members who were not keeping up with maintaining the integrity of the LEGO® sets and the organization of the freestyle materials. After a few late evenings sorting and re-assembling LEGO at the end of the day, I started asking group members to help out with the LEGO room and collections, and then offering to pay them with LEGO points. This wasn't strictly necessary for a lot of the group members, but some might have resented having to clean up messes or repair damage left by other groups, especially the younger groups.

This process got an accidental boost one day when a toddler – the sibling of a client of one of my office partners – wandered into the LEGO room and tried to climb an eight-foot-tall bookshelf loaded with LEGO sets. The bookshelf had been attached to the wall with the safety wire, but the weight of the shelf and the child climbing on it were too much for the wire, and the shelf fell forward. Thankfully, the toddler wasn't hurt – the shelf was made of fairly light material, and it was just LEGO, nothing else – but the results were quite dramatic. The room itself and the hallway outside the door were covered in a spray of LEGO pieces. Approximately 40 LEGO sets were demolished and mixed together in a split second.

The process of sorting out the pieces, using the set directions and by just recognizing the pieces, and then reconstructing the sets, took a couple of months. I handled the situation pretty much the way many natural disasters are addressed: we got some volunteers to start the process, but then as it was clearly too much for them (and me) to handle, I hired and paid freelance re-builders. The natural disaster turned into a boon for the LEGO points economy, and more importantly for me, brought many of the LEGO Club kids together to achieve a common goal. They grumbled a lot about having smaller children in the LEGO room (this was the most extreme incident, but far from the only one), but they supported each other in dealing with the situation. Even participants who had never met each other (from different groups) made appreciative comments, and even left notes for each other about their mutual work on this excavation and restoration project.

At around the same time as this project was finally nearing completion, another trend started to happen which again accelerated and changed the group dynamic process: people started donating LEGO® to the Club. As the membership grew, the Club started getting a bit of a reputation in the community. People heard about it, and there was a generally positive response about it. In fact, at one point, it came up in the Hawaii state legislature. Most of the group members had been referred for the group and their participation was funded by their school district, and, at the time at least, the State of Hawaii only had one school district. So LEGO Club was essentially a state-funded therapy that was exclusively available to those children who were living on Oahu, and mostly, in Honolulu and its suburbs. Someone with an autistic son on the island of Maui complained to the DOE about it, and you can imagine what sort of response he got about that. But the parent on Maui was a stickler about these things. His son was a LEGO fan, and he intuitively understood what a social skills group using LEGO activities would look like. He contacted me, and asked if I would run groups on Maui. Of course, by that point, I was running as many groups as I could (two per weekday and three on Saturdays), and I declined the Maui offer.

The parent contacted his state representative and, sure enough, he brought it up at the next house of state representatives session: Why was LEGO Club, a social skills program for children with autism, being provided on Oahu and not the other islands? I'm sure the inhabitants of the islands other than Oahu had become sensitized to issues like this over the years: by far the bulk of the population of the state lives on Oahu, and the neighboring islands combined comprise only about 25 percent of the state population. So LEGO Club made the news for the first time.

The result of this attention was two-fold: I got my first trainee, and LEGO Club started getting community support.

The outcome of the discussion in the house trickled back to the DOE, and a Maui administrator contacted the local private service agencies about having someone from Maui go to Oahu to be trained to do LEGO® groups. There was a post-doctoral student, Brian, on Maui who was interested in working with this population and he and his agency agreed to have him fly over on weekends so he could meet with me and sit in on my Saturday groups – there were three groups on Saturdays. Brian was the first of what quickly became quite a number of other providers and graduate students who became interested in the LEGO Club methodology, and were invited to join me. I was very glad to have the help, and they helped me sort out more of a consistent methodology. I hadn't really been thinking about what was happening in a systematic way up to that point. But if I was going to be training other people to do this, we had to start coming up with some principles, and a method, not just winging it and going with whatever seemed to be working.

One morning I arrived to find cardboard boxes stacked up in the waiting room with a sticky note: "For the LEGO Club." My secretary said some Boy Scouts had dropped them off. They were filled with used LEGO. Some of it was quite old, and a lot of it wasn't LEGO at all, but random pieces of plastic toys of all sorts, and some nails and screws, discarded crayons, pens and pencils, Barbie shoes, plenty of Megablocks, candy wrappers, and lots of dust and lint. Some of the LEGO contents were complete or incomplete sets that had been broken down or recombined with other sets, and some of it was just bricks. The group members and I wrote a thank you note to the Boy Scouts who had dropped it off, and we talked about what to do with it. We eventually agreed to sort through it and chuck out the non-LEGO stuff, including the fake LEGO (industry knock-offs were just becoming an issue, but we were definitely not interested in what we started calling "Fago" for "fake LEGO," and even made a ceremony of collecting them in a Fago bin, and then dumping them in the garbage once we had a bunch). That was just the start of what soon became a fairly big part of the group's regular activities: sorting through the donations for possible sets like archeologists, and then sorting and storing the rest. Quite often we were able to replace missing pieces from some of our cherished sets, or to recreate older, out-of-date sets, and these were especially prized activities by the older group members who had an appreciation of the history of LEGO®.

So the public attention and growing word-of-mouth referral base resulted in both an increase in the LEGO Club labor force – including Brian and then other adult helpers – as well as a growing need for this labor: restoration projects. We were still building new sets, and there were all sorts of freestyle projects going on, and now there were also boxes and boxes of donated LEGO to sort through and, if possible, re-construct. Some of the donations seemed to be someone's way of clearing up space in the attic or spare room (basements are virtually non-existent in Hawaii, so home-storage space is at a premium). Others were actually brand-new, still-in-the-box sets, or clean and recently disassembled collections. Of course, once the parents of the LEGO Club members realized that the Club was accepting donations, we also got an influx from them. One of the member's mothers decided to have her son bring in his complete collection of Ninja sets – 11 of them – so that they could be displayed in the LEGO room. I had to put up an extra row of shelves just for that collection.

This was actually the start of two new dynamics in the groups: inter-group awareness and competitiveness, and group member labor exchange. As the group projects became more elaborate, both sets and freestyles, there was a lot more direct labor involved, some of which was fairly tedious. All group members shared in both the creative and laborious aspects of the process, but some group members were more interested in designing and creating, or taking on managerial roles, and they were allowed to either pay other group members to work for them, or to barter tasks during a group, or even help each other out across and between groups. For instance, a group member who enjoyed searching for parts in the bins could be asked to pull together a collection of parts of a certain type (e.g. flat pieces, roof shingles, windows, wheels), color or theme, or to find certain minifigs, tools or weapons. For instance, Marla was working on a zoo project, and wanted more animals, as well as anything that resembled bars or cages, and she offered to pay a point for each piece. Some of the group members were busy building parts of the zoo, but some were just lingering on the edges of the project and were happy to be given a role. In another group, a member was building a concert stage and wanted minifigs for his audience, so a couple of kids started putting disassembled minifigs together to be part of the audience.

At times, there were disagreements about what the group would focus on for a given session. If a group member had a particular idea that they were really pushing to have the group work on, they could offer other group members points to go along with their idea, or they would offer to pay back the others in kind, by helping them with their projects in subsequent weeks. This bartering and favor system also extended beyond the group sessions themselves to home-based projects. Some of the group members had elaborate set-building or freestyle projects going on at home that they wanted to finish and eventually bring in to display. We eventually had to add tables in the hall and waiting area to display members' own projects – but this ended after a number of big disasters, some in the waiting area, some in the parking lot, and quite a few in the vehicle on the ride over. We eventually had to agree to bring in photos of the home-based projects which could be displayed in the room, rather than risk having them fall apart during transport. So the bartering and favor-trading started happening in the waiting room and on playdates, etc.

Some group members, like Evan, who were somewhat left out of the process by not having large LEGO® collections of their own, were nonetheless able to access playdates and to receive a lot of social support by putting their skills to work on other members' projects. The value and variety of labor being offered grew considerably once the groups started doing more elaborate freestyle projects, with painted backdrops, and then later, even more so with the advent of stop-motion animated films. Once the groups discovered the stop-motion use of LEGO, the number and variety of roles grew exponentially, and some group member's efforts took on a previously unheard of value. This process, which was quite an amazing development in its own right, will be discussed in more depth later.

In the meantime, though, the group members started to openly acknowledge that the points had taken on additional value, other than in relation to their intended purpose, the prized sets: They were a means to access labor, which became generalized as a type of social control – some members even explicitly admitted they were using their points to buy votes when it came to deciding about activities, etc. They were also a status symbol, and not just because a member had acquired a lot of points. There was status associated with being paid for your input. Some members had exceptionally good part-finding, building or engineering skills and the other members knew they would need to pay them more for their input if they wanted their help with a project.

Some members became known for being able to almost magically find a specific tiny piece, buried in a bin of spare parts, or stashed somewhere among the sets on the shelves. A hat, or a tiny gun, or a head, a clear piece, an unusual shape, etc., could be critical to someone's accurate restoration of a derelict set, or to meet their discerning requirements for a freestyle creation that had to be just-so. This was often a task that I got stuck with, since all the LEGO® was technically mine, and most of the members had this delusion that I knew where every piece in the room was located. It was great to have other members, like Aaron and Keith, who were fanatical about set integrity and keeping track of rare or hard-to-come-by pieces. Some of them came to know the LEGO collection better than I did, so whenever I was asked to find a missing piece, I could pitch it off to one of my "helpers." In fact, this was a strategy that I used almost constantly, but the members I chose to help another member with finding a piece, or quickly assembling something, or helping figure out where building a set had gone wrong, or designing a structure, etc., had to be competent enough at the task, otherwise, the helpee would be grumbling and the helper would be overwhelmed or discouraged.

The groups and I (and Brian, and then others) necessarily had to keep track of who in which groups was competent to help out with which types of tasks. As a fun but also therapeutically relevant activity, we started asking the group members themselves about who was good at what LEGO skills, and we identified the core tasks pretty much the same way we had with the initial division of labor: parts supplier, builder and engineer.

This informal identification among the groups quickly led to a more formal way of keeping track, which was helpful to us all, but also provided another incentive for the prosocial and collaborative participation process: the LEGO® level system.

The levels started out as different roles, without a sense of hierarchy, because some group members were good at or preferred certain tasks: finding pieces and supplying them, putting pieces together into sets or freestyle creations, and then either following directions or designing freestyle creations. But as we started assigning roles and responsibilities to new group members, it became clear that not everyone who claimed to be a whiz at building or designing could actually do the job, or at least not to the high standards of the other group members. The group members themselves actually started challenging each other to demonstrate their competencies if they claimed to be good at one of the tasks. This led to my decision to structure this a bit, and we started assigning LEGO Club certificates, like diplomas, based on demonstrated competence, and having the other group members agree that a member was competent, and then sign their certificate to acknowledge it. The group members immediately vied to demonstrate their competencies and earn a certificate, which came with the recognition of their peers of their competency.

New group members, before they had had a chance to demonstrate any skills to the group, were assigned the role of "helper," which was basically finding pieces for someone else's freestyle project, or supplying parts during a set construction. The new member would be assigned a more senior group member as a mentor to assess their competency at the different building tasks, and the mentor would often give a formal test, like assigning a set for the new member to build (typically, one with at least 100 pieces). Once they had done that, the mentor would present the new member to the group, with the set, and they would review it too, with the mentor's input, to decide if they had shown competence at the basic building skills, accurate parts-finding, brick assembly and following set directions or blueprints. Through the set-building test, or by participating in group projects, the members agreed that someone was now a competent builder, and I printed out a certificate with the group member's name on it, as well as the other group members' names at the bottom, and they all signed it.

Once a member was given a LEGO® Builder certificate, they were eligible to be assigned any of the basic tasks in the building process, but they were not allowed to be a lead engineer or provide design suggestions for freestyles, until they had competently mastered these additional skills. The group members devised two tests for the engineering or "creator" level, which assessed design integrity, and aesthetics or validity. The first test was a group decision which we called the "What is it?" test. The freestyle construction had to be recognizably something, not just a collection of pieces, and the group members had to agree about what that something was. Some of the group members were less stringent about this test than others – some were more willing to accept a description (mostly vehicles or weapons), and like inkblots or clouds, project a little in order to help out a new member. Some were sticklers for design features, choice of materials and functionality. ("There's no place for the driver!" "That door doesn't open.") The second test was what came to be known as the "drop test." A group member designed a freestyle with an acceptable level of complexity (i.e. about 50 pieces), and one of the group leaders would hold it about waist or table top height and drop it (the floor was carpeted). If the set was still recognizable, that is, not just a bunch of pieces, but some semblance of the original design minus a few jet blasters or radar dishes, they had passed the drop test.

The drop test was later dropped in favor of a more in-depth review of the "What is it?" test, which included ratings on novelty, creativity and color choices (random or mixed colors was definitely a negative factor). Some of the group members really struggled with the drop test idea, especially the growing number of girls who often made freestyle creations that were structures or less vehicle-weapon-like items that just couldn't be dropped. Some failed drop tests also resulted in very undesirable outcomes – tears, wailing, tantrums, threats of aggression, etc. Others were younger or had more significant autistic issues which made it difficult for them to come up with novel creations at all. These members could build sets and follow directions, but novel freestyle building was not within their zone of proximal development. For them, we agreed to accept an alternative test, which was to recreate a LEGO® set using an alternative block set. For instance, a group member could take a LEGO helicopter or submarine, and recreate it brick-for-brick from the freestyle bins, or maybe recreate it in a different color or with slight design modifications.

Once a group had agreed that a member's freestyle creation was acceptable, we all congratulated them, and they were given a LEGO Creator certificate. This gave them a considerable boost in prestige among the other group members and allowed them to have input about group freestyle projects, including design modifications, doing drawings, or consulting on someone else's freestyle engineering problems. They weren't, however, allowed to take over the responsibility of leading the group in one of the group projects. Group leaders were all what we called LEGO Masters. A LEGO Creator could contribute ideas to the group, however, such as a new set they wanted the group to acquire, or a freestyle project they had in mind. If the group liked the idea, and the materials were available, the Creator could be offered the opportunity to take charge of the group for that project. Typically, again, there would be a LEGO Master assigned as a mentor who would help them through the steps of implementing the project, like a fledgling project manager being mentored by an experienced manager.

Depending on the proposed project, a Creator might spend weeks getting their project completed. The group was easily distracted from week to week, and if the Master-in-training wasn't diligent, their project could get pushed back in priority behind other projects. They had to advocate for the group to focus on their project, and they had to delegate roles, supervise the implementation, direct the new Helper members, etc. The Master-in-training was challenged to confront other group members who might want to sabotage their project so they could promote their own. Sometimes, there were multiple Master-level training projects going on at once, and group members had only the first few minutes of the group to make their pitch, otherwise the group time would get used up in arguments, and there would be little time left for the projects themselves.

Sometimes Master-in-training candidates would have to trade favors, let someone else use some of their time, or offer up a stash of LEGO® points to get skilled members to contribute to their project and speed it along. There was also an informal hierarchy within many groups, so that some members (e.g. Sam) would be more influential because of their infectious personalities, leadership skills, LEGO skills, or just plain old assertiveness. Alignments and allegiances were made in order to advance a project, and the reward – a LEGO Master certificate – was clearly enough motivation. Many group members would comment to me or to the other therapists that they wanted help with their social and communication skills – they might literally say, "I gotta get better social skills, or I'll never get this project done and be a Master." They would talk to their parents, or to other members' parents in the waiting room, arrange playdates and ask their parents to provide snacks or other enticements, like bringing coffee and donuts to a critical conference meeting, or invite an influential colleague or boss to a lunch.

Eventually, the LEGO Creator's project would be complete, and the group would be asked to evaluate the process – not the project itself, so much, since that had been agreed upon to begin with as worthwhile – and decide if the Creator showed good leadership and project management skills. Were they able to move the project forward, and make sure that it was done efficiently and with integrity? Did the group members feel they were encouraged to participate, or bossed and harangued by the Creator? The group members were not always in harmony with their judgments, and again some were very generous while others were much more critical, but they all typically understood what they were being asked to do: give credit, approval and recognition to another group member for their ideas and management skills. They would also often discuss the Creator's basic LEGO skills, since these were often needed in order for the Master-in-training to demonstrate or model for the Helpers. The Helpers had to agree that they had learned something from the Creator, and appreciated having them as a leader not just for the sake of the project, but for their own development as budding Builders.

Likewise, the Builders in the group had to agree that the project itself was challenging enough or creative enough to inspire them to become Creators. They were looking to the Creator for inspiration for their own projects, and they would often decline to participate (this could get dramatic, like a striking union sometimes) if a project didn't capture them, or they objected to the content. This was notably a problem for some of the girls who faced some prejudice from some of the boys about their Master-in-training projects. It was somewhat surprising that it was not typically the other Masters who were hesitant to give support to alternative or feminine project ideas, but more often the Helpers and Builders, who may have had a narrower view of what LEGO® Club was supposed to be creating.

The other Creators were often a problem for a Master-in-training, since they were in the process of being surpassed, and unless they were freshly minted Creators, they probably had their own Master-in-training projects in mind, or underway. This direct competition for group influence, and striving to have a member's ideas or choice for the group collection realized, could get very heated, especially given the strong egocentric, almost solipsistic, tendencies of the members. Emotional outbursts, destruction of property (LEGO and otherwise), and physical aggression were not unheard of. In later years, when the LEGO Club room also became a film studio, these outbursts could wind up being very expensive (we lost at least one camera every couple of months, for instance, not to mention a number of laptops, and other electronic items). My colleagues and I got quite proficient at crisis de-escalation and quick interventions involving blocking or partial restraint of aggression.

Some projects failed miserably. A few members failed multiple times. For some the issue was the project itself: unrealistically complex, or just un-workable from a practical standpoint. For others, the problem was lack of assertiveness and follow-through. They'd let other members take over, or distract them from the project with ideas of their own. For many, though, the issue was just poor leadership: they got over-excited, pushy and unilateral, or overly demanding and harsh towards other group members, especially the Builders, who were often inefficient and distractible. The group members would spontaneously rebel and stop working on a project if a Master-in-training became angry and loud, or frustrated and tearful. Then they would look to me or another adult group leader to ask for the project to be postponed. Most of the time, we would put it back to them, or to the other Masters in the room, to decide if they could support the Master-in-training to continue, or if we should shelve it for another week.

For some group members, achieving LEGO® Master status was a breeze, and they hardly seemed to notice. They were typically quiet, skilled with the materials, and worked well on others' projects, so they had the respect of their fellow members from the outset. They picked realistic projects within their technical grasp, and kept track of who was skilled at what aspects of the project and made sure to assign roles based on skill, not personal preference. Some group members became close friends outside of the group, but they would not give major roles to their friends on their own projects, because they knew their limitations (practical, or interpersonal). Some group members were a bit resentful about another Creator's rise to Master's level, but we tried to alleviate that by allowing everyone to celebrate a member's graduation. At times like this, we sometimes broke our "No food" rule and had cake or cookies to celebrate a graduation. We had similar celebrations when group members, often after achieving Master's level, were formally graduated from the group.

For a couple of years, the group level system ended at LEGO Master, and the Master's level members often then graduated from the group, usually by my making a formal clinical decision (along with their parents and often their IEP team or at least their IEP team case managers) that the group was no longer necessary for them. Through the process of becoming LEGO Masters they had demonstrated, and were continuing to demonstrate, age-appropriate social competence. Our observational data and records from school staff, as well as ratings on the Vineland, confirmed that the social skills we were observing in the group were also generalizing to other settings. These group members made friends, and maintained relationships fairly independently. They could resolve conflicts as well as endear themselves to others by being helpful and considerate. They were able to share their ideas effectively with others. This was not a universal result, but it was a common enough outcome to be very encouraging about the LEGO® Club process as a therapy approach.

Group members who graduated were not excluded from returning to the group, however. These members often attended on an "at-will" basis, free of charge, as consultants, or Helpers. They were identified by me to the group as such, and often they had a legacy of LEGO projects, and their photos were often on the group's corkboard, so the new group members imbued them with semi-celebrity status. They were often terrific mentors for the newer group members, and were always welcomed with excitement when they chose to come back for a visit. Sometimes, however, the return visit was not a cause for celebration. As is described below, the members were often subjected to changing social contexts (new school, new neighborhood), or changing rules that resulted from the maturation and development of their peer group, and they might find the social complexities of this changed situation a bit too much to handle.

Most of the group members at the Master's level stopped attending for positive reasons, though. Non-attendance of this kind was probably the most common outcome for members who really benefitted from the therapy. Typically, I'd find out that a group member was no longer able to attend consistently because they had other activities that were interfering with their LEGO Club schedule. Their social and adaptive coping skills had improved enough for them to get involved in the school band, or karate classes, or they joined the basketball, soccer or swim team, or Boy Scouts, or a church youth group, etc. Or, often, they just had more friends and wanted to spend more time with them. Some expressed feeling self-conscious about telling their friends that they belonged to this group. While some members naïvely invited their friends to come with them to the group (this happened quite a lot, actually), others had the insight that this was a therapy group, and they felt or clearly understood that they had outgrown it. Whether they slowly stopped attending, or suddenly didn't come back, I would follow up with their parents, and inevitably, it was a pleasant and positive interaction. The parents and the member sometimes felt guilty about not wanting to attend anymore, but I was quickly able to reassure them that this was a maturational achievement.

Some group members left the group, graduated, but then returned years later, and not just for nostalgic reasons. This was common for members who did well in the group and attended for a year or so in elementary school years, but then would run into a whole other set of social complications during puberty and middle school, and they would re-contact us about coming back. Sometimes, the child would have suffered badly at the hands of peers who had previously been accepting and friendly. With growth hormone and testosterone, and the complexities of sexual development and sexualized relationships, there were higher stakes, including more vicious forms of teasing or bullying. Some group members were either badly victimized or had retaliated and were often scapegoated in juvenile court or in school disciplinary actions. Many group members' parents were delighted to find out that the groups were still available to kids in middle and high school age ranges, when the challenges of social coping were so much more complex and subtle.

While I was involved in the slow process of determining whether this social skills therapy approach was having the impact I was hoping it would, the group dynamics changed again, and again this was the result of the group members' initiative, not mine. It was Keith (whose story appears later in the book) who first suggested making a stop-motion animated film using the LEGO® materials. By that point he was a LEGO Master and was attending groups somewhat inconsistently. He was in an advanced studies history class and had been asked to do an informational documentary for his classmates on an historical topic, and he had chosen the NASA Apollo 13 story.

For the class assignment, Keith had done an outline and a storyboard which incorporated images of LEGO sets that were in the LEGO Club collection including the rocket, launch pad and astronaut minifigs. He discussed it with me first, during an individual therapy session, and it seemed like a reasonable project to consider for the group. At the time, he was in the oldest group, teenagers, and they were all ready for a challenge beyond just putting sets together, or building elaborate freestyles. The only worries I had were about the technology involved – the camera and film-editing equipment (this was many years before stop-motion animation computer software was available) – and the time commitment. I hadn't done it before, but I understood the basic concept, and I could imagine that shooting the whole story that Keith had laid out in his outline would take many hours to set up and shoot. I wasn't sure the group members would have the patience and task focus to stay on one large project for that many sessions. Keith was pretty enthusiastic and determined, though. He said he would bring in his own camera and VCR on which he had already been practicing some basic stop-motion, as well as special effects that he had studied from the Star Wars films.

So, I agreed to let Keith pitch his stop-motion film idea to the group, and see if he could convince them all to participate. I had told him that he would need to get the whole group interested in the project, and that he would need to involve them all in the process, not just let them hang out and watch him and a friend or two make a film. I also emphasized that since it was his project, I wouldn't be involved in getting the others to agree to it. The convincing had to be done by Keith. Despite his enthusiasm, Keith had the insight that this was not going to be easy. Not only would the other group members have to agree that it was a worthwhile idea, they would have to participate in hours of fairly tedious and painstakingly detailed work. Keith and I agreed that it would be a good idea to start with having the group members do some simple stop-motion animation sequences to get the feel for it, and then decide whether they felt up to a much bigger project.

The group members turned out to be more receptive to the idea than either Keith or I had expected. One of the girls in the group, Angel, was a big Gumby fan, who had gotten interested when *Gumby the Movie* (1995) had come out, and then she had learned about the original Art Clokey series from the 1950s. Pretty much all the group members had some idea about what Claymation was, from the classic holiday films and the more recent Wallace and Gromit series (*A Grand Day Out* (1990) had been nominated for an Oscar for Best Animated Film). Using LEGO® materials, and minifigs, seemed like an excellent stop-motion material, and we were all quickly piled on top of each other in the LEGO® room with my VHS format camera. We initially set up some flats on a table and had minifigs walk or run through, and then we tried a few vehicles. We also ran the camera over some still scenes to create a "pass-by" effect, which Keith said was used a lot in Star Wars and Star Trek shots. Luckily, the LEGO room at the time had a plush dark blue carpet which was just about ideal for shooting space scenes.

After a couple of sessions of practicing simple stop-motion scenes, the group was not only ready to take on the Apollo 13 project, they were already coming up with some of their own ideas, and were eager to get this done so we could move on. Many of the group members had favorite movie or TV scenes that they wanted to shoot, or do parodies of, using the LEGO-mation techniques we were developing. It took us about four hours of group time to shoot the Apollo 13 sequences, and then a few more hours for Keith and I to edit the video and audio, including the credits and voice-overs, using the VHS camera and two VCRs. The end product was a clumsy but coherent 12-minute stop-motion film that earned Keith an A in his history class, and also sparked a mini-movement and a new level of LEGO Club creativity and collaborative achievement.

This expansion of the range of LEGO Club activities greatly increased the potential complexity and creativity of club member contributions. Participation was no longer limited to the three main set and freestyle building roles of builder, engineer and parts supplier. With the advent of LEGO stop-motion animation, the LEGO set and freestyle building continued – every new film needed a set, or sets, and a cast of characters, which often included innovative creatures, real and imaginary – but to this process was added additional new roles which included the script-writing, story-boarding, voice-acting, stop-motion handlers, cinematographer, director and producer.

In addition to the increased motivation to participate in an exciting and challenging medium, the advantages of including the stop-motion filming also included increasing the age range for participants – many teenagers were hesitant about the idea of participating in a LEGO-building club, but a stop-motion animation club was very attractive to them (even after high school, into their early twenties, many members were hooked on LEGO®-mation). The script-writing component also allowed for inclusion of more complex language-based collaboration and symbolic expression, including the potential for incorporating Social Stories™ (see Gray 1998), which could be developed and implemented as a group (with some guidance from me or the other therapists, of course).

There was also an increased "wow" factor when it came to sharing with parents, siblings and friends what LEGO Club had been able to achieve as a group. Many of the parents and siblings had long ceased to be very impressed with large, complex LEGO creations – the LEGO group members' capacity for sustained focus on repetitive tasks and themes was well known. Even quite astounding feats, such as when one group member built an entire football stadium as a freestyle and peopled it with about 1000 minifigs, could get not much more than a supportive nod from parents who were getting used to this sort of ambitious undertaking. Now, when that football stadium and its minifig crowd were used to film a stop-motion music video, and the crowd did "the wave" to Queen's "We Will Rock You," there was definitely a more enthusiastic response.

The inter-group awareness was also raised to a new level. By the time we started incorporating LEGO-mation as a regular LEGO Club activity, there were nine groups per week using the same LEGO room and materials, including the camera, editing equipment and, eventually, computer and big screen. In addition to catching up on their own last week's footage, in the process of deciding what to do on that day, the group members often wanted to see what the other groups had been working on. They often saw their sets and characters, often with painted or written signs, etc., and they were interested. Sometimes, they even copied from or modeled their own versions of a theme that had been created by another group after watching their videos. The members of one group might try to compete with another group on a particular theme using the new film-based character sets, like Star Wars, Spider-Man, Batman, Indiana Jones, SpongeBob, Thomas the Tank Engine and Harry Potter, or other LEGO action themes that were easily translated into stop-motion animation, such as basketball, skateboarding, soccer, Extreme Team, Pirates, Old West, etc.

Some of the group members also came up with their own original cast of characters and storylines that were used in a series of films like a weekly TV show. For a while we had a "Stuntman Bif" TV-style show with a stuntman who did impossible and invariably disastrous stunts. There was an action-news segment, with "Cindy Brickberg," a hapless news anchor who was also crushed, eaten, burned, blown up or run over in her on-the-scenes news coverage. There was a quiz show, called "Try Not to Die," in which contestants answered scientific questions in order to avoid being killed by a laser beam or bomb. The most popular of the original short animated film series was one that started as an exercise. One group member, Charlie, had chosen a crocodile and a "swordfish" (actually, a saw shark), more or less at random from the creature drawer, and he set them on a blue background to practice moving them around using stop-motion.

Over time, Charlie incorporated other objects, and then started doing simple voice-overs, with slapstick-style interactions. Charlie stayed with this simple pair of characters and began to get more and more elaborate with the storylines he created and then animated, resulting in what became known as the "Crocy and Swordy Show." Episodes of "Crocy and Swordy" were extremely popular with all the groups, and Charlie himself became somewhat of a celebrity among the group members. Along with Allen (see below), who became the well-recognized and highly sought-after voice of Cindy Brickberg, Charlie's straightforward, sincere and unaltered voice-overs of Crocy and Swordy stirred up the curiosity and admiration of the other groups.

Eventually, there was a LEGO® Club staff (other therapists and a media or IT consultant), and a cohort of technically proficient parents, who helped us put together a LEGO Club Film Festival. It was about 90 minutes of short animated films (two minutes to ten minutes in length), featuring many of the Club's own mini-celebrities. The technical innovations at that point included computer-animated special effects (lasers, fireballs and explosions, mostly), careful editing of sound and the usual sort of stop-motion video glitches (heads and hands in the shot). The crowd that attended the Film Festival included so many members, parents, grandparents, siblings and friends that the large therapy room used for LEGO® Club didn't even come close to accommodating them all. Before the Film Festival had even started, there were festival fans waiting all the way down the hallway, so we quickly moved the venue to the building lobby and set up the chairs and equipment out there. The fans were very patient, and most of them carried their own chairs out to the lobby.

Six months later, at the second LEGO Film Festival, there were approximately twice as many attendees as the first, over 200. The event was also covered by both a Philadelphia newspaper and a local television station. Standing at the back of the hall, being interviewed by a couple of newspaper journalists and a TV crew, while Charlie and Allen were down front signing autographs, it was very clear to me that LEGO Club had become more than just a couple of kids in a room putting bricks together. It was especially gratifying to me that the attention and well-deserved accolades were not reserved for the highest functioning (highest IQs) of the groups. Many of the new LEGO Club animation stars were kids with significant language impairment and clearly apparent autistic behavioral rigidity and stereotypies (see Colin's story below). There was a certain "diagnosis blindness" that permeated the creative process in the rooms, which often did not even make it out to the waiting room – parents were sometimes alarmed, put-off or skeptical about the groups when they met or observed children whose autistic features were more apparent than those of their own children. Many of these parents were the first, however, to praise the more classically autistic participants' LEGO-mation creations. Of course, the parents of those classically autistic kids, like Colin's father, Fred, couldn't have been more proud.

# JONATHAN

## INITIAL CONTACT

I first met Jonathan at the Queen's Medical Center in Honolulu, when he was 11 years old and I was still completing my post-doctoral training there at an outpatient mental health clinic. He was referred by his grandmother, at the recommendation of his school counselor. Jonathan had recently been displaying some significant behavioral problems, and he had a family history of mental health problems. He lived with his mother and grandmother, both of whom had been diagnosed with schizophrenia and were on long-term disability. Jonathan's mother, Tamoko ("Tami"), had also been diagnosed with Mild Mental Retardation, and Jonathan's guardian of record was his grandmother, although he also had a guardian assigned by the state. Jonathan was reported to be having difficulties with peers, and had been truanting from school, but he was not a typical behavior-problem student. In addition to missing school, Jonathan had been caught behaving inappropriately at a public beach, and was reported by school staff to have unusual interests (soap operas, family genealogies).

As noted above, his mother and grandmother were both disabled, Jonathan's grandfather was deceased, and Jonathan's father was no longer involved with the family. He was reported to have been quite a few years older than Jonathan's mother, and with not much of a relationship with her.

---

I will quote Jonathan and his grandmother just as they typically spoke to me, which was in "Pidgin," sometimes called "local," which is technically Hawaiian Creole English.

---

"Jonathan's father just one neighbor," his grandmother explained. "He come around whenevers and drink beer." Jonathan had a younger brother from this same father who was reported to be doing fairly well at school and had friends. After the second child, though, Jonathan's grandmother discouraged the relationship. "He didn't do nothing for the keikis. He just come by for da kine, my daughter. I knowed what he want. Same kine every time. Kissy, kissy, on the couch. Never bring no food, no money. Just beer. I told him no more come around our house."

Jonathan's mother attended a state-run day program for adults dually diagnosed with psychiatric and developmental disabilities, and she was not much involved with her children's upbringing. This was left to their grandmother. In addition to having been diagnosed with paranoid schizophrenia, Jonathan's grandmother was functionally disabled by obesity and arthritis. She was wheelchair bound, and used public handicapped-accessible transportation to bring Jonathan to the clinic. She typically brought her daughter and Jonathan's brother with her when they came. She sometimes complained to the staff at the clinic about having to come to the hospital with Jonathan to see me, and asked if I could do home visits, like the social worker. She was also upset with the school district for fussing about the boys' attendance record, and for asking personal questions about the family situation. The school district had initiated a referral of the family to a state social services agency, and a social worker had been assigned to monitor Jonathan and his brother's school attendance, and Jonathan's progress in therapy.

Jonathan's grandmother was well aware of the potential consequences of not attending sessions with me – social services visits, and discussion of custody and guardianship – so she grumbled to the staff but said nothing to me about her concerns. When we did talk about her ability to handle Jonathan and his brother, and cope with her daughter's needs, she was a bit defensive, quickly pointing out that Jonathan's mother was in a day program down the street, and that his brother was doing well. "No problem, that one. Just Jonathan. But he be alright, too." She was angry at Jonathan for misbehaving at school and for inappropriate behavior in public – he had been caught masturbating while watching young surfers in the showers at the beach – bringing them up on the radar for the local social services agency. "He bring shame on us doing all that."

At the same time, when Jonathan missed school, he was typically at home with her, watching soap operas. He helped out around the house, and took his grandmother down to the corner store in her wheelchair to buy groceries and the latest *Soap Opera Digest*. They also watched hula performances and kept track of hula competitions and events, and professional wrestling. Grandma had been a hula dancer and instructor at one time, and was teaching Jonathan hula. She wanted him to get private lessons, but they couldn't afford it. The school also offered hula, which Jonathan attended, although he was one of the few boys who did. Most of the boys preferred ukulele lessons, and they could be seen and heard practicing on their way to and from school. The professional wrestling interest was more age and gender typical, and I asked Grandma if they watched wrestling together. They did, she said – in fact, the whole family watched wrestling together and were avid fans of their favorite wrestlers. Grandma did not seem to understand, or care, that soap operas and professional wrestling were both staged drama. She spoke of them with grave seriousness and unfeigned emotion, as if they were real people, not actors portraying characters.

My initial work with Jonathan was focused on clarifying his diagnosis, and the underlying source or causes of his atypical behavior. A previous psychiatric assessment had indicated a likely diagnosis of Schizophreniform Disorder (an early stage of possible schizophrenia), as well as Oppositional Defiant Disorder. From the outset, it was clear that a major factor in Jonathan's presenting problems was lack of socialization opportunities and appropriate role models. His teacher reported that he did not interact much with the other boys at school, and his grandmother kept him in the apartment at home, worried that he would get into more trouble if left on his own. During recess, he often asked to stay in, and he talked with his teacher about soap operas, or about a family tree he was working on. He also asked about her clothing and shoes, where she'd bought them, etc. If he did go out with the other children, he tended to wander around by himself, or interacted briefly with the girls.

Jonathan was noted by school staff to be physically under-developed and awkward, or clumsy. His walking gait was unaffected, but he did not run easily at all, and could not ride a bicycle or two-wheeled scooter, which were popular ways of getting around for most of the boys his age. He did not do well in PE, and often asked to be excused from it, feigning physical symptoms when it came to more demanding physical challenges like baseball, basketball or soccer. He wouldn't even try flag football, even though some of the girls played. He did not bring sneakers or runners or a change of clothing to school, as had been asked, but typically wore flip-flops, or "slippahs," as his primary footwear for all occasions. His IEP included physical and occupational therapy, and his therapists had reported that he exhibited low muscle tone (hypotonia), and poor motor planning or dyspraxia. His personal grooming was marginal, and typically his hair was clean but uncombed, and stood up at odd angles from his head.

During my assessment of Jonathan, he was very quiet, did not ask questions, and often did not respond to questions or to test items, but just looked around the room as if I weren't there. When he did respond, his answers were tangential, off-topic, and I had to repeat or clarify them. I tried an experiment with him, getting him to look at some Thematic Apperception cards. The Thematic Apperception Test (TAT; Murray 1943) is a projective test, in which subjects are shown black and white drawings which depict intense social and emotional situations which pull for certain responses which are supposed to be indicative of underlying, sometimes unconscious motivations. They are asked structured questions such as "What is the person thinking or feeling in the picture?" Jonathan refused the "projective" aspect of the task. He said he could not imagine what another person could be thinking or feeling, especially since these were just pictures, and black and white at that.

I asked him about the soap operas that he and his grandmother watched. He excitedly told me about "General Hospital," "Days of Our Lives," and "Young and Restless." He said he did not pay attention to the characters' thoughts and feelings, though. He just followed the plots' "comings and goings," especially with regard to the genealogies of the characters and their life events. He made notes about the histories of characters, current and past, and drew genealogical charts of them. He had a similar system for keeping track of the professional wrestlers' matches, wins and losses, and upcoming bouts. Unlike his grandmother, Jonathan did not seem invested in the soaps and wrestling in an emotional way, but he seemed to understand that the characters were important, and that he should keep track of them.

During my initial contacts with Jonathan, he often made excuses to leave the room, to use the bathroom or get something from Grandma, and then he would just stay in the waiting room, looking at the fish tank, or dancing hula with Grandma watching and coaching him, until I came to get him. I did eventually discover that Jonathan's mental illness did not seem to fit the pattern of a psychotic disorder like schizophrenia. He clearly had some gender identity issues, which could have been related to his family situation and lack of male role models, but then his younger brother was not interested in soap operas or hula, and preferred to watch professional wrestling. The behaviors that on the surface appeared to be psychotic were actually just atypical, and he had a social indifference and awkwardness that made him stand out from peers.

Jonathan scored much higher on standard ratings of Asperger's Disorder. He had lifelong difficulties with social interaction, including a flat, monotone prosody and nasal voice tone, minimal eye contact, and an inability to sustain a back-and-forth conversation unless it was on one of his obsessive, idiosyncratic interests, which he would go on about, regardless of his audience or the social context. His grandmother's presentation and demeanor were also generally socially inappropriate, and she denied any history of hallucinations, delusions or other psychotic features. She also admitted that her interest in soap operas was excessive, and included collecting magazines and other memorabilia, and keeping her own diary of the shows, and researching past histories of characters and plot lines to the beginning of each soap that she watched. In other words, Jonathan and his grandmother's behavior wasn't necessarily bizarre, but it was oddly excessive, rigid and repetitive, indifferent to social norms, and lacking social intentions. I had few opportunities to speak with Jonathan's mother, but I also suspected that she might have been autistic rather than schizophrenic, likely suffering from a more severe form of autism than what Jonathan was exhibiting.

In truth, Jonathan's grandmother probably would not have been bringing him to see me if she had not been compelled by social services, but she did seem to care about him, and she had some insight that he was not developing in a typical way. She blamed her daughter for having had an affair with a much older man, and she was judgmental about her daughter's mental status – though she never mentioned her own issues. She seemed pleased that I was getting along with Jonathan, and Jonathan was showing more interest in coming here, and one day she asked to speak with me alone. She brought up the issue about Jonathan and the surfers; it turned out that this had not been an isolated incident, and Jonathan had been teased and bullied mercilessly as a result of his preoccupation with teenaged males. I didn't mention soap operas or hula dancing, but Grandma seemed to get the general idea that there may be some gender identity issues, and was hoping that I would address this with Jonathan and encourage more gender typical interests.

Although I had to tell Grandma that changing Jonathan's sexual object choice, or his gender identity, was not within the scope of my mandate as a therapist, it did make sense to try to encourage some more typical interests for the sake of improving his social adjustment. I encouraged her to consider enrolling Jonathan in a martial arts class, which was a popular activity for boys in their area. There was also surfing, scooter and skateboard riding, and football, but based on the family's limited resources, and Jonathan's limited physical coordination and interests, these were probably a bit out of his range, at least for now. At the same time, I shifted my work with Jonathan away from counseling about his life situation and problems with peers, and towards a more activity-based intervention, with a focus on using the activities to encourage adopting more appropriate social behavior. We focused initially on playing chess together – which became interesting to Jonathan only after we started making soap opera storylines based on the interactions of the chess pieces. I told the story of the board and the action of the players in dramatic soap opera terms, and Jonathan was delighted, focused and animated: "The King is lame. He has the gout, and so he moves slow, but his wife, the Queen, is a dancer, and powerful. She dances all over the board, sometimes she flirts with the knights, then she says, 'Off with his head!' and the knight obey her. The knights protect the King, because he is lame, and he is wise and religious – he consults with the bishops. He is the leader, but the others know the Queen is more powerful, and much more beautiful. The pawns are sent off to war. They are slow but steady soldiers who march ahead, grumbling, but steady."

Jonathan picked up his queen and kissed her. Then he moved a pawn, "Go pawn. Go to your death," and he laughed in a sinister way. We played chess this way for a couple of sessions, and Jonathan seemed to enjoy it. For the first time, he asked me questions about the players, about their motives and their feelings. "Why do the pawns gotta stay two-step, one-step like that? Why do they follow the rules? Why not just run up and down and attack?" I said, "Well, I guess that's like life, Jonathan. We all have feelings, and dreams, but there are also rules that we have to follow."

"Never mind," Jonathan said. "Can we play without the rules?"

I said, "I guess, but it won't be a very fun game. Playing by the rules makes it a game, otherwise, it's just messing around, not very interesting."

"Kay den, you play by the rules. I'm goin' make up my own moves," and he attacked my pieces with his pawn using professional wrestling moves, knocking my pieces off the board. "Body slam! Flying take down from top rope!" Then he knocked down his own, and pushed them off the table to the floor. He danced the pawn on the board, kicking at the strewn players. "Now, I'm the King! Get off you. Get off my mountain. Hah!" Then he sat and looked at the board. He laughed. "Wah! I'm sad. I killed all my friends! This is no more fun."

The next week, Jonathan arrived with a pile of papers stuffed in a paper shopping bag. He had written down names of characters and plot progressions on sheets of paper, and had cut them out. He said he wanted to borrow a large sheet of drawing paper and put all the pieces up to make a big collage, a family tree of "Days of Our Lives." I agreed to get him a large sheet of paper from the front desk. When I came back to my office, I didn't see Jonathan. I poked my head in the door and called him, and out of the corner of my eye I caught a glimpse of movement. I jumped back. Jonathan had stripped, and was standing behind the door waiting for me to come in. He lunged at me, naked, trying to embrace me. I took a step back out of his reach, and held my hand up in his face. "Jonathan! Stop!" He turned away and looked down.

"Jonathan, I'm going to wait in the hall while you get dressed. When you're dressed we should talk about this."

"I don't want to talk." He was dressing himself quickly – he had put his clothes, neatly folded, in the paper bag he had brought. I stood outside the door and waited for him. The chief of social work walked by, a big, cheerful man. "What's up Doc? Lock yourself out?" He looked into the office as he went by and saw Jonathan getting dressed, and he laughed his great big Santa Claus laugh: "Hoo boy! I can't wait to hear this one!"

When Jonathan was dressed, I came in and he sat down, looking at the floor. "Jonathan," I said, "I'm not angry, but you know that was wrong. You can't take your clothes off here." He agreed, and asked if he was going to be in trouble. I said no, but he wasn't to do anything like that again. I told him it was alright to talk about feelings here, even to act them out with toys, but we didn't act out our feelings by getting aggressive, or sexual, for real. We talked about what he had learned about these things at school, and how he felt that here was different, where the rules were more flexible. "Well, yeah," I said, "but we still have rules. And that's one of them, you have to leave your clothes on." Jonathan and I talked about his understanding about sexual relationships, and I made sure he was aware that he was too young for those experiences with other people. I also checked to see if he had any experiences like that with anyone else, which he had not.

We talked more about the rules and therapy, and our relationship, and he seemed relieved that we were talking and I wasn't sending him to the waiting room to meet with his grandmother. We got over it, and I felt like I had a better understanding of Jonathan. I tried talking to Grandma about maybe limiting the soap operas since they might be a little over-stimulating for Jonathan, but she misunderstood. She thought I was recommending a punishment for some reason. "What he do now? I told him!" I backed off a bit, and said, "No, he's not in trouble at all. I just thought, maybe he should mix it up a bit, watch something other than soap operas once in a while." Grandma smiled. "Huh. Like some hula! No mo' wrestling. That give him ideas, and he fights with his brother."

---

Around that time, I graduated from my post-doctoral fellowship, and was invited to share office space with a local child psychiatrist who had a busy practice. I took over a large room that had been a legal library, and converted it into a playroom. I set up areas for reading, drawing and painting, bags of dress-up clothes and masks, water play, a sand-tray table with small figures and vehicles, animals and furniture, a puppet theater and puppets, modeling clay, and a corner for LEGO® building. There were small tables and chairs, big foam cushions, and beanbag chairs. At the time, I was reading everything I could about therapy with children, on interpreting drawings, and sand play, Stanley Greenspan's Floortime, and expressive therapies, creating a holding environment, noticing and reflecting back anything they brought up about me, or about their parents, being neutral and accepting, following their lead in play themes, joining them and allowing them to direct me and observing and commenting about the emotions and relationships emerging in the play.

Unfortunately, many of the children I was working with did not exhibit much imaginative play. They treated the figures as objects, and just sorted them, or lined them up. Jonathan's version of that was more elaborate – arranging and re-arranging soap opera characters – but it was the same mode of play in a way. There was nothing emotional or dynamic about it. Just a reflection of a system he had come to know and felt comfortable with. During our chess games, Jonathan had started to be more expressive, but even then, he was not acting out anything emotional or social. He was just commenting on the social context of the game, in a way that I had started doing. It didn't seem very productive, although he did seem more animated and engaged at least, and was willing to come and see me.

Jonathan did not show that much affinity for LEGO®, at least not initially. He seemed bored, and was willing to participate with me in building sets or some basic freestyle creating, but he was always more animated about spending time talking about soap operas. One day I suggested we try building a LEGO film studio, and try to recreate one of the sets from a soap opera, including some of the characters. By then, I had a fairly large freestyle LEGO collection, including a large drawer of LEGO minifigs, and suddenly, Jonathan was much more animated and engaged. He quickly dug around in the minifig drawer, and mixing bodies, heads, hair and head-gear, he came up with a collection of characters from his favorite soap, "General Hospital." He identified them for me, heroes and heroines, and villains, and asked me to help him create a couple of scenes for him. He wasn't able to give me much of a description of the sets he wanted, but we kept at it, and eventually agreed to try having Jonathan draw some floorplans. Jonathan was very fussy about the layout and the details of the sets, including props, and looked closely at the sets from all angles to make sure they looked right.

Over the next few sessions, Jonathan and I worked on building the "General Hospital" sets, and he was eager to come in and work on it, and he did not leave the room as he typically did. In fact, he was adamant about staying longer than our one hour sessions, and wanted to bring the sets out to show his grandmother when they were done. He included cameras, lighting, a film crew, stage hands and a director. He had recreated two specific scenes, and wanted to show his grandmother, and remind her about the scenes, and the importance of the scenes with regard to the plot line. Jonathan was breathless with excitement when we brought the scenes out to show her, and Grandma was suitably impressed. "What you got there? Oh, very fine. Yes, yes, I see. I remember that one!"

Jonathan showed his brother, Sam, who said "LEGO®, cool!" and tried to touch the set, but Jonathan pulled it away. He took one of the scenes over to show the receptionist at the desk, and she was also very supportive and encouraging about it. Jonathan said, "It's just like 'General Hospital'…look, look," and he explained all the characters, etc. "Next week, I'm going to do 'Days of Our Lives'! You wait and see. You will love it." Jonathan stood in the middle of the waiting area admiring the LEGO creation, with his brother peering around his elbows and getting rebuffed. Then his grandmother told him it was time to go. He went to leave with the LEGO, and I suggested that it would probably be safer if he left it here with me. "Okay, Dr. Dan. But put it on a shelf, up high. I don't want anyone messing with it." At the time, I recall thinking this was progress in a way; at least he was showing some pride in something he had accomplished, and wanted to share this accomplishment with others. On the other hand, his response to his younger brother was a concern. He showed no empathy in his response to his interest, no willingness to share the excitement with him, and no awareness of his role in this relationship as the older brother.

## LEARNING THROUGH LEGO

The following week, Jonathan and I did work on a set from "Days of Our Lives." He had brought a floor plan with him, with a list of characters, and a written plot excerpt from the series. He was excited to get going, and came breezing into my office, dropped the papers on my desk, checked on his "General Hospital" set, which was intact, and went straight to the LEGO® corner and started digging around in the "people drawer." I said, "Hi, Jonathan."

He said, "What? You got another hair like this? With the ponytail?" He went back to digging while holding up the piece for me to see.

"Jonathan, I said hi."

"Oh, yeah. Well, hi. Do you? Got another one like this? Brown, not black." Digging, searching. "I'm pretty sure I saw one here last week, unless you used it. Did you use any hair?" He started looking up on the shelves where there were other LEGO creations, and immediately found the hair piece he was looking for, brown with a pony tail. He took the minifig, pulled off the hair, and tossed the minifig back on the shelf. "Great." He sighed with relief and turned back to the people drawer.

"Jonathan."

"Mmm?" Digging and searching.

"Jonathan, can I have your attention for a sec?"

Jonathan didn't look up. "What? Dr. Dan, I need your help. I need to make…"

"Look at me." I smiled and tried to look patient. "Don't we usually talk a bit when you come in? You tell me about your week, we talk about school, and soap operas. You know, talk."

Jonathan sighed loudly, and sat down. "You mean talk story? You like my grandma and my teacher, you all want to talk story."

---

Talk story is a tradition in local culture in the islands. It is a part of daily life that can be a bother to mainlanders who just want to get through the check-out line at the grocery store, or the bank, or the post-office. To the locals, however, it is an important and necessary part of the joy of island life – sharing experiences and ideas with your family, and neighbors, who are often treated like family. Being in too much of a hurry to have time for talking story is a mainlander problem, a sign that they have not accepted the concept of "Hawaiian time" – events happen when they happen, not always according to clocks and schedules, and people and their lives are more important than clocks and schedules.

---

"Okay, sorry, Jonathan, but that is pretty normal. When people haven't seen each other for a while, they say hi, and they talk story for a bit. Did anything happen this week? Anything you want to talk about?"

Jonathan thought about it, then said, "Grandma gave Stephen a lickin'." Then he laughed, a stilted, forced laugh. "He ask to come play LEGO®s, and Grandma told him no, he had to stay wait. He sassed her, and say he bored, no want to come if no play LEGO. She licked him and he cried. Ha!" He turned away and started rummaging through the people drawer again.

---

This was getting complicated. Although it was positive that Jonathan was identifying and describing a relevant social event, he was again devoid of empathy for this brother, and seemed to be enjoying his pain and misery. I understood Stephen's point of view entirely, without having had that much contact with him. He had to come to the clinic every week so that his brother could get adult attention and play, while he had to be dragged away from whatever he was doing at home, to do his homework in the waiting room. He was not interested in soap operas, but had to watch them on the TV with his brother and grandmother. I could only imagine what life was like for him at home, with his disabled mother and grandmother, and aloof, odd older brother. Jonathan seemed to have no awareness of how his behavior could be contributing to his brother's misery.

Making the situation more complicated, Jonathan had just told me that his grandmother hit Stephen, probably spanked him. Physical punishment from parents was a significant cultural conflict in Hawaii at the time. Local parents "gave lickins," even though they understood that this was not acceptable to many mainlanders and to the teachers, social workers and doctors who tried to interfere with their parenting styles. The family system, the ohana, is at the core of local culture, and this family was on thin ice with the child and family services agency. Jonathan and Stephen could easily wind up in foster care, which would have been devastating to his grandmother and mother, and likely lead to significant complications for Jonathan and Stephen as well – the foster system was overburdened, and there was a long history of negative attitudes towards social services' intrusion into the lives of the locals. So, there were two goals that were very apparent in this situation: first, changing the parenting strategies and helping Grandma to be more effective with Jonathan and Stephen so that she did not feel the need to resort to physical punishment; and second, improving Jonathan's capacity for empathy and understanding another person's point of view.

Jonathan and I spent the rest of that session working on being more aware of other people's perspectives, needs and feelings, starting with the idea of having to share the LEGO® materials with other clients whom Jonathan had not met. I asked Jonathan to put the LEGO hair piece he wanted back on the minifig and put it back with the set on the shelf. It had not occurred to him that the set was someone else's creation, and, just like he didn't want anyone messing with his creations, he should respect theirs, even if they had pieces he wanted. When I pointed this out, it seemed like it was occurring to him for the first time, though I thought he surely must have known the creations were made by children similar to him. He looked at the shelves for a while, and then he said, "So other keiki built them? Not you?"

"No, Jonathan. I didn't build them," I said, and laughed.

"Oh, I thought these was yours. So who else coming here? Do I know them?"

After that insight, Jonathan was more willing to compromise on the hair piece, and in the end, he was fairly happy with his "Days of Our Lives" creation. He was excited to bring the set out to the waiting room to show his grandmother, and I reminded him to share with his brother as well. When we came out, Grandma was talking story with the receptionist, and Stephen was sitting with another client of mine, Keith, watching him play "Pokemon Red" on a Gameboy®. Jonathan seemed to be stalled there for a second, not sure who to approach, then he went over to his brother and the other boy, and showed them his set. He got a mild response from Stephen, but more enthusiastic praise from Keith. He didn't seem to know much about soap operas, but he liked the idea of re-creating a TV show scene, especially one that involved weapons and a murder plot. Keith showed Jonathan a "Star Wars" set that he had built and brought from home. Keith said he wanted to freestyle some scenes from "Star Wars" and from "Dragon Ball Z," a Japanese anime cartoon. Both Stephen and Jonathan seemed impressed, and Keith seemed happy to have an appreciative audience. Keith, Jonathan and Stephen talked about LEGO®, "Pokemon" and anime, and Star Wars for a while, while their parents waited. Lisa eventually came over, cheerfully greeted Grandma, and told Keith it was his appointment time. (Also see Keith's story, later in the book.)

When I met with Jonathan and his grandmother, mother and Stephen, the atmosphere was tense. Grandma especially seemed tense and defensive, and bossy with her daughter and the boys. I had heard her earlier from down the hall, talking to the receptionist about the family meeting in a low, grumbly voice, anxious. I worked towards building an alliance with her initially, being deferential and acknowledging her many contributions to the family. She seemed pleased to have her responsibilities acknowledged. Eventually we got around to talking about the family's challenges, her daughter's mental illness and Jonathan's, her disability, the tenuous situation with social services, their relative lack of extended family support, and the lack of male role models in the family. Grandma opened up the discussion about physical punishment on her own: "When my husband was here, he would not put up with this kine behavior. He would, oh!" She swung her hand. "Do it or else!"

We also talked about the demands the boys and their mother put on her, asking for help at home and wanting things from her, things she could rarely afford on her disability income. I got the boys and their mother to chime in on this topic, and we agreed that although the family had limited resources, their best strategy was to cooperate and pitch in together, and all reap the benefits. They were all willing to consider working out a home-based economy system where positive contributions – doing chores, homework, staying out of trouble, following directions and listening – could be rewarded with simple and inexpensive rewards (snacks, toys, outings, TV time, or small amounts of money). Likewise, not listening or following rules and direction from Grandma could result in costs or deductions from these rewards. I wrote the basics of a home-based economy and behavior contract down, and we all agreed to sign it, and abide by it. I asked them to agree to follow it for at least the coming week, and if they wanted any changes, that we could discuss that next week.

After the family session, I had a talk privately with Grandma about what Jonathan had told me about "lickins." I reassured her that I was aware of the cultural differences regarding physical punishment, and I did not consider her spanking Jonathan or Stephen grounds to contact social services, but I also told her I didn't think it was a very effective parenting strategy. I emphasized that what we had discussed today, in terms of settings rules, rewarding compliance and helpfulness, and using restrictions or delays in the availability of rewards (using terms she understood and could identify with), was a better strategy. We talked about needing to stay ahead of predictable situations, and not wait until she was caught in public or in a rush to get somewhere, before having to deal with a non-compliance situation by yelling, threatening or spanking. Grandma had been very patient with me, and she sighed. "You got kids, Doc? Yeah, I know you do, and you no give 'em lickins? 'K den. I gon' give it one try. Pay them for being good. Like you say, not a bribe, a reward. I gon' give it one try and see." I supported her in that, again acknowledged how brave she was in taking on the head of the household and maintaining the ohana despite all the odds, including not having transportation. "'K den," Grandma said, "I appreciate that. Now if you would share this with the social worker lady, please! Mahalo! If I have to hear one more time about she going take the kids, oh!" She wiped a tear from her eyes with the sleeve of her muu-muu. "Ah! I can't even talk about that." I gave her a hug and took her out to the waiting room.

The next week, before I'd had a chance to arrange a therapy group for some of my pre-teen male clients, Jonathan and his family came for his session loaded with positive news about their family contract. Grandma was making it work, offering rewards and incentives to her daughter and the boys (snacks, movies, special meal requests, spare change, etc.), and withholding them, or delaying them, contingent on the completion of chores, homework and activities of daily living (ADLs). "Alright, I not going smack 'em, but if no ready for school, shower, backpack, the whole nine yard, I keep the Rice Krispy treat out. I keep it. They can have when they get home and do they homework, they chores." She had shared what she was doing at home with the school counselor, who had also apprised the family's social worker. All were pleased with the results, except Jonathan.

According to Grandma, Jonathan was unhappy because his brother Stephen had adapted to the system very quickly, and now was being rewarded consistently, and even setting up deals with his grandmother for additional, bigger rewards. He wanted a snorkeling mask and fins, and was willing to forgo his allowance and other rewards in order to more quickly earn it. Grandma was delighted: "I don't care if he want me buy him new surfboard. He keep it up, I goin' buy him whatevers, what we can afford." For Jonathan, it was more of a struggle. Initially, he liked the idea – I had suggested to Grandma that she start out the system being rather generous, in order to get the boys and their mother to commit to it more readily – and was pleased to be rewarded for getting ready for school on time, doing his homework, helping his brother with his homework, etc. But within a few days, it started to feel more routine to him, and he didn't want to comply when Grandma withheld the rewards. He didn't want to accept her authority. "She not my boss. I don't need one boss."

We talked about Jonathan's respecting his grandmother, about her efforts to keep the family together and use their limited resources efficiently. Jonathan saw this as an opportunity to negotiate: "I can just leave. You know, I don't have to do this, and what she going do? I run away, and they going give me a new family. One with the big TV and all da kine." He resented his brother's success at this new system, and didn't see it as fair that his brother was more often rewarded. "He gets everything! And more." Stephen had even tried talking to Jonathan about the need to help out, to keep the family together, but Jonathan did not see the value of the family unit. Ohana was still just a word to him, or worse, a social system that put expectations and restrictions on him. Without that value, Jonathan did not experience the benefit of being a part of the family, let alone accept his role as the big brother, a role model and a positive influence for Stephen and his mother. Underlying his lack of respect for his grandmother, and his lack of empathy for his brother, was the absence of a sense of value attached to being part of a social system, being a social person. In order for him to eventually get that, we were going to have to extend the range of positive social experiences, and the value to him of those experiences, but the family system was maxed out. So, I offered to make a deal with Grandma.

By this point, I had started the small group with Aaron, Sam and Evan, and I had allocated a budget for LEGO® purchases. As the available LEGO materials grew, the LEGO fan base grew, and they became more involved with the LEGO system – we had new

142

catalogues and copies of the *LEGO® Mania* magazine in the waiting and playrooms. Jonathan expressed an interest in sets other than the freestyle soap opera creations he had been working on, and he knew already that Grandma could not afford most of the sets he was asking for. I had arranged to put aside a number of LEGO sets of varying themes and sizes as rewards for my growing group of LEGO kids, and Jonathan was one of the first to notice this. He was especially intrigued by a set with Robin Hood figures. I discussed with Jonathan and his grandmother the option of setting up a reward system (token economy), so that Jonathan could earn points towards getting LEGO sets from the clinic.

They were both excited about the idea, so it was just a matter of working out the details, and following through with it week after week. In this way, the issues at home were fairly well resolved. Grandma gave me an account of Jonathan's behavior each week, and we tallied up his points, discussed his goals, and the LEGO sets he was potentially able to earn. Jonathan was well motivated by this system for a few months. After a while, though, he seemed to have enough LEGO at home, and had enough access to LEGO through the group, that he was less interested, but he kept up with positive behavior at home, which he acknowledged with a shrug, and he seemed to have accepted his grandmother's authority at home, and the less concrete benefits of being a family member.

---

I subsequently used a similar strategy with a number of clients whose families were struggling to come up with consistent "motivators," in reward-based token economy or positive reinforcement systems at home. Many of them had histories of domestic violence – often carrying forward with problems of aggression, disruptive behavior and property destruction in the kids themselves – where clearly the family support network and parenting strategies were just not working. Some of these children had problems which were clearly autistic, while others would have been diagnosed with Oppositional Defiant Disorder or Conduct Disorder. For the most part, though, there was a common ground of miscommunication and a breakdown of the social contract inherent in family units. Parents who had themselves grown up in families in which respect for parents was an unspoken rule, and violation of that rule was quickly and forcefully responded to with threats or actual physical punishment, seemed lost without this as a fallback position.

The change, at least in the immediate social environment of my practice at the time, had happened very quickly – one generation. Luckily, many of these parents appreciated the opportunity to discuss openly the lack of options they faced in trying to influence their wayward children. The option of using financial or other incentives seemed reasonable to them – the carrot rather than the stick – except in some instances in which the parents resented having to concede that they were no longer allowed to threaten or intimidate their children. Most of these parents, after some convincing, were able to understand that there had been a sudden change in societal attitudes about parenting, and that focusing on the positive was in the end a more effective form of influence. This was especially the case for many fathers of clients with autism/Asperger's who were mystified by their sons' difficulties with social situations, including sports, school dances, family functions and making friends.

Many parents, especially fathers, seemed to resent having to change their parenting strategies to accommodate their child's needs. "I'm not going to pay my kid to do the right thing... Why do I have to bribe him to just do what he's supposed to?" The difficulty, as I saw it, was that the child was no longer adequately influenced by the underlying fabric of the family unit. Many of them had experienced so much disapproval and failure during opportunities for positive feedback – sports, social relationships, academics – that they no longer cared about disapproval. They expected it. I called it the "black hat syndrome." These kids put on the black hat – the bad guy identity – when they got up in the morning, and accepted the role offered them by their parents, their teachers and coaches, and their peers. They were the trouble-makers. The ones out of step, late, out of bounds, called last, valued least, picked on and teased or excluded, or feared, vilified, challenged and punished. It seemed to be a form of learned helplessness, but even more negative. They hadn't given up trying to escape a painful situation – they had identified with it and, in so doing, elicited the punishment and pain willingly.

This was another important piece of the puzzle for my understanding of clients like Jonathan. Somehow we needed to reverse the course of a negative identity formation, not just add social skills. Time after time, I was confronted by behavior that went beyond a skill deficit – it was overtly negative, destructive and provocative. For most of the clients I was working with, by the time I got to see them, they were well along the "black hat" path. Not only did they not care what their parents, siblings, teachers or peers thought of them, they were also tired of feeling helpless and frustrated in social situations. They were no longer feeling inferior when compared with siblings and peers at home and at school, and they had stopped trying to compete – in fact, they had stopped trying to participate altogether. Once they had decided on wearing the black hat, they were free from the rules and values that applied to the "white hat" crowd. Being a good son or daughter, being a good student, being a good teammate – none of that applied anymore. They were now focused on self-interest, getting what they wanted, willing to accept the consequences of criticism and rejection because these consequences no longer carried any meaning.

So there was this layer of resistance and self-sabotaging that was both functional – it worked in most situations – and ego-syntonic. There was no conflict about it, no cognitive dissonance. Over the years so many of these clients' parents brought them in, exasperated and deeply angry at them, completely unaware that their anger and disapproval was just making them worse, pushing them further along the path. At least for the client, they were able to feel some sense of power and control when they elicited predictable negative reactions in the adults and peers in their world. I often compared it with flicking light switches. Why would a child bother flicking a light switch on and off? Or push all the buttons on the elevator, or make the windows go up and down in the car, or mess with the radio and the heater/AC controls? They are sources of control. They make predictable events happen. It didn't matter that the room was light or dark, or that their parents or teachers were annoyed or happy – what mattered was that they made it happen.

Unfortunately, while it was difficult enough helping the parents have some insight about this dynamic, with the kids themselves, it was virtually impossible. I learned the hard way that insight about these entrenched patterns of reacting to one's social environment did not change them. It was only through direct, sustained, repeated and personally meaningful experiences that the "Oh yeah? Okay" insight was transformed into a realization, and a capacity to perceive, feel and respond differently. As my supervisors had often taught me, change needed to come through corrective emotional experience, not insight alone. The trick was creating enough of these key experiences, in the context of a stream of ongoing negative experiences – ones that sustained the pre-existing "black hat" system – to nudge them towards seeking out these experiences on their own, essentially reversing the negative vicious cycle that was working for them well enough up to that point.

I should point out that the "black hat" dynamic was far from universal among the kids I was working with, although it was common. Luckily, many of the kids – including most of the girls – had not had the sustained and pervasive negative social experiences that led to this defensive reaction, and were therefore still open and responsive to social overtures and social influence. Without this oppositional overlay, children with social development difficulties were often still innocent of the gap between them and their peers and siblings in terms of social adaptation. These different experiences of social context sometimes made the LEGO® Club interventions more complicated and difficult to nuance.

As I became more aware of this, and had a larger cohort of children to choose from, I was able to assign clients to different groups based on the "darkness" or tone of their social interactions. Black hat kids tended to victimize and take the role of aggressor (in dynamic terms they were exhibiting identification with the aggressor), and became dominant and belittling towards the more innocent and compliant clients. Not an impossible situation, and at times it was useful in a "grist-for-the-mill" sort of way. But parents were not at all happy to learn after a group that their child had been subjected to the same sort of verbal "bullying" in LEGO® Club group that they had been exposed to on the playground, or lunch room at school, or in the community. So, although I was now considering introducing Jonathan to other children with similar interests in order to provide opportunities to exercise and shape his social interactions with peers, I was already aware that there would be inherent dangers, both for Jonathan and the other children. This was especially so considering his history of impulsive sexual acting out. I knew I would have to be monitoring and predicting Jonathan's reactions carefully with other children who might be deeply affected by his aggressive and sexual tendencies. I was also more than a little anxious about how the other parents might react to Jonathan and his family.

## JOINING OTHERS

Jonathan's grandmother had whole-heartedly agreed to the suggestion of having Jonathan join the LEGO Club group, which at the time consisted of Sam, Aaron and Evan. The other boys were a couple of years younger than Jonathan, but Jonathan was somewhat delayed intellectually and socially relative to these peers, and was small for his age, so the difference would not be very noticeable. Of course, there was the issue of pubertal development, which I was just hoping to keep out of the situation by focusing the group on the LEGO activities, and carefully monitoring any intrusion of intimidation or sexualized content. That turned out to be less of a problem than I had anticipated. Jonathan was eager to participate, and he seemed happy to have some peers with whom to interact. I had also been concerned about how well Jonathan's grandmother and mother would get along with the other parents. Although the boys all seemed to have quite a bit in common, in terms of their social adjustment difficulties, obsessive interests and rigid, self-centered styles, the parents had much less in common.

Luckily, I had underestimated the generosity and good-heartedness of the parents, and at the first group session with

Jonathan and the other boys, Louise and Max were very welcoming to Grandma (Jonathan's mother did not attend the first session, but she did come to later sessions, with Jonathan's brother Stephen). Sue was a little harder for everyone to figure out. She would typically arrive just a little late, with Evan out of breath trying to keep up with her. She paced in the waiting area, or sat by herself by the door, quickly pulling out papers she was reviewing or exams she was grading, and didn't interact much with the other parents. While I was busy with the group, the parents apparently did quite a lot of communicating, and within a couple of weeks, they had developed a lot of familiarity and knew each other's children's histories, their educational and social struggles, and the issues with siblings. Sue remained fairly aloof to all of this for a while, but eventually she was drawn in, especially when Aaron's father Jim was there. They were familiar with each other from the university, and there was definitely a spark of warmth in Sue towards Jim that I would not have predicted. Fairly soon, the LEGO® Club parents were sharing food with each other – Max and Grandma almost always brought snacks for themselves, the other parents and the siblings that hung out while their brothers were in LEGO Club.

Jonathan's slightly odd appearance and effeminate inter-personal style were apparently not noticed by the other boys, or at least they didn't say anything. They were a little surprised when they learned that he had created the little Soap Opera scenes, and didn't know what to make of them. They had assumed that they were just random creations, or personal, like a family scene. In the first session, each of the members introduced himself, and then I had them talk about their interests and show the other members the projects they had been working on. Jonathan was at a disadvantage since the other three had met already, and Sam and Aaron had already established a personal bond and had the common interest in marine and space exploration, but Evan was clearly looking for more of an ally, and he spent quite a bit of time in that initial session interacting with Jonathan and asking him questions. Jonathan didn't seem to mind that many of Evan's questions were inappropriate or intrusive – he was just glad to have some attention, and he seemed to be able to tell that Evan was also an outsider. They were all outsiders, but in that context, Aaron and Sam were somewhat higher on the pecking order.

I cringed a little when Jonathan introduced the boys to his latest "Days of Our Lives" creation, and began cataloguing the characters and their histories, in a monotone voice. Evan knew nothing about it, but feigned some interest, and Sam said, "My mom watches that show. I know what you're talking about." Aaron was completely uninterested, and a little confused about the topic: "So, these are characters in a 'Soap'?" He seemed a little more interested when Jonathan told a bit about murder plots, but he still couldn't understand the LEGO® creation aspect of it. There was nothing very interesting to build – no ships, no weapons, no technology – just people and some rooms. The conversation and activity ground to a halt, and the boys started looking to me for input as to where to go from there.

We had finished the Robin Hood set, and had started building a race car set with three race cars and a car carrier truck, so I suggested we get back to building that. We had the cars built, and were working on the truck, and we had bought a number of road plates to set up as a race course, so there was a lot for all of us to do. Sam and Aaron worked on the truck, while Jonathan and Evan started putting a race course together. None of the boys had a particular interest in the race car theme – it was actually one of my interests for a change – but they were being diligent about the project. The room got quiet and was busy with active building. Jonathan and Evan put in some traffic signs and pit areas, course obstacles, and then a small grandstand full of spectators. Sam and Aaron were still working on the truck, which was fairly involved and delicate.

Towards the end of the session, they created a scene all together, and set the race cars out on the track. They made a lot of race car and cheering fans noises, as they moved the cars around the track. This type of scene was one that later captured their interest when we started doing stop-motion animation, and we recreated the race with a range of comedic or tragic outcomes many times. Years later, the boys got to re-enact this scenario using the "LEGO Racers" video game (1999), which was a big hit with the whole LEGO Club gang. For the time being, the best we could do was a Polaroid photo of the scene with the boys hamming it up around the table. When we were done and headed out to the waiting room, I let Jonathan take the picture out to show the parents. When Grandma saw them running out to the waiting room to tell their parents what they'd been up to, and Jonathan showed her the picture of the racing car scene, with him in the middle of it, there were tears in her eyes. "Good job, Jonathan! Did you build this?" Jonathan sat on her lap in her wheelchair. "Yes, Grandma. I built it with my friends." The other boys crowded around Jonathan and his grandmother to get another look, and then Grandma passed the picture around the room. Max brought Sam over to introduce himself to Grandma, and she asked him how Jonathan had done in the group. Sam looked over at Jonathan. "Just fine, Auntie," Sam said smiling, "He is welcome to come back."

At his individual therapy session that week, I congratulated Jonathan on his success with the other LEGO® Club group members, and he seemed pleased with his first experience. He said he enjoyed the group, but thought the project was boring. I told him I sensed that during the group, and he suggested coming up with something more interesting to build. More soap opera scenes were probably not going to cut it with the other group members, I suggested, and Jonathan said he wasn't thinking about that. He said he wanted to try building a wrestling ring, with pro-wrestlers. This sounded more promising, and since there weren't any pro-wrestling LEGO sets, this would be a good freestyle project. We started looking for some suitable materials, and minifigs, and put them aside.

At the next LEGO Club group, there was more than the usual hubbub in the waiting area. Aside from the four boys, there were many parents and siblings, Sam's cousins, and then Jonathan's mother, Tami, his Grandma, his brother Stephen, and their case worker, who had brought them and wanted me to fill out paperwork. I felt distracted and overwhelmed when we came back to the therapy rooms. I didn't feel like I'd had time to prepare a plan for the group, and had this sense of dread about that. I had to put the social services paperwork on my desk, and when I came into the LEGO room, Jonathan already had the attention of the boys. He had presented the idea of building a wrestling ring and re-creating a professional wrestling scene, along with a crew of wrestlers, managers and an audience. The other boys clearly approved of the idea, and were excited about it. Jonathan brought out the materials that we had set aside for the ring and the minifigs and they were busy looking for more pieces and starting to assemble it all.

They were also all talking at once, over the top of one another, and beginning to argue about who would do what, and which characters to include, or how to create their costumes, etc. I could readily see that the week before I'd made a mistake by imposing my own interest – racing cars – assuming that they would be excited about it; the group had been uninspired and not very playful or engaging. This week, without really intending to, I'd let one of them choose the activity, and they all seemed more animated and excited about it, but the group was now a bit unmanageable, and the social interaction was not good. They were being unilateral, pushy, loud, rigid. They weren't acknowledging each other. So I got them to stop and back up, so I could impose a little order, remind them about the LEGO® points, the group as opposed to individual goals, etc. This was one of the first times that I initiated the group "check-in" process as well, which had a calming effect on them and got them to focus more on each other, rather than on the LEGO and their own building ideas. I started with Sam, since he looked fairly calm, and was always eager to talk. Once Sam started, and I showed attention to him and thanked him for his update, the others were eager to share as well. I ended with Jonathan, so it would be an easy segue back to the project, which was Jonathan's idea.

The other boys seemed impressed with Jonathan's knowledge of professional wrestling. Similar to his encyclopedic knowledge about soap operas, though Jonathan's understanding of wrestling was thinly spread: he knew a lot about the history of it, the various championships, winners and losers, and who had a grudge match with whom, or KO'd someone with a chair, but when the boys started horsing around, and Sam started doing a loud impersonation of Cactus Jack (Mick Foley), Jonathan looked uncomfortable. The boys did manage to settle on a cast of characters, including some "good guys" and "bad guys" and some managers and others, which they arranged around a ring, along with an audience and TV crew. The building process kept getting interrupted by sudden outbursts of impromptu battling by the minifigs, but they eventually settled on an action scene, which warranted another Polaroid shot, and then they asked to show it to their families.

Jonathan ran out to the waiting room to invite his mother, grandmother and brother to come back – their case worker came with them, pushing Grandma's chair. Stephen smiled and seemed a little proud of his big brother, as well as envious. Evan had contributed as best he could, but he really didn't know anything about WWF (World Wrestling Federation), etc. (neither did I, actually), but he pretended, and I thought he pulled this off fairly well. I could tell, though, that Sue wasn't too pleased with the theme. Aaron's dad, Jim, didn't seem to quite share the group's enthusiasm, but he smiled and nodded appreciatively, and that seemed to help Sue to accept that this was something socially normal. Max was a big WWF fan herself, and was loudly praising the ring and all the details that the boys had included, like the TV crew and the managers. They could tell that this had been fun for the boys, and they could sense the common interest and bond that was developing among them, including Jonathan.

Tami asked me on the way out if Stephen could participate: "He feels left out. He doesn't want to wait out there when his brother is having fun with the LEGO®s." I told her I would have to check with Jonathan about that. Jonathan overheard me, and he said he thought Stephen would fit in well: "He can build LEGOs better than me!" I also checked with the other group members, and it was agreed to let Stephen come in and demonstrate his LEGO skills. He was the first sibling included in the group. Having typically developing, or similarly affected, siblings participate in the group, when appropriate, became fairly commonplace over the next years, since not including them often created more problems at home, and the siblings were often excellent role models and a good source of support for me. The siblings allowed me at times to interject some typical peer feedback about social norms, such as clothing and hairstyle choices, use of slang or idioms, and gestures. Stephen was an avid LEGO Club attendee for years, and he was always included in the extra activities (birthdays, holidays) that were hosted by the families of the other members.

# KEITH

## INITIAL CONTACT

Keith was a ten-year-old boy who was referred by his parents, although he had already been seen by a number of private mental health providers. His family background was not typical for the public health setting I was working in at the time. I was more than a little intimidated when I saw the referral packet full of assessments and consultations by a number of well-known developmental, psychiatric and neurological specialists in both Hawaii and California. Keith's father, Peter, was a successful hotel and resort executive, and Keith had been attending a large, prestigious private school up until just prior to my seeing him. The list of prior diagnoses included ADHD, Oppositional Defiant Disorder, Conduct Disorder, Mood Disorder and Bipolar Disorder.

As I normally did at that time, I met with Keith's parents first to get some of the background and to identify goals for my involvement. The first thing I noticed about Peter and his wife, Lisa, was how angry and frustrated they were. They had been taking him to various specialists for a few years now, but Lisa indicated that he had been a difficult child from infancy onward. Regarding coming to see me, Peter explained that the family was "sick of paying these huge bills for nothing, no offense. If he isn't going to put in some effort and try to get better, what's the point?" Keith had two younger brothers, Andrew and Jeffrey, and it was only after they were born and his parents had some experience with them that they became aware of how aloof and self-absorbed Keith had been. Lisa said, "We never bonded. After the other two came along, I realized, there was something wrong with him. They were so easy compared to him. He was just never happy, no matter what. Never. The other two were so easy after him!"

Peter had noticed that it was difficult to get Keith's attention when he was small, and he didn't seem to want to play. He rarely laughed, and most of his play was repetitive, or destructive. "You let him have anything, and he'd throw it, or just drop it and watch it fall. He tore up paper and threw it. He smashed up his food and threw it. We had to watch him all the time, and if you tried to stop him, he would cry and fight you. Really hit and try to bite and scratch." Later, they noticed that he did not want to play with other children, and could be aggressive with them if they tried to engage with him. He was that way with his brothers when they were born, and his parents were alarmed that he would be so aggressive with small infants, even hitting them with objects, throwing things at them, biting or slapping them, and pushing them down when they were toddlers. Needless to say, his brothers, who were close in age – one year apart – were close with each other and played well together, but were not fond of their older brother.

Keith's father and brothers, like many boys and men who grew up in Hawaii, took full advantage of the beautiful climate, the mountains and the ocean, and enjoyed snorkeling, spear fishing and outdoor sports like soccer, baseball, football, golf and tennis. Keith was pale and hated having to be outside. He avoided going in the ocean. He also did not dress in shorts, flip-flops ("slippahs") and t-shirts like his brothers and most of his peers. Keith typically wore collared shirts (golf shirts or button-down oxfords), long pants with a belt, and either sneakers or hiking shoes, even when his family went to the beach or the park for a picnic. Most of the times I saw him, he was wearing his school uniform, so his atypical appearance was less noticeable.

Keith's behavior at school with peers was more restrained than it was at home, most of the time. He was not big for his age, but could still be very animated and would quickly escalate from minor conflicts to threats and then aggression, even with much larger peers. His father observed, "Definitely a chip on his shoulder, just touch him, or anything even close to him, and he goes off. It doesn't matter who you are, the teacher or even the principal, he'll come at you, yelling and threatening." His educational career, even at the best private school, included a long list of disciplinary actions and sanctions, including meetings with parents and referrals for evaluations. The school emphasized athletics, and had its own tennis courts, a competitive golf team, and one of the best football teams in the country. Keith was more academically oriented; he enjoyed reading and was rarely without a book in his hands, but he was not doing well academically. His psychological and academic testing showed that he was in the gifted range cognitively and he was more than a year ahead of his classmates academically in all areas. According to his father, "He just doesn't care. He'll be sitting there in class, reading what he wants, usually Star Wars, and he ignores the teacher and everybody around him. Except maybe Art. That's where they let him do more of his own thing. So he draws pictures of weapons and Star Wars stuff – space ships and light sabers."

Keith was finally given an ultimatum by the school administration: he would participate in class and not get into conflicts with his peers, or he would be expelled. A week later, he was sent to the principal's office for threatening a classmate with "a pen." When the principal told Keith he would need to contact his parents, Keith threatened the principal with the same pen: it turned out to be a pen with a built-in letter opener, which was a three-inch slender steel blade, rather flimsy, but it qualified as a lethal weapon according to the school's policies. Luckily, the school did not pursue charges. Instead, Keith's parents and the school administration met and agreed to refer him to another private school, with less strict academic and behavioral policies, and he was accepted. The school he was referred to had a more student-centered learning approach which emphasized individuality and creativity. The classes were smaller, and Keith would be allowed to express more of his own interests in the context of the curriculum. At the time I first met him, he had been enrolled there for a month, and there had not been any incidents.

When I met Keith, he was seated in the waiting room with both of his parents and his two younger brothers, Andrew and Jeffrey. He was a strongly built boy, of mixed racial background, with thick black hair and dark eyes, wearing a baseball cap, windbreaker and jeans, and carrying a large, heavily stuffed backpack. He was immediately anxious and upset when I asked him to come in by himself. "Mom, Dad, you're not going to send me in alone with this guy are you? He could be some kind of pervert!" His parents sighed and his father stood up. "Look, we're going to be right here. This is Dr. Dan, he's not a pervert, I promise. Just go and talk to him, and when you're done, we'll all go out for dinner." Keith looked at me suspiciously, and followed me to my office. He sat down in a chair near the door, still wearing his backpack. When I suggested taking off the backpack, he said, "No way. I might have to run out of here." He put his hand on the doorknob.

I had the feeling he was testing me, and I decided to avoid picking up on this, but instead to use humor, and help him to feel safe and that he could express himself here and be accepted. I said, "What do you have in that backpack anyway? Weapons? A bomb?" He glowered at me. "I wish. You'd be dead by now if I did." He didn't seem very sincere about this, so I just kept joking with him, but in a deadpan way, using a paradoxical strategy, still trying to break the tension and get him to see that I was no threat and we were on the same team. "No weapons? You mean you're defenseless?" He stood up and walked over to my desk, picked up a pencil and pointed it at me. "I don't need weapons to kill you."

I said, "That sounds like something Darth Vader would say."

Keith smiled a little. "I know a lot about the dark force. Do you even know what the dark force is?" By this point, he had moved over to a white board, took a marker pen, and started drawing a Darth Vader helmet on the wall next to the board. He looked over his shoulder at me, but I ignored his doodling on the wall. He then drew a stick figure with the head chopped off by a light saber. He wrote "Dr. Dan" under the figure.

Luckily, I did know about the dark force. I had been a bit of a Star Wars fan myself. I told him I'd seen the first Star Wars movie when it came out in Canada, in the late 1970s, at a drive-in. He didn't know what a drive-in was, so I explained. He asked if I had seen the other Star Wars movies, which I had and I could name them. They had been in the theaters before he was born, and he seemed impressed that I had seen them on their original release. He asked if I had read any of the Star Wars books. There, I was a novice. He unloaded his backpack on the floor, and started sifting through the pile. There were a couple of textbooks and notes from school which he stuffed back in, but the bulk of it was Star Wars-based novels, action figures and model vehicles, as well as crumpled pages of notes and well-worn notebooks full of his notes about the books and movies. He excitedly explained about the storylines of the books, showed me the figures, and read from his notes about them, which were mostly peripheral to the movies. He seemed to be especially motivated to show me that he knew more than most people about the Star Wars trilogy – esoteric details about weapons, planets, technology, lineages and backstory. I let him fill me in, and as he went on, he got more and more excited, took off his jacket and hat, and pulled his chair up next to mine. He reminded me of some of my university professors when I'd shown an interest in their particular field of study: books would appear along with sketches and diagrams on the blackboard, revered names were repeated, the concepts and their histories explained. Keith had become my professor, and I was his student, and in that way, we had established the basis for some kind of relationship.

Of course, by the time we got back to the waiting room, Keith was back in his glowering character. While I spoke briefly with his parents, he tipped books off the shelf in the lounge, threatened his brothers, and doodled on the wall. His parents seemed puzzled that I wasn't reacting to his behavior. His mother went over and grabbed him by his arm, pulling him over to us. I focused on the positive and said he was obviously a very bright, creative and complicated kid, and I would be happy to see him again. In the meantime, I said to Kevin, "Try to stay under the radar at school. You do not want to go to public school, which is the next option after this." He looked at me and nodded. "You're right, Doc. I'll be murdered in public school."

In the following few months, Kevin and I met weekly, sometimes just the two of us, and sometimes with his parents. The initial focus for me was trying to clarify his diagnosis, so I got some more background from his parents, looked more carefully at his school records, and did some psychological testing. I confirmed that his IQ was as high as had been reported; he tested in the Very Superior range on both Verbal and Performance (visual-spatial) abilities. His parents' and teachers' ratings of him on standardized behavioral rating scales were elevated on practically every scale. It was hard to pick out the key issues from the background noise of complaints, but I was struck by just that – how willing everyone was to be negative about Keith. I recalled vividly how detached and critical his parents had seemed about him even as an infant: "We never bonded." The teachers at his new school, which espoused a very supportive and accepting philosophy, were objective and generally critical of Keith. He wasn't making friends there, he didn't seem motivated to participate, he was aloof.

At the time, there weren't very good measures of autistic conditions, but I had been developing some feel for this population – Asperger's Disorder and high-functioning autism – using certain projective tests, including the Thematic Apperception Test (TAT), the Rorschach inkblots, and human figure drawings (Draw-a-Person Test, Kinetic Family Drawing, House-Tree-Person Test). I was interested in the responses that these children gave, which tended to be both unusual and asocial, with few responses that indicated an interest in other people and relationships, which is typically a dominant theme in most children's responses to these tests. Of course, if the test is to draw a person or a picture of your family doing something together, or look at pictures of people and say what you think about them, it's hard to imagine how one would not give a response that did not include people, but Keith did just that.

When I showed him the first TAT card, a lone boy looking pensive, and asked him to tell me what he thought was happening in the card, he said, "How am I supposed to know? It's your card, Doc, you tell me." I persisted a bit, and encouraged him to imagine what the boy might be thinking or feeling. "Thinking or feeling? No way. It's a picture. Not even a photograph, it's a drawing. Looks like something from an old movie, you know, black and white. Depression era." When he was asked to draw a picture of a person, he drew his favorite Star Wars character, Boba Fett the bounty hunter, in very great detail – the drawing took him over half an hour to complete. He talked about the details of the character's armor and weapons, his "back story," from the novels he was reading. The drawing showed the character with a helmet, no face. Boba Fett, Keith explained, was later cloned. "His DNA was used to make an army of clones." Keith was fascinated by this idea: "You didn't have to give them all commands – they all thought and behaved the same way."

When asked to draw a picture of his family, he drew stick figures of different sizes, his father, mother and brothers, watching TV at home. He did not include himself. When I asked him why he didn't draw himself in the picture, he said, "Because you asked me to draw a picture of my family doing something. That's what I did." I realized he wasn't being oppositional or argumentative. When I asked him to draw a picture of his family, he thought of them, but he did not think of himself as part of that family. It was something that his teachers had commented about as well. Whenever they gave an instruction to the classroom, he would ignore them unless they addressed him specifically as well. "Everyone, put your Math books away, we're going to get ready for lunch. You too, Keith. Put your Math away and get ready for lunch." Keith did not see himself as part of any social group, even his family. He was deeply separate.

Over time, Keith and I were developing something of an alliance, which I felt was key to us making some progress. I was careful not to align myself overtly with his parents, so that he would not feel that I was just an extension of their influence over him, which he rejected. I sensed it would be important for him to have this relationship with me and trust me, before he was willing to consider bridging the rift between him and his family. But it was hard for him to identify any personal goals for the therapy. He still didn't see the point of his coming to see me, but he was fine with it as long as we spent some time talking about Star Wars, or some other interests he was willing to share with me. These included Japanese anime, manga and the emerging Gameboy® series. He was interested in Dragon Ball Z, Pokemon and Super Mario.

Although Keith's ancestry included Hawaiian, German and Chinese, he identified most with the Japanese part of his descent, which came from both his mother and father's lineage. There were many aspects of Japanese culture and traditions that appealed to him, especially anything related to the history of the Japanese military, the samurai. He was less fond of what he described as a "mainland" concept of the ninja. "Ninja were spies and assassins. Samurai were proper warriors. They were knights." Again, I found myself in the role of student with Keith teaching me about Japanese culture and history, but our conversations were often useful ways for me to connect with him, and to help him develop some insights about himself and his relationships, including with his family.

Keith was openly critical and contemptuous of his parents, and only a little less so towards his younger brothers. He was often offended by what he perceived as intrusions into his private world when his parents would ask him to do his homework, or clean his room. He resented having to share the television and had insisted that his parents get him his own TV for his room. He had his own room, while his brothers shared a room, and he became very angry and threatening if any of his family came into his room for any reason. He was especially sensitive to intrusions by his mother, who was a naturally affectionate and emotional person. Peter was a tall, assertive and intimidating man. His German and Hawaiian ancestry were evident in his size, and it was clear that much of Keith's exceptional analytical and verbal abilities came from him. Keith was not tall like his father, though, and he showed his mother's emotionality and quick temper. Keith complained about his father's dominance at home, and he admitted to being afraid of him, but his father worked long hours and would often be away on business trips.

It was during one of his father's absences that Keith became challenging for his mother, and she got angry with him and slapped him. In previous family sessions it had come out that there were often conflicts between Keith and his mother about food. Lisa was less than five feet tall, and admitted that she struggled with her weight. She enjoyed cooking and shopping at traditional Japanese, Korean and Chinese bakeries, but then would be angry with herself if she gained weight. Keith shared her taste for sweets, but had no concern about his weight. His mother tended to fuss about his eating, though, and she was often upset and frustrated with Keith that he would eat a lot of sweets and junk food and not seem to care. This day, Keith had eaten a lot of cookies that his mother had been saving for a tea with friends, and when Keith reacted indifferently about it, she slapped him. Keith picked up a kitchen knife and threatened her with it. Lisa took the younger boys with her to a neighbor's house and called the police.

Keith was not afraid of the two police officers who arrived at the house. They were apparently a little amused when they were dispatched to a domestic violence call in a prestigious area of old Manoa and a diminutive 11-year-old boy politely answered the door. Keith asked them about the guns they carried, and whether they had other weapons in the car. Lisa was overwrought, and wanted him arrested, but the police explained that he was too young to be taken into custody. His mother was referred to a crisis intervention agency, which was run from the clinic where I worked. Based on the crisis worker's assessment, and the fact that Lisa was not feeling safe with him until his father came home, Keith was taken by the police to a youth psychiatric crisis unit for the next few days; in the end, Keith wound up staying there for two weeks.

Despite his long history of previous evaluations, and the fact that he was in therapy with me, the crisis unit undertook an intensive evaluation of Keith, including additional psychological testing, neuro-imaging studies and behavioral observation. His parents reported that they were not happy with the services being provided by me, and they did not feel that I was focusing on the family's needs adequately. This feedback was given to me by the attending psychiatrist who was also in charge of my division. He recommended that I needed to focus more on parenting and behavioral strategies at home, and included a recommendation for home-based family and crisis involvement, and the use of psychiatric medication.

I explained to the psychiatrist that I was fairly convinced that Keith's primary diagnosis was Asperger's Disorder, and that the other features – inattentiveness, oppositional and disruptive behavior, emotional outbursts – may be secondary to this condition. He agreed with me, and was interested in the Asperger diagnosis, which was fairly new at the time, but he left the other diagnoses in place. Keith was discharged after two weeks, on a mood stabilizer and an antipsychotic. A home-based behavioral specialist was assigned, and a crisis plan was developed so that the family could call them, not the police. I continued to see Keith and his family on a weekly basis, and also met with the home therapist and crisis team monthly to review progress and discuss any problems.

By the time I saw Keith again, I had moved from the Department of Health offices to a private practice setting. I had a much bigger office and a very large playroom, with a LEGO® corner. Keith was not impressed, and he was quite surly – he blamed me for the trip to the psychiatric facility, and the home-based behavior therapist. I had been seeing a number of other kids his age who presented with somewhat similar issues, and had been diagnosed, by me or others, with Asperger's Disorder or Pervasive Developmental Disorder, Not Otherwise Specified (PDD-NOS). These were boys who had also shown similar interests to Keith, including LEGO, Star Wars, electronic games and Japanese animation – which was not unusual relative to the non-affected population of boys that age – but, like Keith, their interests were either extreme in intensity and focus, or included other, more idiosyncratic topics, or both. It was also noticeable that most of them, including Keith, lacked other common interests of boys their age, particularly anything that involved the outdoors, or teams. But there in my playroom, they were free to explore and discuss their own interests safely, with no pressure from me or anyone else, to get outside, kick or throw a ball, get in the ocean, or sweat.

---

Often I had to rein in my own enthusiasm for the outdoors and physical exercise when setting goals with these kids. I was, and am, a big believer in being active outside as a buffer against depression and social isolation. I also just loved being out in nature whether it was on the ocean, in the mountains, or just pedaling down the road. A big part of the reason I had moved to Hawaii from Canada was so that I could indulge in outdoor sports year-round. I usually got in a surf session before or after work, and weekends, I was all over the island running, mountain biking, hiking, surfing, snorkeling or kayaking. I was well aware that this was a bias of mine and I tried not to be judgmental or to push them towards my own interests. It did make it hard for me at times to identify with a group of kids who preferred to be inside, even in such a glorious setting as Hawaii.

---

Keith's interests were typical of the indoor type, so it took me some extra effort to find common ground. This was especially an issue in the therapy, since it seemed clear that we needed to repair our alliance after he had been subjected to the psychiatric setting and the intrusion into his home life, for which he understandably held me accountable. It was a dark moment for our relationship. He barely looked at me as he wandered around the playroom, scoffing at the toys, puppet theater, water station, sand-tray, easel and paints: "What's all this crap? Are we going to play with puppets now?" This seemed like displaced anger to me – he wasn't angry at my playroom, he was angry at me.

Rather than defending myself or my playroom, I acknowledged that he was angry with me, and had a right to be angry about his experience. I didn't particularly want to accept responsibility for that – I was leaning towards blaming his parents and the crisis response team for the hospitalization, but I knew he needed to get angry with me, and have that turn out alright. It didn't have to escalate the way it did at home, or at school. I did feel responsible for not having been more active with his parents. I could have anticipated the crisis, and had a crisis plan in place, especially given his history of aggression and the threats he had made to his parents, teachers and school staff in the past. But he hadn't introduced the underlying reason for his anger yet, so I said, "Yeah, a lot of this is kiddie stuff. I'm just getting it set up." I thought I might try to lift his spirits and bring up some positive aspect of the experience, but not steer away from the topic: "I heard you got arrested. HPD."

Keith sneered. "I've been arrested before. This time it took two cops, both with Glocks."

I didn't want to buy into the theme of getting arrested as a positive experience, but I could tell for him it was something he had probably planned on bragging about: "Yikes. Were you scared?"

"Nah. They left their side arms holstered. I was more worried about the handcuffs." He had wandered over to the LEGO® corner, and noticed some of the sets and creations on the shelves and table. He picked up a LEGO pistol. "Who the heck made this?" he said, and sat down at the table, rummaging through a bin of parts.

I said, "Another kid who comes here. So, how did you know they had Glocks?"

Keith was more animated and looked at me incredulously. "Don't you know what a Glock looks like? Not like this!" he said, and flipped the LEGO gun to the floor. He started putting black and gray bricks together. He turned his attention to the gun he was making and I sat across from him.

"You know," I said, "that whole thing, with your mom, and you getting arrested and going to the psych unit, that was kind of my fault…"

Keith looked up again. "Kind of? Where were you when all this was going on? Why didn't you get me out of there? It was definitely not fun."

"Yeah," I said. "I let you down."

We talked for a while about the incident with his mother. He agreed that threatening her with a knife was "overkill," but he said he felt threatened by her. "She slapped me, just like that, right across the face."

"Well," I said, "I guess you know by now, adults aren't perfect. We make mistakes, too."

Keith was focused on the LEGO gun, digging around for pieces. He stood up, putting another piece on the gun. Then, adopting his pedantic tone, he said, "I'll say. Don't let that happen again, okay? You got me?"

"Yep."

"Alright," he said, looking at me closely. "I'll let you live…" and he pointed the half-made gun at me, aiming it with both hands, "…this time." Then he sat down and started looking for more pieces.

## LEARNING THROUGH LEGO®

Over the next few weeks, I met with Keith individually. His mother brought him and dropped him off, running off to a soccer game or tennis lesson for one of the other boys and picking him up later. Keith usually seemed indifferent or bored when he came in, but I had been getting some new LEGO sets that sparked his interest, Ninja LEGO. He noticed the first set, already under construction and sitting on the shelf. "Woh. What's this?" It was a small castle with ninja and samurai figures with detailed costumes, swords and bows, and armored horses. He gave me a critique of the genre, but he was also fascinated. He wanted to finish the LEGO set, but I told him that another client was working on it and we would have to work on something else. He gave me a peevish look, but then I pulled out a box containing another, even bigger, Ninja castle set.

Keith grabbed the box out of my hands, and went to the table, already trying to open it. "Hold on!" I said. "We can build it, but we have to talk about some rules first."

"Rules?" Keith said, incredulous. He stopped tearing at the box. "Okay. Like what?"

I sat down with him. "First, we're building this together. I'm not going to just sit here and watch you, okay?"

Keith looked at me and at the set. "Yes, alright. You can help." He turned away to the box again.

"Fine. Next rule: We're going to talk, alright?" I reached out and took the box from him, and made eye contact.

"Talk. Talk? Like now?" he said, reaching for the box.

"Yep, like this. You know, we'll talk about whatever is going on, while we build. Will that work?" I held on to the box.

"Yes. Now can we build, please?" Keith moved his chair over to give me and the LEGO set more room, then he held his hands up and bowed, and I gave him the box.

For the next half hour or so, Keith and I opened the set and started organizing some of the pieces. I picked up the instructions and we looked at the first few steps together. Keith reached for the figures on the table, but I picked them up, and opened the bag they were in. He held the instructions and we looked at them together, then I handed him the pieces of the human figures and the two horses. He jousted and had a miniature sword battle between a samurai and a ninja. Then he got the platform out and counted the bumps along each side to make sure it was the right size and to determine where to put the first bricks. The whole time, we talked about what we were doing and the set, and when we were quietly building together, I asked him about his week, how the home therapy was going, and how things were with his parents. He answered me sincerely and without being defensive or exaggerating anything.

When our time was up, the set was not even half finished. Keith wanted to keep working, but I said I had another client to see. He said he would just stay and build. "I don't care. I won't say anything. I promise I won't bug you. Just let me stay and finish this." I told him I couldn't do that, and his mother would be waiting to get him. I reminded him that we could finish it next week. He clenched his fists and tears appeared in his eyes. "No. Someone else will see it and finish it."

I reminded him about earlier in the session when he had wanted to finish someone else's work and I didn't let him. "It'll be like that, Keith. I promise. No one will even touch it. We'll put it on the shelf, and we can even put your name on it if you want."

He slumped in the chair and growled, but then he shrugged and stood up. He put the LEGO® set and the remaining pieces in the cardboard tray. He put the box and instructions on the shelf, and put the tray on top. Then he went to the table and got a sticky note and wrote his name on it with a marker. Then he took another sticky note and wrote, "Don't touch!" – and in the corners he wrote, "or...you... will...die." He went to the door, and when I came over, he gave me a quick, formal handshake, stood back and gave me a salute. "I'm counting on you, Dr. Dan."

The next week, the Ninja LEGO set was still on the shelf, just as Keith had left it (it had been saved from interference a number of times in the intervening days). He was accompanied by his new home-based therapist, Mike. He had originally been assigned a young woman, but apparently Keith had been so uncooperative and rude to her, making frequent misogynistic comments, that she finally recommended getting a male therapist. Mike was a young graduate student from UH who worked part-time for the state-contracted family services agency. He had played football for UH, and was still a big, athletic young man. Keith seemed proud to be coming in with Mike. They both seemed to be getting along very well. At first, Mike sat across the room from us, answering questions from me about the home-based behavior plan, and Keith's progress at school. Eventually, Keith waved him over to join us at the table, and he did.

Keith showed him the Ninja set we were working on. He held up a samurai sword. "Cool huh?" Keith nodded. "Nothing like the LEGO® I had when I was a kid." I chimed in about the rudimentary LEGO I'd played with, bricks and wheels pretty much, and we all worked on the set together. I wound up holding the directions, and Mike was sorting through the pieces, looking over at the directions when I showed him the next pieces, and Keith was busy building. "Come on, come on you guys! What's next? Let's see if we can get this done today."

I reminded him about the rule about talking, and he said, "Fine. Talk! But let's just keep on building. I need the roof parts, uh, about ten of them, hold on. One, two, four, eight. Okay, no, eight, like this..." He held up a piece for Mike to see. Mike looked for them.

"So, Keith, what's it like having Mike around the house?" I said, and they both looked up.

Keith was still building. "It's okay. It's good. He talks to the parental units, but mostly it's just us. We do some fun stuff. But my mom keeps wanting to talk with him. She gets all, 'Mi-i-ke,'" he said in a high-pitched voice, and batting his eyes. Mike said, "She's concerned. She's worried mostly about how Keith is getting along with his brothers, which you know, he's not." There had been a lot of arguing at home, mostly between Keith and his brothers, then his parents would get involved, and sometimes this would start an argument between them. Mike explained that Lisa preferred to finish arguments: "She thinks you have to get it all out, and then it can be over. Keith's dad doesn't like the yelling, and he will just walk away, or he'll even get in his car and drive away. He doesn't think they should be talking to Keith about it, treating him like an adult."

Keith was building but he was also listening. He nodded and smiled. "I am like an adult. But my brothers are kids. They play games, and snuggle with mommy."

I said, "What's wrong with being a kid? Once you get to be an adult, that's it, no turning back. Enjoy it while you can, Keith. I loved being a kid."

Mike chimed in, "Yeah. I already miss it. Seriously, everyone when they're like this, you know, or in their teens, they want to be grown up. Look grown up, act grown up, drink, smoke, get a girlfriend. Then you get grown up and you wish you were a kid again. Hanging out with your friends, no bills to pay, mom and dad take care of everything."

"Okay, okay," Keith said, working on the set, and nudging Mike for the next piece. "I get it. You guys had fun when you were kids. It's not fun for me, alright? I don't have friends. I don't play sports. I hate my family..."

"Hang on," I said. "You *hate* your family?"

"Hate. H-A-T-E, hate. They'd be dead if I thought I could get away with it." He turned away from the set and started digging in the small bin of minifigs.

I said, "Keith. You gotta be careful about saying things like that. They're your family. And we're working on improving things for you all, helping you get along better, right Mike?"

Keith returned to the table with a small group of minifigs. He took the samurai figure on its horse and had the samurai attack the small group, pulling their heads, hands, arms and legs apart and scattering them. Mike said, "You gotta see this, Doc." He pulled a sheet of paper out of his backpack, and put it in front of me. It was one of Keith's drawings. Mike had asked him to draw a picture of his family doing something together, and he had drawn them in front of their house, being slaughtered by two samurai with swords. He had labeled the samurai "Me" and "Mike." His brothers had their limbs and heads cut off and blood was spilling out. His father was depicted being beheaded by Mike, and the "Me" samurai was stabbing the only female figure. I pointed at that, and said, "I guess that's your mom." He was busy pretending to chop up the minifigures with the samurai sword, but glanced over. "Yep. That's mom. Cha!"

The issue of anger and resentment towards his family lingered on for years with Keith. Clearly, it had become a vicious cycle, with Keith struggling to accept being part of a social unit, and inevitably offending and alienating his parents and brothers. When they would react to some of his offensive remarks, or self-centered aggression and entitlement, this gave more fuel to the fire of his resentment towards them. Luckily, the LEGO® activities we engaged in allowed Keith and me a basis for communication about these issues, both through direct talking, as well as through symbolic expressions, as described above.

Keith became fond of building elaborate scenes using LEGO, and then enacting improvised plays, often involving his family or his teachers and classmates, and later, his friends. He enjoyed the role of "director," getting me, his stage crew and sometimes part of the cast, to participate. He was a demanding director, but he got much quicker at recognizing my efforts and thanking me. One day, he asked me to videotape a scene, with his parents and brothers. They were all having Thanksgiving dinner together, and Kevin got to say "grace," and blessed the food and his family. Then an argument and a food fight ensued, but it was a good-natured dispute and Keith laughed a lot off camera. Mostly the scene was one of acceptance and love, but with recognition of the underlying tensions that were still there, but eased and even released by using humor. Keith's dark sense of humor continued to develop and became a valued characteristic of his among his school friends and teachers alike.

Mike and I both worked with Keith's parents to try to make their reactions to Keith more objective and less emotional and angry, and we set up rules and structure at home that was designed to minimize the amount of negative affect being expressed. Mike had developed the view that Keith might still turn out to have something more ominous than Asperger's Disorder, like Bipolar or Schizophreniform Disorder. But Keith's moods stayed fairly stable, and he did not develop paranoia or other psychotic symptoms. Over time, he became less angry, and although he was always fairly aloof and judgmental towards both his parents and his brothers, he was never again aggressive and he rarely threatened anyone. Keith's parents learned to deal with him more objectively and by following a plan, rather than reacting with strong emotions. This led to more harmony at home – less stress and lingering resentments – and their relationship as a couple improved as well.

Keith and his brothers developed something of a truce, mostly through staying out of each other's way, but they were never close.

Their parents, Lisa and Peter, had hoped for more. They had wanted the boys to get along and enjoy each other's company, but they accepted the outcome they got, which was a collegial relationship: not quite loving, but not hate, either. Once they had accepted that Keith was always going to be different from Andrew and Jeffrey, and stopped trying to get him to be like them, they were in conflict with him much less often. Keith's brothers continued to be successful at school, in sports and socially, and as they moved into their own social lives with peers, they crossed paths with Keith less and less. In the meantime, Keith had discovered a new social circle, one unlike any he had had before – the LEGO® Club.

This was an important opportunity for Keith, but also for his parents, who got to see him as accepted and even valued by other LEGO Club group members for his creativity, humor and leadership skills. It was a great experience for us all that Keith's parents got to hear other parents talking about Keith in positive ways, and sharing what a positive influence he had become for his peers: in the Club, Keith was sincerely admired and he was a mentor for other teens who were less assertive than he was. Once he felt accepted there – which was not an immediate result of his joining – he seemed to be less resentful and reactive at home. He seemed to be more accepting of himself, and therefore, more willing to let his family live their lives without his relentless negativity.

## JOINING OTHERS

Lisa and Peter were not all that receptive to the idea of group therapy when I first suggested it. At the time, they were still angry with him, and invested in making all of their problems, including their marital problems, Keith's fault (sadly, they weren't entirely wrong). They said they were worried that Keith might become agitated or aggressive with the other boys, or alternatively, that he might learn some new problem behaviors from them. At times, I felt that they were committed to being long-suffering martyrs, and Keith was their cross to bear. If he got better, there would be no one to blame but themselves and each other for their unhappily successful lives. At other times, they seemed very sincere about wanting Keith to get better, or to change in some way, but they had become cynical about the offerings of healthcare professionals. They had taken him, often at considerable expense, to so many established and well-known providers, I couldn't blame them for being pessimistic about the idea of Keith improving as the result of playing LEGO® with other boys who had similar problems. Their objections to the group therapy proposal weren't far-fetched either. The thought of Keith and some of the other group members in the same room for an hour or so also made me cringe a bit, not to mention the thought of Peter and Lisa chatting in the waiting room with some of the other parents.

On the other hand, Keith was showing a persistent interest in the LEGO activities and in the mysterious group of children who had by now completely transformed the playroom into a busy LEGO-creation workshop. He was also failing to make friends at school and was almost constantly bickering or physically fighting with his brothers, despite the efforts of his home-therapist, Mike. It was actually Mike who convinced Keith's parents to give it a try. They had had a meeting with Keith's new school to review his progress, and they made it clear that Keith was teetering on the brink of being asked to leave. Although there had not been any serious incidents, and Keith was doing fairly well academically, he was not participating in the "cultural" aspects of the student community. This meant that, aside from generally making everyone around him uncomfortable, he was not sharing his ideas or participating in group projects, which was a core part of the school's academic mission. Keith had also been dismissive and critical of the other students' work, and was even critical and argumentative with his teachers. Mike had attended the meeting, and he brought up the idea of having Keith attend a social skills group, which the school staff supported whole-heartedly.

Later, Mike and Keith's parents discussed the idea with Keith, and they were surprised that he was excited about the idea. Keith's motivation for joining the group wasn't exactly what they had been hoping for – according to Mike, Keith had the idea that he would be more or less in charge of the group, and that the others would be enlisted to help him with his projects. He said Keith used the word "minions" to refer to the other members. Mike had heard a bit about how the group was going from me, and he felt confident that the structure of the group and its objectives and rules would be helpful for Keith. I wasn't so sure. Even though I supported the idea in general, I was worried about how introducing Keith into the mix would affect some of the other members, especially given his initial response. Since he was open to it, and his parents were willing to give it a try, I thought it was better to go ahead and at least try, despite the many disaster scenarios I envisioned.

In addition to the potential for Keith trying to dominate the group, and possibly getting into serious conflicts with Sam, or being belittling and hurtful to Evan and Jonathan, I wasn't sure I would be able to stay on top of all the LEGO®-focused details as well as the interpersonal dynamics with six kids in the room: Aaron, Sam, Evan, Jonathan and Stephen, plus Keith. Luckily, Mike was interested, and since he had supported the group idea with Keith's parents and the school, he was also invested in having this work out well. So, Mike became my first LEGO co-therapist. He and I and Keith met to discuss the group rules and objectives, and Keith seemed quite receptive to the whole package, although with his typical egocentric interpretation of things. He liked the idea of discussing the group activities at the beginning of each group, and sharing ideas about what the group would be focusing on: "So, if someone wants to do something really sucky, we can all just say that and do something else, right?" I said yes, tentatively, but that we don't say someone else's idea is "sucky."

Keith seemed to want to be provocative, as usual, but he also seemed open to compromising a bit: "Alright, but what if it really is a sucky idea? At school, we can't criticize at all. They might want to do something stupid like raising chicks, or making rag dolls, or baking cookies. They freak out if you say that's just dumb – it's been done. Anyone can do the same thing that's been done over and over. Where's the ingenuity in that?" At first, I tried to explain how those activities invariably involved some creativity – not every chick, rag doll or cookie was the same as every other – but I could see Keith was glazing over, and he was making the "blah, blah, blah" gesture he used when he didn't want to hear something, using his hand as a puppet, so I shifted tactics. "The focus in LEGO Club is on creativity, and sharing our ideas, even if it involves doing something that's been done before. Sometimes we build sets, which is like following a cookie recipe, but we do it our way, and we have our own reasons for doing it. We try to stay open to each other's ideas, because most of them are really good. But if you don't like a project – if you think it's going to be boring, or impossible to build – you can suggest something else." We talked about the way the group members had started taking turns helping each other with projects, trading favors, and using LEGO® points to pay for labor. Keith's Machiavellian wheels were turning. He looked at Mike and then back at me. "So when do we get started?"

Mike brought Keith to the group the next week, so the waiting room wasn't any more of a zoo than usual. I was a bit surprised by Keith's reaction to the group, and vice versa. Keith was more tentative and quiet than I expected, and the group hardly noticed him, since they were more interested in Mike. They hadn't had another adult attend the groups up to that point, and they all seemed to think it was very important to orient him to the group procedures and activities. Sam was doing most of the talking, and I could tell Keith was sizing him up as the "alpha male" in the group. He was showing Mike and Keith some of the group's creations, and was proudly telling them about our latest freestyle innovation, the pro-wrestling ring, which Mike appreciated. Keith wasn't very impressed. He pointed out a few of his own projects, and the group members then realized that he had already spent quite a bit of time in the LEGO room. Since Sam and Aaron had already said quite a bit about the group process to Mike and Keith, I asked Evan to go over the rules for us. He did this very well, with a pedantic flair, and citing examples of infractions of each rule by some of the members, but he did include himself as well. Keith then took the opportunity to suggest a project for the group: he was interested in getting some more Star Wars LEGO. Jonathan seemed to want to stay focused on the wrestling ring theme and he told the group that he'd been watching a TV show called "Robot Wars," which had a new spin-off show called "Battlebots." I hadn't heard of it, but the group members were suddenly excited and were talking about it all at once.

Keith jumped in on the topic with the rest of them, and even Mike seemed to know something about it and was talking about his favorite 'bot, along with the rest of them. The group needed to settle down and focus, so I called on the ever-calm and studious Aaron to fill me in. He explained the basics, with multiple interruptions, but it was good for him to be a bit assertive and remind the others that he had been asked to speak. I eventually got back around to each of them and got their input, and they all seemed to want to try making their own versions of the battling robots – bins were open and parts started coming out onto the table – and design strategies were being bandied about. It didn't seem likely that we were going to be able to agree on one design or replication, so I suggested teams. Aaron, Sam and Evan quickly agreed to work together, and Jonathan, Stephen and Keith were left looking at each other. Keith got hold of Mike (literally, taking his arm), and volunteered him to be their team leader, and Sam said, "Fine, we'll take Dr. Dan!" So we started our first intragroup building competition.

The groups initially wanted to try making LEGO® versions of the TV show robots (which were remote control motorized robots with mechanical weapons), but these seemed a bit out of reach of the group's materials and engineering skills, so I suggested we come up with our own versions. The group members agreed, and soon we were all busy pulling out parts and trying different strategies to get something that would hold together, move around on wheels or tracks, and have some kind of menacing-looking weapons. Mike was right in the fray, and was good about following my recommendation not to get too involved in the project, but stay focused on the communication and group dynamics. From that point on, Keith and Mike were part of the group.

# MOVING TO NEW JERSEY AND DEVELOPING A DEEPER UNDERSTANDING OF AUTISM

Towards the end of 2002, my wife and I made the painful decision to leave our idyllic island home in Hawaii and return to the mainland, to be closer to both of our families, and to provide our children with better educational opportunities. My wife's family lived in Southern New Jersey, just outside of Philadelphia, and so I made inquiries with colleagues about possible opportunities in that area. I had been thinking of re-establishing my private practice in the area, but that would take a while, and as I soon learned, there was a lot more competition there than in Hawaii. The area hosted a large number of major universities and medical schools, and so there were a lot more healthcare services available, and there were also a lot more people involved in providing "best practice" autism and neurodevelopmental services. Setting up and running a practice in that setting was going to be a lot more complicated and challenging than it had been in Hawaii. Needless to say, I was the laughing stock of my friends, and many of my family members, for leaving a successful practice in Hawaii to move to New Jersey.

Southern New Jersey was actually a pleasant surprise, though. The region we were looking to move to, Gloucester County, was mostly rural or suburban, and had lush small orchards and vegetable farms (corn, tomatoes, blueberries, etc.). There were many streams and lakes, and both the Pine Barrens National Forest and "the shore," New Jersey's Atlantic shoreline, with its beaches and boardwalks. It was nothing like the industrial and dense urban areas of North Jersey, around New York City. South Jersey was a quiet country setting, with small towns, Fourth of July parades, hayrides, kids trick-or-treating, barber shops, mom-and-pop corner stores, hardware stores and butchers. South Jersey also has four full seasons, each one full of traditions.

In order to have some continuity of employment income, I applied for and accepted a job at a venerable educational and healthcare institution in Haddonfield, one of the older, wealthier and more developed small towns in the region. My main role there was in an outpatient center up the road from the institution's main campus. At that setting, I was working closely with a pediatric neurologist who had been my initial contact in New Jersey. Although I was primarily expected to be doing neuropsychological and developmental evaluations, and to help the main facility to develop intervention programs for children with developmental and acquired neurological conditions, I was also doing some of my own individual and family therapy. As I got used to the system, and started developing referral sources, I began to see more and more kids who could have benefited from the LEGO® therapy program.

I had mentioned the LEGO-based therapy program to the neurologist, and as our joint practice got busier with children who exhibited a range of autistic features, he was more interested in starting a LEGO-based therapy program. Although the increase in rates of milder forms of autism was even more evident in New Jersey than in Hawaii, there was also a much longer history of educational and behavioral interventions having been available in the area. One of the benefits of having moved to New Jersey was some well-needed downtime from my very busy clinical practice and the related business paperwork. While I was waiting through the credentialing process, I had the time to start digging through my boxes of clinical files, and I found I had access to some fairly complete and useful data sets reflecting the outcomes of children who had participated in the LEGO Club groups, as well as many who had not. Again, due to the advent of IDEA law and the higher need for accountability in provision of services, the clinical records I had for children

I was seeing in Hawaii – many of whom were referred by the school system – were fairly complete and included annual updates for IEP purposes. Many of the children I had seen had been referred to my practice and then put on a waiting list for up to six months or longer, but the data was available for them from the date of referral. As a result, I was able to pull out a lot of the data that was used to evaluate the kids for their IEPs, and to use that to determine their functioning levels before and after participating in LEGO®-based and other therapies. This post-hoc analysis, which utilized the participants themselves as their own controls in a waiting-list control group design, was the basis for the first LEGO-based therapy outcome study (LeGoff 2004).

In the context of my new setting it was even more important that what we were offering as therapy had research-backed evidence to support it. The institution was already well known as a bastion of "evidence-based treatment" and Applied Behavior Analysis, by the time I arrived. When we introduced some of the educational and behavioral intervention program administrators there to the idea of LEGO-based therapy, they were receptive, but not very encouraging. They were polite to my face, at least. I heard through more supportive colleagues later that in fact a number of the senior program directors openly scoffed at it, and one ABA-devotee asked if we would also be offering "Barbie® Therapy" for those who weren't so interested in LEGO.

Once I had convinced my colleagues using the data that I had available to me, I eventually got permission from the administration to give it a try, and they even offered to do some PR work for me to get it up and running. At this time, the first article (LeGoff 2004) had been published and reviewed by some of the bigger names in the field, including Ami Klin and Fred Volkmar, Lorna Crisp and, of course, Simon Baron Cohen. One of the best pieces of feedback I got, aside from some encouragement from Dr. Volkmar, was a note from Dr. Klin regarding future directions, to consider expanding the data set to include Vineland Adaptive Behavior Scales scores. Luckily, I happened to have been using the Vineland as an outcome measure and was able to provide those data to assess more generalized outcomes, and to compare those with the group of children from Hawaii whom I'd been following for assessment and consultation, but who were not attending LEGO®-based therapy – my second control group. With the help of Dr. Michael Sherman we were able to put together another longer-term outcome study, which was the basis for the second publication (LeGoff and Sherman 2006).

By the time that article came out, however, I had made a running start on LEGO Club in New Jersey. I had assertively gotten hold of an infrequently used conference room at the institute, but it was not a very conducive setting. The long center table made the room almost useless, and the long, dark wood panels on the walls made it very serious and drab. So, one weekend in the summer when things weren't too busy, I took a handful of LEGO bricks to my local building supply store, and asked them to give me a gallon of paint in each color. Then I spent the rest of the weekend painting the conference room in LEGO colors (basically, primary colors), and putting up bookshelves. I summarily disposed of the conference table and chairs, and scavenged children's chairs and small tables from the basement of the nearby autism school (thank you, Matthew Sharp, administrator). The room started to look very interesting and fun, and quite a few noses were poked in to what used to be an intimidating and very adult space.

Now, all I needed was a lot of LEGO. I had left most of the LEGO I had used in Hawaii at my former office – another child psychologist took over the space, and had offered to continue the program. This was a big deal for the kids who had been part of the initial LEGO therapy groups – in fact, the most common question they asked me when I told them I was moving to the mainland was: "Are you going to leave the LEGO here?" I had brought with me a few boxes of what I considered to be my personal, irreplaceable collection, but that was not going to nearly fill the need for what I was planning at the institute. Luckily, with an organization of that size, there is always the possibility for staff support. I advertised internally for staff who might be interested in helping out – Dr. M had convinced the administration to give me a staffing budget, so I could hire whomever I wanted from in-house and pay them overtime to work after hours in the Club – and also advertised for LEGO® donations.

It seems fairly commonplace to me now, but at the time, I was shocked and happily surprised by the generous response of the institute's community to my call for "old LEGO." Boxes piled up at the reception desk in week one, and by the end of the first month, we were stacking them in the LEGO room in every available space. LEGO collections arrived, many of them with rare, vintage LEGO, decades old. There was a lot of work involved in turning these generous donations into useable LEGO, however. Most of the collections were dusty, full of hair and some insects, Playdoh®, plastic soldiers, GI Joe® and Mechano® parts, broken crayons, all kinds of plastic bits, rubber bands, coins and candy wrappers. But all of this was grist for the mill: we started our first LEGO Club groups focused on sifting through, organizing, sorting and cleaning about two dozen storage boxes of LEGO, of various vintages and in various states of disarray, but all valued and much appreciated.

As I mentioned above, most of the staff at the institute, who were generally highly trained and scrupulous ABA followers, were skeptical to say the least. They wanted to know how the data was being collected in the groups, how the target behaviors were identified, and what sorts of reinforcement schedules were being applied. I did my best to translate LEGO therapy into terms they would accept: naturally reinforcing activities, peer-mediated social learning and behavior interventions, token economy with short- and longer-term reinforcers, etc. It seemed completely out of place in that setting to say something like: "You get a bunch of LEGO, and you help the kids do it together. And while they're having a lot of fun, they learn to be part of a group, and even listen to feedback from us and each other. It just works."

So the LEGO groups started again, and my experience of it was just as it had been in Hawaii. The kids loved the room and the activities. They showed up early and almost never missed a week. I found out at one point that some parents used LEGO Club participation as a reward for "good behavior" during the week. Unfortunately, on bad weeks, they restricted them from coming: "Okay, that's it! No LEGO Club this week." I had to gently dissuade them from that behavior change strategy. They often didn't want to leave. The groups were scheduled for an hour, but it took at least an hour-and-a-half to two hours to get them into the room, participate, and back out again. I frequently found some kids and parents camped out in the parking lot – forming impromptu parent support groups.

# ANTHONY

## INITIAL CONTACT

Anthony was one of the first LEGO® club members in New Jersey, at the new LEGO Club setting at the Institute's education and outpatient consultation center. At that time, he was 12 years old, from an intact family, with an older brother, Jordan (14), and a younger sister, Angela (8). His parents were fairly young, in their thirties, and physically and socially active. They owned a small business together, a local beauty and tanning salon, and were active members of their community as well as having large extended family support on both sides. Anthony was born just 18 months after his brother, but four years before his younger sister: "She was a surprise! But so what? She's perfect, and she's great with Anthony."

Anthony's early childhood development was fairly unremarkable, with no problems with labor or delivery, and he walked and talked at about the right times. But, his parents reported, "He cried a lot more than Jordy, he didn't want to sleep, didn't want to nurse. Just cried. And he didn't crawl. He didn't crawl, and we were starting to get worried about him. It was, you know, 10 or 12 months, and then one day he pulled himself up by the coffee table, and he started walking just like that. Just walked. Then I couldn't keep track of him. He was into everything. Thank God for Jordy, he was an angel, just playing and keeping himself occupied."

When he started preschool, Anthony's teachers reported that he was easily frustrated and upset, and didn't like to do things in groups, would leave circle time, didn't want to hold hands, etc. His mother, Terri, had to come pick him up a number of times when he got upset and wouldn't calm down: "He would go off, and scream and yell and throw things. They called me at the boutique and told me to come get him. We were lucky they didn't kick him out, but they remembered having Jordy, and Jordy was so easy, so they figured Ant would come around." In Kindergarten, his teacher reported similar problems: he had the usual sorts of problems at school – not paying attention or participating in group activities, being disruptive, periodic tantrums, fights with other boys at recess, etc. At home, he was often "needy," in the sense of crying frequently, asking to sleep in his parents' bed at night, wanting his parents to solve conflicts with his brother, and not wanting to play with the neighbors, or his cousins when they were over. "He was always clingy, and he wanted things his way. Wouldn't eat a sandwich unless it was just so. Not like his brother at all. Fussy!"

Anthony's school district had asked his parents to have him evaluated for possible ADHD when he was in 1st grade, and he was diagnosed by his pediatrician and started on a psychostimulant medication, Adderall®. Terri said this medication "made him bounce off the walls like a trapped squirrel. He went nutso, ballistic!" They tried adjusting the dose and using different versions of it, but the results were always hyperactivity, sleep disturbance, loss of appetite, and increased frequency of emotional outbursts. His father, Dale, said, "He was an emotional wreck on that medicine, happy and running around one minute, and then sobbing and wailing the next." The pediatrician recommended an anticholinergic, Tenex®, which did seem to make Anthony calmer, and he was able to sleep at night, but it didn't help him stay focused at school, or at home. "He was always off, looking out the window, or into one of his comic books. Anything but what he was supposed to be learning."

Anthony's teacher was reporting that he was falling further behind academically by the summer before 3rd grade, and he was put on another medication, Strattera®, which seemed to help for a while. Then he starting having suicidal thoughts – he was still only seven years old when he told his parents during a tantrum that he wanted to jump out the window or suffocate himself with a pillow. His pediatrician referred the family to a child psychiatrist, who recommended Ritalin®, but when Anthony's parents found out it was a psychostimulant similar to Adderall® and Strattera®, they wouldn't go for it. The psychiatrist settled on prescribing him Wellbutrin®, an antidepressant, which seemed like a safer bet, and there were no further unusual side effects. Anthony seemed a little calmer, and the school district finally referred him to a developmental specialist and the Child Study Team for assessment to determine if he was eligible for special services.

The developmental pediatrician, Dr. L, interviewed Anthony along with his parents, and reviewed his educational and health records. She concurred with the diagnosis of ADHD, and felt that the medication side effects needed to be tolerated for now and would wear off after a few weeks. She also noted that Anthony had features of a Pervasive Developmental Disorder, which Anthony's parents took to mean cognitive delays. They privately disagreed with this assessment, but didn't say anything to Dr. L, as the assessment was being conducted for the school district. As Dale reported to me later, "People always think that Anthony's a bit slow because he cries and doesn't know how to behave, like on the baseball team and soccer team. He'd just melt down right in front of everybody. I don't blame them for thinking there was something wrong with him, you know, development-wise. He'd have a tantrum in the grocery store about getting a comic book or a magazine, or freak out in the swimming pool if some little kid touched him or splashed him. And you could tell, everyone just thought he was retarded. But we know he's not. He's as smart as his brother, and smarter sometimes, and Jordy's in gifted classes now, AC classes."

At that time, in order to meet the selection criteria for special services under IDEA, that is, in order to get an IEP, the child had to show evidence of a significant learning disability, in addition to any other identified disabling condition. In other words, your child might have visual or hearing impairment, or autism, but if their objectively assessed academic achievement test scores were not at least 20 points lower than their assessed cognitive abilities (IQ), they might be offered an ADA Section 504 modification plan, but not an IEP.[1] Anthony had been diagnosed with ADHD, so he was already eligible for a 504 plan, but he had not yet been diagnosed with either an

---

1    An IEP is an individualized education plan that is implemented for all students with special needs that impact their learning and therefore the extent to which they may benefit from publicly available education. It specifies the type and extent of special education supports and services that will be offered based on a student's identified educationally relevant disability, according to a federal law, the Individuals with Disabilities Education Act (IDEA). A Section 504 modification plan refers to a documented need for accommodations or supports for a student with an identified disability, whose access to education is impacted by an identified disability, but who may not need more than certain modifications rather than needing additional services or special education classification. It falls under separate federal laws (the Americans with Disabilities Act, ADA, and the Rehabilitation Act) which regulate individuals' rights to access publicly available services, rather than showing benefit from receiving educational services as under IDEA.

autistic condition or a learning disability. But by the time he was evaluated, his classroom behavioral issues had interfered with his learning long enough that he was no longer even close to where he should have been academically.

Once the Child Study Team determined that Anthony had a learning disability (he was more than a year behind in all academic areas, with an IQ in the average to high average range), they needed to meet with his parents to determine the best eligibility category for him. The diagnosis of ADHD, combined with the learning deficits, suggested that Anthony should be classified as "Multiply Disabled" (now, he would probably have been classified as "Other Health Impaired," or "Specific Learning Disability"). His parents had no idea what the school district was recommending when they offered to have Anthony placed in the "MD class" for the fall of his 4th grade year.

At first, Anthony was pleased with his new classroom. It was smaller and had only eight students in total, and only one girl, which was fine with Anthony. He didn't get along very well with his younger sister, who was just as bossy as his mother. The academic level was a lot lower than the mainstream 4th grade curriculum, and Anthony got to see his former classmates at lunch and during assemblies. Otherwise, he was with the MD class throughout the day, including recess, PE and library. When Anthony first complained about the classroom, it was about some of his classmates, who were being disruptive and weren't listening or complying with the teaching staff. Most of Anthony's classmates had been classified as MD based on a combination of developmental delays and behavioral problems. Anthony's parents were not aware of this until Jordan came home from school one day and told them that his brother was "in the retard class."

At first, Terri and Dale explained to Jordy that Anthony was in a self-contained special education classroom, but it was for students who had learning problems, and it was helping Anthony to catch up academically. Jordy told them he knew lots of students with special needs, but they were mainstreamed and were pulled out for special education help in academic topics, or for speech-language or OT services. Dale told him they would ask their IEP case manager about Anthony's placement, and, in the meantime, told him not to refer to anyone, especially not his brother, as a "retard."

Anthony's case manager was new and was not that familiar with Anthony. She knew that he had scored low on the Wechsler Individual Achievement Test, Second Edition (WIAT-II), and had been diagnosed with ADHD, so he met the criteria for MD placement. She reassured Terri and Dale that it was the best setting for Anthony, as the curriculum could be individualized for him, and there was a classroom-wide behavior support program – positive reinforcement for classroom participation using tokens. She did not mention that Anthony's teacher used a single curriculum guide for the whole classroom, and that Anthony was now working at a 1st grade level on reading and spelling, and was doing 2nd grade math. His IEP indicated "Progressing" in all areas. Since being in the classroom, he had also exhibited some uncharacteristic behaviors, such as cursing at and threatening his teachers. The following year, the IEP team recommended continued placement in the self-contained MD setting, due to learning and behavioral deficits.

By the time Anthony was 12 years old, in 6th grade, and facing a transition from the elementary school to the district's middle school, he was still two to three years behind academically, and his behavior at home and at school had deteriorated significantly. Anthony had continued to have conflicts with his peers, and was now more intimidating and aggressive towards his sister, Angie. He had also been openly defiant and menacing at times towards his mother. His father, Dale, had come home one day to find him throwing his school books at her in the kitchen and cursing. Anthony threatened her, and Dale grabbed him by the arm and took him to his room, where he pushed him onto the bed and then slammed the door behind him. Anthony reported this to his school counselor the next day, and she was required to alert the Department of Youth and Family Services (DYFS – which was subsequently renamed the Division of Child Protection and Permanency, DCPP). A case was opened and an investigator was assigned. DYFS was also required to initiate home-based behavioral counseling services for the family, which they accepted.

Luckily for the family, the behavior consultant assigned was from the Institute team, which had a home-based behavior services contract with both DYFS and the school district. She was the first person to carefully review the record and to question the "Rule-out PDD" diagnosis made by Dr. L. Neither the case manager nor the parents understood that that meant "Rule out autism." Initially, Dale and Terri were sure that this was incorrect. They knew what autism was, and Anthony certainly didn't fall into that category.

As Anthony's parents read more about pervasive developmental disorders, and the emerging autism literature, they began to recognize characteristics of Anthony's as related to Asperger's Disorder. For example, his behavioral rigidity and difficulties with change and disappointment, changes in schedule, and his obsession with certain comic books and literature about comic books, including the "Captain Underpants" series and spinoff literature by Dav Pilkey. Most obviously, though, Anthony didn't seem to know how to get along with peers. At school, on the soccer field, basketball court and baseball diamond, in the pool, at the beach, in the mall...anywhere Anthony went, he made enemies of his peers. He was loud, he talked too much, talked over other people, didn't look at them, and ignored how they responded. Even his gifted and good-natured older brother found him challenging and annoying most of the time. The more Anthony's parents read about and talked to other parents about Asperger's Disorder, the more convinced they were that Anthony had had it all along.

By the time I got to meet Anthony, which was in the summer before he was to start middle school, 7th grade, his parents were on a mission, and Anthony was a handful. The behavior specialist who was involved in the home arranged for the school district to offer Anthony a comprehensive assessment by me to clarify his diagnosis and cognitive abilities. Anthony presented at the initial interview with just Terri (Dale was working at the salon). He was a pale, mildly overweight youth with brown curly hair, with colorful highlights (thanks to his mother), wearing a spiked leather bracelet and a "Captain Underpants" t-shirt. He had braces on his teeth and mild acne, but was a handsome boy, with strong cheekbones and bright green eyes. He spoke in a loud voice, almost explosively, and he tended to pace or fidget while he talked. Anthony came in to my assessment office (which was sound-proofed for neuropsych testing), and looked around, then at me. "You Dr. Dan?" I said yes, and that he must be Anthony, and he replied, "You got that right. Good for you. Now just diagnose me with Asperger's and tell my mom I'm not retarded and I'll be on my way."

By this point, I had gone to the University of Michigan for ADOS and ADI-R training, so there was a lot more to the assessment that day than chit-chat. Anthony was very engaging and had a quirky sense of humor (Dav Pilkey would have approved), but he was also extremely loud – in the small, sound-proofed room, it was like he was yelling or using a microphone and amplifier – and he persistently interrupted his mother and me, and dominated the conversation even after being asked repeatedly to hold off and let me get his history from his mother. Inevitably, Anthony also tried to turn the conversation towards his obsession with comic books, especially the Archie Comics series ("Archie," "Betty and Veronica," "Josie," and then, "Sonic the Hedgehog"). He wasn't subtle about this. His mother might be answering a question, or I might be asking her one, and Anthony would suddenly say something about the Archie Comics series – not the characters or the plot of a comic book, but about the publisher, or the number of publications in certain series, or when a certain character was introduced. I had a quick flashback to Jonathan's obsession with soap operas – he'd had no interest in the actual content, but was obsessed with the behind-the-scenes factual details, the actors, directors, production crew, etc.

Following that initial assessment, there wasn't much doubt about Anthony's diagnosis. He had scored in the "Autism Spectrum" range on both the ADOS and ADI-R, but also in the high-average range on the IQ test I gave him, so the most appropriate diagnosis was Asperger's Disorder. Some mental health practitioners would have added a co-morbid diagnosis of ADHD, given that this had been a previous diagnosis, but, in my view, this was a misdiagnosis – the "ADHD" symptoms that Anthony had exhibited were actually the characteristic learning and coping style of a child with Asperger's. The DSM system also precluded the diagnosis of ADHD when there was a Pervasive Developmental Disorder diagnosis (a rule that very few of my colleagues paid much attention to).

On the academic achievement testing, he was not so far behind as we'd feared: close to 6$^{th}$ grade on reading and spelling, with age-level achievement in math and listening comprehension, but his writing was very poor – 3$^{rd}$ grade for sentences and essay. He just couldn't put his thoughts into sentences when he tried to write. His speech, in terms of diction and syntax, was fine, even advanced, but he really struggled with generating novel sentences or paragraphs that made any sense, especially when they weren't on a topic of his choosing. So, he had a writing problem, and Asperger's Disorder.

The behavior specialist, Virginia, fully agreed with my assessment, and was willing to bridge the gap between the parents and the IEP team, as well as to communicate with DYFS about the family situation – there were no further incidents of aggression at home. Unfortunately, the school district didn't want to budge about Anthony's placement. They were worried about his being disruptive in a mainstream classroom, and they felt that he would do better academically in the small classroom as well.

My assessment of Anthony had also included the Vineland Adaptive Behavior Scales, and Anthony's results on that were much lower than his cognitive or academic scores. This has become a fairly standard part of my assessment procedures, and sadly, a typical finding for most children with autistic conditions is that cognitive development and academic functioning are high, age level or above, but adaptive functioning is much lower. This assessment is based on parent or teacher interviews, or both, and covers three domains: communication, socialization and daily living skills, with subdomains within each. Measures of adaptive functioning are much more predictive of long-term outcomes than educational, cognitive or other clinical measures, in part because of content validity – questions about current adaptive functioning are just better predictors of future adaptive functioning, relative to related but different content domains, such as intelligence, academic skills, or ratings of clinical symptoms or personality traits.

Given that the interfering factors (i.e. the aspects of a given mental health diagnosis that have a negative impact on adaptive functioning) in autism/Asperger's cases are focused on the particular issues with cultural adaptation, as I have mentioned above, it is not surprising to find that these individuals' IQs and academic test scores are especially bad at predicting how well they will do as independent adults. In terms of being able to support themselves and function in the world without additional supports, their cognitive abilities and academic skills are masked by their deficits in social and "common sense" areas. This has been a very thorny issue for educators to address for kids like Anthony: adaptive functioning is not typically a part of the educational curriculum, except for students who have the sorts of disabilities that directly interfere with adaptive coping, such as developmental delays, or sensory or motor impairments. So what I was hoping would be a part of Anthony's IEP were some social life skills and adaptive coping goals, but the focus in the MD classroom was remedial academics and behavior change.

---

Adaptive functioning, except for students with global developmental delays, was typically left up to the families to address. If your child was in special education, you normally had to teach them how to use the phone, an elevator or public transportation, or to make a friend, on your own. But what if your child's particular disability affected their natural mechanism for learning those things the way most children do, by imitative play and modeling of adults and peers? What if your child had no interest in using the phone, the elevator or public transportation, let alone making friends? This was the situation for Anthony and his family.

---

Aside from the fact that Anthony's primary area of need – adaptive functioning – was not going to be addressed in his IEP, the other big problem with the MD classroom was the social milieu. It has been my experience that while children with autistic conditions tend not to imitate peers when it comes to daily routines and habits, like their physical appearance or communicative gestures, they are more likely to notice, and be fascinated by, low-frequency, high-intensity behaviors. Incidents. Outliers. When these happen, for whatever reason, children and adolescents with autism seem to be very affected by them – they perseverate on them, and for many, this often leads to a desire to imitate or repeat the unusual (and often offensive) behavior. Unfortunately, the child with autism is often poorly equipped to choose the right moment or context for this imitative attempt. They wind up trying out their first curse word in class, or at a family function, or they imitate a threatening gesture with their parents, or some other authority figure, instead of trying it out on the playground or in the locker room.

Anthony had learned some inappropriate language, and attitudes, from his peers there, and the situation in the middle school didn't seem like it was going to be any better. In fact, as it turned out, most of the students from Anthony's MD classroom in the elementary school were going to be attending a new county regional developmental school, and the MD classroom at the middle school was to be primarily students with a combination of behavioral and learning problems. There was an "autism" classroom at the school as well, but that was for students who met the IDEA eligibility criteria for classification as "autistic," which was not the same as the diagnostic criteria for a PDD. This classroom was also being phased out after this year, and those students were being referred to the district special needs regional school.

Difficulties with appropriate classroom placement were apparent for many of the clients that I was evaluating and developing programming for at the time. Students with mild autism (HFA), or PDD/Asperger's, were not well suited to either the self-contained autism classroom or the mixed behavioral/learning problems classroom. They were also often unable to attend the mainstream, regular education classroom setting because they were either disruptive, overwhelmed and inattentive, or subject to bullying and harassment. The alternative was to seek an out-of-district placement in either a small private special needs school, with classrooms specifically for HFA/Asperger's students, or just a smaller, more flexible and tolerant private school, but this was usually at the parents' expense. Even if parents could afford it, the private schools which met the needs of this particular cohort were often full, and there were long waiting lists for the better schools – that is, those with social skills and behavioral programming.

What we had to offer as an outpatient clinic at the time seemed to be almost futile, but out of necessity, we started doing as much as we could to supplement the educational system with social learning opportunities in the LEGO® Club format, as well as coaching parents, and doing direct individual therapy, to improve adaptive coping at home and in the community. Anthony was a good example of a coordinated approach, too, since he had the behavior specialist involved who was also on my staff, and we were able to get the school to agree to some in-home and community-based instruction after school to help address some weaknesses in his adaptive functioning identified by the Vineland scales, such as community mobility, peer relationships, and recreational activities. Having the home-based consultant available to Dale and Terri alleviated a lot of their anxiety, and even helped with the relationships between Anthony and his siblings. We were also able to generalize some of the things we were working on in LEGO Club to the home setting, and vice versa. Anthony's home therapist would often alert me to issues that were coming up there, and I was able to introduce these into the group for discussion, or to probe or test out Anthony on difficult dynamics, like sharing resources, enjoying someone else's success, accepting critical feedback, or providing appropriate critical feedback.

Working with Anthony and others in New Jersey introduced me to an interdisciplinary and multi-provider model which soon became the norm. While I was in Hawaii, I had gotten used to often being the sole provider on a case other than the physicians (pediatrician, neurologist or psychiatrist) and the teaching staff at school. In New Jersey, the available resources were so much better that I would often be joined by a school psychologist, behavior analyst and/or behavior specialist, home-based therapist, family therapist, speech-language pathologist, occupational therapist, clinical social worker, and educational consultant. Although in many instances I was still the only mental health provider, much more frequently I was either sharing responsibilities with staff from my own clinic, or with those from other agencies, and we needed to be more aware of each other's input, advice and interventions. Over the years, many of the other providers took it upon themselves to come visit the LEGO® Club groups, and to talk about what we were working on in there. Participants like Anthony often talked a lot about LEGO Club outside of the group sessions, to their parents and siblings, of course, but also with their teachers, classmates, other therapists, grandparents and neighbors, and anyone else who they could get to listen. Some of the therapist visitors wound up sticking around and getting an informal training in LEGO-based therapy, which they then took into their own practices.

So my role with Anthony was necessarily somewhat narrower than it had been with previous clients in Hawaii. I had completed the comprehensive assessment, and then I saw him for a few individual sessions while the LEGO room was being set up, then he joined the first New Jersey-based LEGO Club at the Institute. After that, my individual contact with him was limited to crisis situations, and consultations with his parents and other treatment providers when there were transitions or incidents at school or at home that warranted a "whole team" approach.

The first issues I got to address with Anthony, along with his family and behavior specialist, were his voice volume and tantrums. As the reader may recall, I had dealt with the issue of voice volume with Sam. Sam was loud, but he could moderate his voice to some extent, and he was aware of it, so he was apologetic, and disarmed people with his sense of humor, including making fun of his loud voice. Anthony had a sense of humor, like Sam, so his loud, bombastic communication style was often tolerated – he was annoying, but he made you laugh, too. But unlike Sam who tended to get quiet and withdrawn when he was anxious or upset, Anthony got louder when he was unhappy, and his voice took on a whiny, needle-sharp edge to it. When he was very upset, his voice jumped an octave and he literally wailed, and words poured out of him as if he were keening. He even rocked and paced like a bereaved parent, wailing and keening, tears would stream down his face, mucus would run, and he would slap himself in the face, pull his own hair, gnash his teeth, foam at the mouth and saliva would fly out with every word. Unlike Sam who was willing to moderate his voice and had the self-awareness to at least acknowledge the volume of his voice, Anthony's response to corrective feedback was escalation.

## LEARNING THROUGH LEGO®

During one of my first individual sessions with Anthony, I'd gotten an update from Terri, and Anthony was starting to get edgy and upset about me talking with her: "You're using up my time with Dr. Dan, Mom! Get out!" He was very motivated by the idea of sorting through the donated LEGO boxes, and helping me put the room in order for the Club, and he wanted to get to the sorting. His motivation was not entirely disingenuous, though, since he had an alternative agenda – Anthony wanted to find superhero LEGO (Batman, Spider-Man, etc.) – and assemble comic book scenes, which he envisioned having some prominence on the empty shelves, with the scene title and his name displayed. Basically, pages of a comic book in 3D. He used the "helping Dr. Dan with the LEGO" as an excuse to get access to the boxes.

Terri had been telling me about an incident at school in which some other students had been teasing/harassing him, but Anthony hadn't really noticed; in fact, he thought they were being playful with him. Anthony's brother, Jordan, had seen some of this going on and he knew they were not being playful. One of the themes that some of the other kids had used to pick on Anthony was that he had a list of names of kids he wanted to kill, and was going to bring the list and an automatic weapon to school someday. Mass-shooting incidents like this had been in the media a lot recently, and were a major concern to both parents and teaching staff, but it was fair game for teasing among middle schoolers. Like most of the kids I worked with, Anthony had difficulty distinguishing playful teasing from mean or harmful teasing. Dale had noticed that Anthony would get very upset and "go into one of his deals," if he or Jordan tried playfully teasing him. But in this instance his peers were clearly trying to target and exclude Anthony, and possibly provoke a reaction from him; he thought it was funny, and that they were paying him some kind of compliment by saying he might be dangerous.

I worked with Anthony on reciprocity in the LEGO® room; I knew it would be important later in the group, as well as being a bigger issue for him in relationships in general. I helped him search for superhero-related materials in the boxes, and he helped me sort the mass of the material into drawers (cheap, plastic bins on coaster wheels with see-through plastic drawers – perfect for LEGO sorting and storage). We engaged in our LEGO archeological dig, and I noticed that Anthony's voice was much lower when he was concentrating. I complimented him on using a more appropriate voice tone for the setting and our proximity. Anthony smiled, and said, "Yeah, I don't always talk so loud, especially when I chew gum." It turned out that he had had the insight that he didn't talk too loudly when he was concentrating, and when he chewed gum, but he hadn't bothered to tell anyone. Soon after this session, gum and hands-on activities (e.g. Gameboy®) became a mandatory part of car-rides, restaurant visits, trips to the library, family get-togethers, etc.

The following week when Anthony was scheduled to join three other boys for the first LEGO Club group session, Terri called and asked if we could have an emergency family session. Both Terri and Dale arrived, with Anthony and Jordan, and they all looked upset. It turned out that Anthony had been talking to the boys who were teasing him at school, and he had joked along with them, indicating one boy in particular by saying, "I don't have a list, but if I had one, your name would be on the top of it." He had said this, in his loud voice, within earshot of a staff member. The boys happily confirmed for the staff that Anthony had threatened him, and that he had a plan to come to school with a weapon and kill a "list of students."

The school administration suspended Anthony pending further investigation, and a mental health assessment regarding "homicidal ideation/statements." They also alerted the police, who interviewed the other boys involved, and wound up charging Anthony with terroristic threatening. I interviewed Anthony and got the details, and wrote a brief assessment indicating that he was not a threat and did not have thoughts or intentions regarding hurting anyone, but the school administrator indicated that Anthony would be suspended from school until after the court date, which was three months away. They indicated that the risk to other students at the school was too high to allow him to return unless he was cleared of all charges.

Anthony's parents were angry, of course, and blamed the school for allowing Anthony to be teased and picked on at school. They were never as trusting or supportive towards their school district as they had been before this incident, and they subsequently advocated for Anthony to be placed in a private special needs setting. They were eventually successful in getting the district to fund Anthony at a private school, but until then his parents had to pay for an attorney, and a private tutor to teach and watch over Anthony while they were at work. The attorney filed for a manifestation hearing, during which he argued that the incident at the school was a direct manifestation of Anthony's Asperger's Disorder (I had written an expert opinion for the hearing on this topic), and they won that case, so the charges were dropped. In the meantime, though, the local press had published an article about the incident, citing the school's "vigilance against threats of violence," and vilifying Anthony and his parents for trying to put Anthony back in school despite his "terroristic threats against fellow students." The article did not mention that Anthony had a disability.

None of this bothered Anthony, at least not directly. In fact, his parents had to ask him to stop mentioning the incident to family members, and even strangers – he had been carrying around a copy of the newspaper article and showing it to anyone who would look at it. There was no press coverage of the manifestation hearing in which the judge dismissed the charges, and admonished the school district for allowing the other boys to tease Anthony and essentially instigate this incident, clearly picking on him because of his disability. Anthony, however, perseverated on the topic, and then started making up lists at home – lists of students, then other lists of names of famous murderers and serial killers, mass shooters, superheroes and comic-book characters, and lists of family members. Then he started rank ordering the lists of names as the "Top Ten Family Members" and "Top Twelve Archie Comics Characters," and so on. This preoccupation with making lists lasted for years, similar to many other examples I'd seen of how children with autism responded to significant events by repeating them in some form. Eventually, he got over it, though, as he did the loudness and tantrums, largely through the development of other strengths and self-confidence. Anthony eventually learned that he was not only no "retard," but he was an intelligent and creative person, and having that insight, he began to behave in a way that was consistent with his new self-image.

## JOINING OTHERS

Introducing Anthony to a LEGO® Club group was significantly different in a few ways from the way this process had gone in the past. In Hawaii, the group process had been more new and more plastic, so there wasn't as much of a structure to familiarize the new members with. With Anthony and the other group members whom I was planning to put together in New Jersey – see Allen, Charlie, Paul and Colin, below – I was able to give them some expectations about the group process, rules, activities and expectations. I was also planning to include higher-order group activities; given that the members I was working with were somewhat older and had a lot of LEGO experience already, we were hopefully going to move through the level system (Helper, Builder, Creator, Master) fairly quickly, and get on to some bigger projects, including stop-motion film-making and the organization of larger freestyle building projects as film sets, or even a miniature film studio. Having those pre-set plans and an idea about what to expect from the group activities also helped me introduce the idea to Anthony's and the other group members' parents.

In Hawaii, the level of available services had been so low that the parents and school districts were very accepting and happy to have any kind of autism/Asperger's services, especially a social skills group. Even if it seemed a little unorthodox to have a social skills group based on LEGO play, it was never really questioned.

In New Jersey, the parents were much more critical as consumers, and they had options. There were a number of social skills groups for children with autism/Asperger's already up and running in the area when I introduced LEGO® Club. The school districts and other providers were also anything but naïve about what I was offering. Although they were willing to adopt a "wait-and-see" attitude, some were outright skeptical, as had been many of my colleagues at the Institute. So, clearly, I wasn't just "winging it" anymore – in New Jersey, I had a structure to follow, there were expectations about outcomes, and there were plenty of well-informed, critical observers.

The first day that we all got together for a LEGO Club group – our grand opening – everything just flowed. The parents and participants arrived on time or early – they were eager to get started. The building had plenty of parking, and a large, nicely furnished waiting room (thank you, the Institute!), and so the parents and siblings had room to sit and discover each other. The painting and decorating of the room was finished, and we had lots of space, chairs, table surfaces and shelving. There were still stacks of boxes full of unexplored donated LEGO, as well as bins now half-full of sorted LEGO, quite a few completed sets on display, and some early freestyle projects well underway. I had asked one of my graduate students, Sarah, to participate, and she was a big hit with the group – mainly because she claimed to know nothing about LEGO, so the members had someone to teach, and also because she was young and very pretty. The boys were more focused on the LEGO overall, than on me, Sarah or each other, but I asked them to introduce themselves, and share their interests and ideas for the Club. They got excited and talked over each other, and Anthony got loud, of course, but it was a very positive experience.

The following week, we started getting more focused, as we engaged in the "Helper" level tasks of sorting through the LEGO and organizing it, labeling the bins and identifying parts from sets that we might be able to complete. That was a particularly thrilling activity – someone would find parts in a box that they recognized from a familiar set, some of them quite old, and sometimes there would even be a remnant or complete set of directions along with it. This really was a bit like an archeological dig. We'd isolate any of the "set" pieces, and slowly go through the rest of the box or bin, and any other containers that might have been donated along with it, to see if we could get a complete set.

As jazzy as this process was for me – discovering an old set, and pulling it together based on partial set directions, or even just an image from an old LEGO® catalogue – some of the group members, including Anthony, had their own agendas. Anthony's, of course, was the comic-book topic, and he would quickly veer off from a group activity if he came across any superhero parts. This was a good example of a behavioral tendency that was not covered by the "LEGO Club Rules," which the boys had been happy to review and post in the room, and to remind each other about. No one really had a problem with the rules, except occasionally taking parts from each other or, of course, yelling or loud voices, and we had not had to implement any "LEGO points," or other formal behavioral intervention strategies, at least not for this first group.

What we did introduce were the "Rules of Cool," which were informal and unwritten social rules, which the members all seemed to agree were relevant, even though they had difficulty following them; for example, "Look at people when you talk to them," "Join in, don't do your own thing," "Don't put down someone else's work," etc. Staying with the group and not doing your own thing was a very common theme with this group, which was good practice for them that had direct relevance to their social interactions outside of the group. It also created lots of opportunities for the trading of favors – which included me. I frequently offered to help Anthony find superheroes, or to build superhero scenes (and later, work on superhero movies), if he would help me sort parts and look for set pieces. It was even easier for Sarah, for whom the group members would do anything just to get her attention.

We eventually had enough of the donated boxes sorted out to start adding some sets, and for the first time, we introduced the LEGO Club Level System. They had all earned their "LEGO Helper" diplomas, and now were asked to demonstrate their LEGO Builder skills, by putting together a medium-sized LEGO set on their own – without mistakes, without losing pieces, and within a reasonable time frame. This was easy enough for most of the group members, and even Anthony scoffed at the task, saying it was too easy for him, but then, he really struggled: he couldn't stay focused on the set long enough to get it done, and then he kept missing steps or dropping and losing pieces. We had long since introduced the cafeteria tray method for keeping LEGO® pieces on the table, but Anthony kept moving pieces off the tray, dropping them on the floor, etc. After the first session when he failed to get his LEGO Builder level (only Allen had also failed, but his problem was poor fine motor skills, as is discussed in Allen's story below), Anthony held it together through the group, then had a "meltdown" in the waiting room with his mom and little sister. Terri and Angela were not a particularly sympathetic audience. Sarah tried to intervene, and was supportive about his chances for next week – she promised to help him get it done. Angela said, "Anthony's really bad at LEGOs, you know. He says he's good, but he's not. Jordy always has to help him. I'm better at LEGOs than Anthony." Luckily, Sarah and I were there to intervene.

The next week, rather than having Sarah help Anthony with the LEGO Builder challenge, we had Anthony and Allen work together – Allen prompted Anthony back to the task and helped him keep track of the pieces, while Anthony did most of the building. Together, they were able to complete two medium-level sets (about 200 pieces each) in an hour and a half, and both earned their "LEGO Builder" certificates, which the other group members were happy to endorse and sign. This was also the start of a significant, long-term relationship between Anthony and Allen, who wound up staying friends outside of the group for years, and both families were very happy to have the other family over for various functions and share holidays, etc.

Anthony progressed through the LEGO Creator level with the group's support quite easily, as his LEGO Superhero comic scenes were well liked and even admired, and his attention to detail and focus for these projects was very good. He had an incredible memory for detail, and could recreate comic-book pages, or scenes from movies, including camera angles, buildings, vehicles and other props, without any visual aids. Anthony desperately wanted to shoot some stop-motion animated footage of Spider-Man and Batman scenes, but first, he had to get to the LEGO Master level. He tried, every group session, to convince the other group members who were at the Master level to take on a superhero project, but they all had their own ideas and projects. In order to get the Master level, Anthony had to get a large set (over 400 pieces) or a large freestyle project done, with the group's involvement and support, and have the other members agree that he had been a good leader on the project. He initiated a number of large building projects, but each time the project was underway, and especially if it looked like we might run out of time, and he would have to wait another week (or more) for the project to be completed, he would get impatient. Then he would get louder, angrier and frustrated, and finally, he would start pacing, cursing and using his "siren" voice, as the boys called it. "Why can't you all just do what I tell you? You're not getting it done fast enough! This isn't good enough! I'm not going to get my Master level because you're all too slow! You have to listen! Stop talking and focus. FOCUS!" He'd be crying by the middle of the group, and the other members would all just stop what they were doing, tell him they wouldn't work with him anymore and move on to something else.

This kept happening to Anthony for months. Allen was keeping track for him: "You've tried for Master 11 times, Anthony. I think you should just give up." Anthony had a mild tantrum about that, but then, in a fit of tears and wailing, said he would give up, and would just stay at Creator level for the rest of his life. A few weeks later, we were working on a cityscape set for one of Charlie's films, and Anthony had been leading the group on the scene, which he had a good mental image for. Charlie liked his ideas and let him run with it – a city street which featured an intersection, and the back and front of a bank building that was the scene of a robbery. Towards the end of the session, we were starting to shoot some of the stop-action footage, and I suggested that we give credit to Anthony for the set design. Allen and Charlie both said Anthony deserved LEGO® Master for the project, and the rest of us agreed. Anthony just looked around in shock. He'd done it without even trying. We printed out his LEGO Master certificate, and everyone signed it and congratulated Anthony, who was in tears by then.

Anthony's achievement of LEGO Master made a great impression on his parents, who had his certificate framed, as well as on Anthony himself. He seemed more confident, calmer and more resilient after that. He seemed to realize that he didn't need to try so hard to accomplish things; he could just use his abilities, talents and creativity, and not worry so much about the outcome. He was eventually given "LEGO Genius" status for his participation in group animated film projects, including his own series. He wrote and directed over a dozen short animated films, and participated as a voice actor, stop-motion controller and cinematographer on many more. He struggled with the writing of scripts, but he was highly motivated to get his ideas on paper, and often used a comic-book format for his stories and story-boarding of films. His projects showed off his quirky sense of humor, and he learned to share and enjoy the equally unique storytelling and visual jokes of his peers. By the time Anthony finished middle school, and was ready for the transition to high school, he had formally graduated from LEGO® Club – he had many friends outside of the group as well as within, and was busy with participating in his school's drama club – it turned out he had a talent for acting. He joined the ranks of an illustrious group of LEGO Club members who became the first "LEGO Legends," a designation that was invented by the Club members to recognize those who had contributed a significant body of work to the LEGO Club community – sets, freestyle creations and short films.

# ALLEN

## INITIAL CONTACT

Allen was fairly typical of the new types of referrals I was getting since relocating to New Jersey. He had already received a diagnosis of Asperger's Disorder, and he and his family had already received some appropriate services, including a very good IEP and educational placement. His neurologist was a colleague at the Institute, Dr. M, who thought he might benefit from the LEGO® Club groups, and his parents and IEP team agreed that this seemed to be a good fit for a missing component of Allen's services array.

Allen presented as a slender 12-year-old youth who looked like he spent most of his time indoors not doing anything very vigorous. He had reddish light brown hair and freckles, and had a striking resemblance to what Bill Gates must have looked like at 12, and Allen not only acknowledged the resemblance: he was proud of it. He wore glasses, which I assumed he must have picked out because they looked just like the ones Bill Gates wore at the time – frameless rectangles. He knew his own diagnosis, and in fact, he owned it, and had a certain confidence about himself that was not typical, in my experience, for a pre-teen with Asperger's Disorder. His parents were also very proud of him, and they seemed relieved to be able to talk to someone who also seemed to see the positive side of children with autistic conditions.

During the initial interview, Allen's parents recalled many negative experiences with the educational system, and in other social settings, where Allen's behavior and social awkwardness had not been welcomed. He had had the usual initial diagnoses from his pediatrician and then child mental health specialists of ADHD and Oppositional Defiant Disorder, due to his apparent indifference to social rules and expectations, and difficulties with peer relationships.

What most people found off-putting about Allen, however, was his pedantic manner of speech and his self-confidence, which, combined with his unusually well-developed vocabulary, seemed like arrogance to them. Cognitive and academic testing had been done on Allen when he was younger, and he had scored in the Very Superior range (gifted) in all areas, especially language-based abilities. His reading level was years ahead of age and grade level norms, and he was often difficult in class simply because he was bored: most of the work he was given at school was just tedious clerical work – he wasn't learning anything at school that he hadn't already learned on his own.

## LEARNING THROUGH LEGO®

What I discovered, though, after spending some time alone with Allen, was that a lot of his self-confident air was a bluff that he put on in front of his parents and siblings. He admitted that he was intelligent, but he was also very socially anxious and highly self-critical. He felt he had a lot to live up to, partly because of all the praise that his parents, and more recently, his teachers, had lavished on him. He was secretly jealous of his younger brother who did not appear to have his gifts, but made friends more easily, and seemed to "get" social and play situations intuitively, in a way that Allen did not. So, in a way, Allen was aware that he was bluffing in social situations, and he lived in fear of being discovered to be what he secretly thought he was: socially awkward, anxious, unsure of himself. He had been feeling less and less competent in social interactions with his peers at school or in the Boy Scouts, which he attended regularly, since they were developing more complex, multi-layered communication patterns that involved sarcasm, idiosyncratic insider jokes, and sexualized humor. These little bits of communication – as well as what Allen called "the girl thing" – made him feel more like an outsider than usual, and he wanted to know the secrets; he wanted to be part of the in-crowd. His strategy to this point had simply been to be seen to be very smart, and an admitted geek, and his peers were okay with him in that role.

One of the nicest traits that Allen had was his honesty and frankness. This made him fairly typical of kids with Asperger's, and also made him easy to work with. There are few social situations in which unadulterated honesty and frankness are more functional than in therapy. Even though most people value honesty and we have a lot of indoctrination throughout childhood to encourage children to be honest, most socially successful adults accept that honesty is a relative concept, and that pure, unmodified expressions of your true inner thoughts and feelings is not public fare. For Allen, as for many of the kids I've worked with over the years, learning when, where and how to be honest is a very confusing process. Most parents will agree that at some point – if not at many or even most points – they've had to remind their child with Asperger's or autism that too much honesty is not a good thing. But even they had a tentative understanding of what all the rules are that apply to self-disclosure or to social commentary that is "true but not appropriate."

It was one of my first insights about social development when I started working with this population – HFA and Asperger's: I had to tell them that there were rules that most people followed in social situations that they themselves didn't even know were rules, until you broke them. It was one of those intuitive "swim with the fishes" kind of things. It made me realize that there were a lot of questions about social development in typical children that science did not have clear answers for. Language acquisition has this mysterious, genetically determined neurological substrate that allows for not only rapid acquisition of a vocabulary and syntax, but also unspoken, unwritten and even unacknowledged rules – or exceptions to rules – that are acquired through exposure and some kind of intuition. Novel, creative uses of language are not completely novel, or random. Early childhood language acquisition violates the structure of language at times, or predictable sequences are uneven (e.g. over-generalization of words, or grammatical rules), but still predictable. Similarly, social development – the acquisition of receptive, associative and expressive elements of social interaction, relationship building, and socially mediated goal achievement – follows a culturally defined, idiosyncratic path or map that doesn't exist in real terms. It was a social map or rulebook that Allen, and many children like him, asked for, and which I did not have.

Although I didn't have an answer to all of his questions about the when, how and why of social interactions, we did have some basic rules, and these were brought out and discussed in LEGO® Club, as the "Rules of Cool." Sometimes we also just talked about social expectations and insights regarding these as a group, and as things came up for various members. I'd hear about a painful, or successful, experience from a member's parents, teacher or therapist, and I'd try to incorporate that experience into the side-bar conversation that was always going on in the group, while we were building. Sometimes, during check-in, or at times just whenever it seemed appropriate, I'd ask a member to tell us about something that happened, or I'd remind them and they would take it up with the group to get their input. Often, other group members would have had similar experiences, and could relate to the conflict, or shared a sense of accomplishment about a similar challenge.

Allen's openness, his blunt honesty about his experiences and his terrific communication abilities allowed him to be a very effective conduit for group discussions about the challenges that adolescents with Asperger's Disorder faced every day. He was also very insightful about knowing when the other group members were not being fully honest, or were presenting events in a self-serving way. It was hard to get any sympathy from Allen, and he was just as hard on himself as he was with his peers. For instance, he was often brutally honest with Anthony about his "meltdowns," and would tell him if he thought he was just trying to get his way by becoming emotional: "Anthony, I'm going to let you do your thing today, because I know otherwise you're going to cry and do that horrible screaming thing. But I just wanted you to know that was why I was doing it, not because I care about you." He would comment on the other boys' hygiene, like body odor or hair and skin conditions, looking them straight in the eye, as he always did: "Yes, you're pubertal. You've got greasy hair and acne, and you smell musky. You should talk to your parents about skin care and deodorant, and maybe change your diet."

Allen was also open to feedback about his communication style, and he was actually very humble about his LEGO® skills, so he did want to enlist the help of his fellow group members. He was especially open to feedback from Sarah, although he would also solicit input from me, especially about situations at school or at home. Allen had a quality that many of his cohort did not, which was that he sincerely wanted to be liked. He was not cynical or indifferent, and he was very aware of his own shortcomings, so that often made him hesitant in the group, since he knew this was not a setting to be bluffing. He didn't want to be in charge, and often didn't want to be the leader, because he knew his LEGO® skills were not as good as some others. But he did feel he could step up as a mediator or to provide emotional support, when there were conflicts between group members, or, as was the case so often with Anthony, they were just frustrated with themselves.

Some of this prosocial attitude seemed to come from Allen's parents, who were kind, generous, helpful people. Both of them were involved in activities with Allen as well as their other children – Allen had a younger brother and sister – such as soccer and swimming, or the PTA, etc. When one of the other parents was having difficulties getting their son to the group, Allen's father volunteered to pick them up every week, and so Allen and another group member car-pooled to the group together every week. This included stopping on the way for a quick meal, since the group was scheduled in the later afternoon. Allen's mother was employed in the healthcare field, and was often answering questions from other parents on health-related issues, and was always ready to wipe a nose or watch a little one in the waiting room.

It was a complete shock when Allen's father stopped coming for a few weeks, and then arrived, looking miserable and unshaven, and admitted that he and his wife had separated. Allen's father admitted that the break-up had been his fault, and that he'd had an affair, and had been asked to move out. Allen and his brother and sister were struggling to assimilate this and his mother was uncharacteristically edgy, on the verge of tears, quiet and tense in the waiting room when she brought Allen. She found some support from the other mothers that were there. Allen's father, when he came with Allen, just dropped him off and left, looking tired and a bit disheveled. It was a very hard time for the family. Anthony's parents helped out by having Allen over for playdates and weekend sleepovers. Eventually, Allen was able to talk about the situation at home with the group.

Allen was bitter, and I recognized his mother's tone in his voice when he talked about his father's affair and then his leaving and getting his own apartment. For the first time, he sounded more cynical and disappointed about his father – he had always been openly admiring of him, which had been clearly a mutual thing. Allen's father had always bragged about him, and even supported the "next Bill Gates" view that Allen expressed sometimes. Although some of the group members were unsympathetic and unhelpful in their response to Allen, others were more empathic and they seemed to be taking it to heart, perhaps even realizing that this was something that could have happened to any of them. Some of them had already experienced their parents getting divorced, and knew how unsettling it was to have the family disintegrate like that.

Luckily, after a few months of tension and Allen expressing anger and fear in groups about his parents' situation – anger at his father, and fear about the home-situation and having to cope with changes in his schedule, maybe even a relocation – Allen's parents went to marital counseling, and they eventually got back together. They had asked Allen not to discuss these family issues in the group, and they did have family therapy and an individual therapist for Allen, so I was not as much involved in the details of this process. I was very happy for them all, though, and it was really nice to see them getting through what would have taken apart so many other families. Allen didn't talk about it much, but he didn't seem to need to: he was back to his usual cheerful, blunt and chatty self.

## JOINING OTHERS

Unlike most of the LEGO® Club participants I had worked with in Hawaii, the individual, one-on-one time that I spent with Allen was much more limited. He also did not require a comprehensive evaluation in order to clarify his diagnosis or educational needs, so my experience of him was mostly through the group, and the incidental contact that I had with him initially and then with his parents and siblings in the waiting room. I was somewhat worried at first about this decreased level of contact and opportunity for individual and family therapy. I wasn't sure that the LEGO group experience, and efficacy, were going to be the same without these extras. For instance, I had gotten used to being able to review challenges or issues before a group, or discuss them afterwards, in individual or family therapy, in order to more thoroughly process and even rehearse alternative social strategies or ways of communicating.

Although this was a worrisome and unsatisfying arrangement for me, the new LEGO Club members were naturally oblivious about the issue. In some instances, parents would seek out my input about issues at home or at school, or in the community, and would schedule individual or family sessions. Some families did ask for ongoing family sessions, especially when there were difficult behaviors at home, adolescent development issues, sibling conflicts, or co-morbid problems such as depression, anxiety or OCD. But for a lot of the group members, including Allen, the family had other providers, and the school setting was doing its appropriate share, so there was just less for me to do. That took some getting used to, especially with participants and families that I felt a strong connection with, such as Allen and his family. Happily, the LEGO® Club groups continued to have a beneficial impact on children's social functioning and their lives in general, even with considerably less of my input.

What Allen did appear to benefit from in terms of his LEGO experience was the awareness of other abilities – what some would call "right brain thinking." Allen was such a natural "left brain" talent – language-based reasoning abilities in the gifted range – that he tended to perceive other children, and many adults, as mere mortals. It was when he was confronted with LEGO that he became more aware that he actually had some limitations, and that other people had abilities or talents that he could admire. Allen also had the insight that LEGO Club was a social skills group, which he tended to be more aware of than the other group members. They usually had some idea that this was not just an ordinary youth group – for instance, it was held in a medical facility – but were too distracted by the LEGO and the activities to give it much thought. Allen actually studied the group process at times, and seemed to be monitoring his own progress. "I'm not very good at this, Dr. Dan. No one seems to want to listen to me, even though I have pretty great ideas. I'm going to have to get better at social skills or I'll never get to be a LEGO Master."

Allen's younger brother, Will, was naturally sociable, like his parents. He was quiet and rather serious, but he could also be endearingly goofy and silly. He was dead serious about LEGO, but he was also a big "Calvin and Hobbes" and "SpongeBob" fan, and liked to act out scenes from these cartoons. Will had mild speech-articulation and speech fluency problems, so he tended to be action-oriented, rather than a natural-born lawyer like his older brother. He would look for opportunities to "show" me what he was thinking about or engaged in – turning a hand-held screen my way, or putting a LEGO set together in the waiting room, without directions.

He probably felt burned that his big brother got to go to LEGO® Club, and he was excluded. He visited the room after every session to see what "the big kids" had been working on, and more than once he commented that he would be able to do any of the LEGO skills necessary, and it was a very sad situation to keep him out of the group. It was probably a relief for Allen, since Will probably would have outshone him quickly in LEGO building finesse. In fact, Allen often spent most of a LEGO session off to one side, talking with Sarah, and commenting on the process, or offering directions from the sidelines. We had to keep after him to stay engaged in the process. As was mentioned in Anthony's story, he and Allen eventually had to team up in order for the two of them to pass one of the easier levels, LEGO Builder. With Allen, the difficulty certainly wasn't with attention span or comprehension – it was visual-spatial analysis and simple mechanical know-how that slowed him down.

This humbling experience, and appreciation of the talents of others, was an important experience for Allen, and he even had this insight and acknowledged it. "Dr. Dan, you have to admit, my ego would be really a problem if I didn't really suck at LEGO. So this is good for me." He smiled. "Now I'm brilliant, and humble!" It also had a beneficial impact on his willingness to engage with peers, and to respect their input. There were a couple of group members who clearly struggled with verbal communication, and Allen could talk rings around them, but they were very skilled LEGO builders and creators. Their visual-spatial abilities, hand-eye coordination and speed were quite remarkable when building, but they also showed a lot of visual cleverness in solving engineering problems, finding novel ways to use LEGO mechanically and visually.

In the film-making process, Allen was quickly found out to be an excellent (and very funny) writer, as well as voice actor. He was excellent at creating storylines and scenarios that were wonderful short skits to animate, but he would have been lost trying to create the sets and scenery on his own. He had come up with the idea of having a news hour – which expanded on Paul's weather report segment (see below). He created the character of Cindy Brickberg, a female news anchor who was invariably injured or killed during "at the scene" news coverage. Allen had initially invited Sarah, the only available female voice in the room, to do Cindy on camera, which worked wonderfully. But then, Sarah left us for other venues, and

Allen took over as the voice of Cindy. His falsetto news reporter was very funny, and the Cindy character remained a hit with LEGO® participants for years. When Allen eventually graduated from the group, the character of Cindy Brickberg lingered on, and Allen, like Anthony, was inducted into the esteemed company of LEGO Legends for his many creative and hilarious Cindy episodes. Even Will was beaming with pride at the first LEGO Film Festival when the Cindy Brickberg episodes were aired to a larger audience.

# CHARLIE

## INITIAL CONTACT

It was Charlie's mother, Cindy, who initiated his referral to LEGO® Club. She had been advocating on behalf of Charlie for his educational and healthcare needs since he was in preschool, and despite not having more than a high school education herself, Cindy had become well versed in the autism/Asperger's treatment and education literature. She also had good judgment about his needs, and about people in general. She was like Allen's mother, always helping out a neighbor or a relative, and was always doing special favors for the group and the other kids and their parents, whether it was baking Christmas cookies, or taking a group of kids to the movies or the pool. She was always giving, and had an intuitive understanding of the value of social support for getting through life. She and her husband had three boys – Charlie was the middle one – and they were both blue-collar workers who lived in a small town. They made sure that Charlie was included in all the activities that his brothers did – baseball, soccer, swimming, Boy Scouts, etc. When Cindy heard about LEGO Club, she knew it was the right thing for Charlie, and she had to harangue her health insurance company to cover it. It was also quite a trip every week to get him to the groups, but she and Charlie, and Charlie's younger brother, were there every week.

Like most of the other boys in this group, Charlie was 12, and was transitioning from elementary school to middle school (6th grade to 7th grade). Charlie had attended a very small, supportive and well-run elementary school. The family lived across the street from the school, so Charlie's mother was always over at the school helping out with functions, and keeping an eye on her boys. She had spoken to the school staff and administration when Charlie first started there in Kindergarten. At that point, he had been diagnosed with PDD-NOS, and had been receiving early intervention services through the county. Cindy was grateful for the help she had gotten from the Early Intervention Program (EIP), but she didn't want to have Charlie attend a self-contained classroom or a special needs school, both of which were offered to her by the school district. She wanted Charlie to attend the mainstream school, and a mainstream classroom, just like his brothers. The school was small enough and had enough flexibility to make accommodations for Charlie, and so his elementary school experience was very good.

Cindy had not heard good things about the middle-school experience. This was a completely different kind of setting. The middle school was a regional one, and was located on the same campus as the regional high school. There were four towns that attended the regional school, and so Charlie would be meeting a large number of new students there, which worried Cindy. "What if they don't get him? I can't be there to protect him, or to keep an eye on those brats. I know, because of my older one, there's some tough ones there – parents don't give a rip, and they're smoking already, doing drugs. I saw a kid in the parking lot the other day with a tattoo! He couldn't have been more than 15. And there's girls there with babies. I don't think Charlie's ready to have a discussion about that."

Cindy had the option of having Charlie attend a regional special needs program, but she wanted to continue with his mainstreaming. She just wanted to make sure he would be able to "fend for himself" in that setting. She thought LEGO® Club would be a great opportunity for him to get used to interacting with kids his age that he didn't know well, and learn to "keep up" socially. "He does alright with the academics. He can read and do math right there at grade level, but he's not too savvy with the social part. At our home, the kids know him and know not to tease him or test him. His brothers also look out for him, and no one messes with him at school. We live right across the street and they know I'll be over there like a momma bear if anything happens. Ah. This middle school thing is stressing me out."

Charlie was quiet and reserved, and he moved and spoke a little hesitantly, like he wasn't quite sure what he wanted to do, or say. He was slender, fairly tall, and had short-cropped blond hair and blue eyes. His speech was a bit indistinct and he always sounded a bit congested (he did suffer from allergies), but his voice was also somewhat high-pitched, and breathy. Charlie was naturally polite and conscientious. He was also rather private, and although he had his share of unusual pre-occupations and certain rigidities and rituals that he engaged in at home, he didn't do much of this in public. Charlie seemed shy at first, but then I realized it was more like aloofness. Cindy told me: "Charlie just likes to do his own thing. If you don't bother him, he'll be off building with his LEGO®s, or drawing, or making up his own game, happy all by himself."

## LEARNING THROUGH LEGO

Charlie had LEGO at home, as did his brothers, and they would sometimes work on projects together, so Charlie was well prepared to join the new LEGO Club group. He had some mild fine motor difficulties, though, and this made it difficult for him at times to manipulate some of the smaller and more mechanical LEGO pieces (e.g. LEGO Technic). Charlie was not particularly self-aware, and so he was often unaware of what sort of impression he was making. Not that he didn't care – he would have been horrified to think that he was being rude to someone – but it just seemed like too much for him to keep track of. This was a "theory of mind" weakness that was a core feature of his atypical autistic presentation. The fact that he was so well adjusted emotionally – very accepting, patient, tolerant, easy-going – had a lot to do with his parents, and the fact that he had gone to a small school where everyone knew him, and included him in every way. He was such a nice, gentle, good-natured kid, it naturally made me anxious for him, the way Cindy was anxious. How was he going to handle middle school and the adolescent social world?

One of Charlie's strengths, though, which made him seem different from most of the other group members, was that he was athletic. Charlie was one of the few HFA/PDD-NOS kids I'd met who could participate in township or inter-scholastic sports, without any accommodations or supports. In my view, that pretty much ruled out Asperger's Disorder, which always seemed to be associated with some level of physical coordination problems. Charlie had fine motor difficulties – slow and poorly formed handwriting, difficulties with small LEGO, and even some difficulties with buttons and shoelaces. But he could catch and throw and run. He could do a layup in basketball, dribble a soccer ball at a full run, catch a grounder or a fly ball, and dive off the three-meter board. Most of the other kids in LEGO® Club couldn't even dream of doing these things, and Charlie did them without even thinking much of it. But Charlie wasn't assertive. He wasn't anxious, he was just, as Cindy said, more into doing his own thing.

Charlie and I had a few sessions alone together. I had met with Cindy and his younger brother a few times as well – Charlie's younger brother, Benjamin, was a huge LEGO fan, and it was torture for him to come to the group sessions with his brother and not be allowed into the groups. Ben did wind up making a good connection with Allen's younger brother, and they often had their own little group going in the waiting room, with their mothers chatting nearby. Charlie said he felt bad that his brother wasn't allowed in, but then he let it go. He was cooperative with me, building a few sets, and searching for some missing pieces in the bins, etc., but he seemed listless. Charlie was less interested in set-building than in doing freestyle, and mostly he liked to reproduce Super Mario characters using LEGO bricks. He told me he had made all of the Super Mario characters at home, and had them all over his room. He quickly made a few for me in the LEGO room. Rather crude, but appropriately pixelated creations. Charlie had a good eye, and the regular building bricks were easy for him to manipulate. We put some of his creations on display in the freestyle area of the room, and Charlie was very pleased.

Having met and gotten to know some of the other group members by that point, I was a bit concerned that Charlie might get a bit lost or overwhelmed in the crowd. Sarah, who had also met Charlie, tended to agree with me, but we were also both confident that we could support Charlie to navigate the challenges, and that it would be good for him to have a safe, supportive setting in which to do that before he started middle school in the fall.

## JOINING OTHERS

The first group session at the facility included Charlie, Anthony, Allen, Paul and Colin, and then Sarah and me. There were more members later, but we started with those five. Charlie and Colin (see below) were definitely the quietest members of the group, but

Charlie stayed involved and didn't try to withdraw, while Colin was in and out of the group. In the first session, we introduced ourselves, and I helped facilitate that by giving a bit more background on each kid, highlighting their strengths, and their LEGO® interests. Then we talked about the rules. I got them to talk about what they felt would be important rules for the group first, then I introduced the list that had become standard with previous groups, and they all agreed that it seemed complete, except for Anthony, who had a lot of rules to add. Anthony seemed to just want to have the group's attention. "We should have a rule about not bringing in bugs. And no spitting. I don't know about you guys, but I really don't want anyone spitting in here, or bringing in bugs. Okay, nothing toxic. No toxic materials. No spitting, no insects and no toxic materials, Dr. Dan. Can you please add those to the list?"

Charlie thought this was funny. "And, Dr. Dan," he laughed, "no dangerous, wild animals. Like lions, tigers and bears." The other group members laughed, too. It was the first time Charlie had said much, and they seemed to appreciate his sense of humor. Anthony wasn't sure whether Charlie was making fun of him, so he looked seriously at Charlie. "No one in here has access to wild animals, but they might bring in insects, or spit, or bring in something toxic..."

"Like a can of insecticide spray," Allen said. He seemed to be getting impatient with Anthony and this topic. "How about a rule that says, No Dumb Rules?"

Colin moved into the group, laughing, and said quietly to himself, "No dumb rules!" and then loudly, "And no spear guns! Or battle axes. Hah! No spear guns or battle axes or swords."

Allen was being patient, but barely, and he said, "And no pointed sticks," a Monty Python reference, which cracked up Anthony – "Pointed sticks!" he cried in his best John Cleese voice, and then, "Come at me with this bah-nah-nah. Be as vicious as you like." Allen and Charlie laughed, and Charlie got it: "That's Monty Python." Paul laughed and hopped up and down, and began reciting the lines from the rabbit scene in "Holy Grail." Anthony countered with lines from the black knight scene, which got Colin acting out the scene, both sides, and Paul jumped up to join him, holding his arms behind his back and hopping on one leg: "Right. I'll do you for that. I'm invincible."

Charlie then quietly went over to a drawer of minifigs and started getting out some knights, armor and weapons. Colin had stepped up and was loudly reciting the bridge of death scene, voicing both Sir Lancelot and the Bridgekeeper: "Who would cross the bridge of death must answer me these questions three…" Charlie quietly said, "Look, Dr. Dan." He had quickly assembled King Arthur, Lancelot and Sir Robin, with men carrying flags, pendants and a cask. Allen was watching Charlie and seemed amazed at how quickly he had pulled out the pieces. Anthony meanwhile was howling loudly, "Bring out your dead!" with Paul and Colin chiming in, "I'm not dead yet," etc. Needless to say, the group decided to follow Charlie's lead, and to recreate in LEGO® a number of the "Holy Grail" scenes, in advance of eventually doing stop-motion recreations of them.

We didn't have the camera equipment or computer, yet, but we were expecting that equipment at some point. Charlie had initiated the building, so over the next couple of sessions he was more-or-less in charge of set design, and he quickly laid out what the various scenes required in terms of minifigs, props, structures and scenery. They all agreed that the French castle scene was a must: "I fart in your general direction. Your mother was a hamster and your father smelled of elderberries," Colin recited in his best John Cleese annoying-French-guy voice. Charlie was focused: "We need a castle with a turret." The others started rummaging in the bins and boxes for castle pieces; Colin was doing most of the building. Charlie found a gray and blue landscape platform to put the castle on. Charlie worked on the castle with Paul, and helped the others by finding parts. He somehow knew exactly the right pieces to recreate the scenes in the film using LEGO, and he and Colin were definitely on the same page. They seemed to communicate by mutual vision – they would look at the pieces and the half-built project, and then with hardly a word, they would add pieces, exchange some, and look for something else. Just as the other boys in the group could recite lines from the movie, Colin and Charlie could recreate the scenes.

Eventually, the video camera and editing software arrived, and we introduced the group to the equipment, and to the basics of stop-motion animation. Right away, there was a power struggle to get use of the camera, but Sarah and I were able to get them to discuss their ideas ahead of time, and agree to have them share responsibilities for the camera and the software, and then for building and controlling the scenes and characters. Anthony wanted to shoot a mid-air WWII fighter plane dog-fight. He showed the rest of us how he would have the planes circling around and attacking each other, with loud machine gun fire. This sparked a competition for "best machine gun," which Colin thought he should have won, but none of them were actually very good, according to Allen. Sarah patiently explained to Anthony that he couldn't hold the fighter planes during the scene, but he was having a hard time with this."Just don't shoot my hands in the picture. Just take that part out." Charlie tried to explain to Anthony how stop-motion worked, but then Allen tried to help Charlie explain, and Anthony felt attacked and he started getting louder and his pitch went up. "Look, I think I had a good idea, and everyone is just criticizing my good idea, instead of helping me." Charlie said, "Anthony, we need a green screen for that. We don't have a green screen, so you can't be in the picture."

Colin got a couple of vehicles – a small truck and a police car – and put them on the table. "Let's start with something like this," he said. Charlie brought over some road plates, and put them down in front of the camera, and Colin put the vehicles on the road. We practiced the simple action of having the cars drive through the scene, and then played around with it a bit, having the truck stop suddenly, and the police car crash into it, then the truck's driver walking back and demanding the police officer's license and registration. We did a variety of car crash scenes, and in later stop-motion pieces we often incorporated car chases, since they were simple, action-packed and the boys enjoyed doing the sound effects of engines, tires and sirens screeching, etc. At first, though, the shots were jumpy and full of heads and hands. It took us forever to set up a shot and to move a vehicle through it. There was a lot of communication involved in just getting a clean sequence of a vehicle or figure moving across a scene, but we were slowly getting better at it. There was a writer/director who envisioned the scene and decided on the parameters of vehicles, scenery, direction and speed. The set-builders and animators had to build and lay out the scenery, and find or build the vehicles or other props (animals, traffic lights, etc.), and then move them in the scene according to the director's requests. The cameraman took the series of shots, with the director watching over his or her shoulder, and telling everyone to be quiet – "Quiet on the set" – and to get their hands and heads out of the shot: "Clear the scene."

One day, while some of the others were busy building a scene, Charlie practiced stop-motion with Colin as cameraman. Charlie had grabbed a couple of animals out of the drawer, a crocodile and a swordfish (sawfish, actually, but Charlie called it a swordfish). He just moved them around a bit, and then had them chasing each other, and then they got into a fight. Charlie narrated it, in a comically flat tone, using the same voice for both characters. Later, he introduced some more props and bits of scenery but kept the crocodile and the sawfish. The others watched his little animation trials, and they really enjoyed them. They were visually simple, but evocative, and Colin did a great job with the camera, making sure the camera and scene didn't move in between shots. The feedback from the group was encouraging to Charlie, so he continued to make what came to be known as "The Crocy and Swordy Show." The two characters were friends, but also fought with each other, and Charlie had them involved in many adventures, often involving Allen's Cindy Brickberg character as well, or Colin's favorite character, Stuntman Bif.

Charlie did a number of other stop-motion film creations, including large-scale LEGO® versions of various videogame characters, mostly from Super Mario, as well as Pokemon figures. Throughout his productions, he remained his usual calm, focused, quiet self. The others in the group came to admire him for that. Even Colin, who was very talented visually and with LEGO the way Charlie was, had to admit that Charlie was better at staying calm than anyone. Charlie was terrific at saying helpful things when the others were upset, which was pretty much every group session. All of them seemed to take turns having tearful, frustrated episodes, except Charlie, who was always saying, "It's okay, we'll get it done another time."

Once there was more than one group running, the groups often watched each other's stop-motion productions, and checked out the other groups' LEGO creations. An intergroup competitive spirit developed, and the groups learned about who the other group members were by their creative projects and films. For some reason, Crocy and Swordy were some of the most popular characters, and other groups even borrowed the characters to use in their own productions. This flattered Charlie, but some of his group-mates were outraged and wanted me to hide the sawfish and crocodile – I had to remind them that they were fairly common LEGO figures and we actually had a few of each. Allen wanted to pay tribute to Charlie for his production, so he came up with his own film idea in which he had Cindy Brickberg do a celebrity interview with Charlie, Crocy and Swordy. Charlie's "Crocy and Swordy Show" was a mainstay of the subsequent LEGO® Club Film Festivals, and was a hit with all the group members, as well as the siblings, parents, grandparents, etc., who also followed the LEGO animation productions. Quiet, unassuming Charlie had become a LEGO Club celebrity.

# PAUL

## INITIAL CONTACT

Paul was initially referred specifically for the LEGO® Club group, which was good timing, since he fitted right in with the other boys: same age, same issues. Paul was having some difficulties with educational placement – he was getting teased and bullied in public school – so I also got involved evaluating Paul and helping with educational recommendations. Similar to many children with Asperger's Disorder, Paul was very intelligent, with an overall IQ in the Superior range with commensurate academic achievement scores, but his Vineland Adaptive Behavior Scale ratings were significantly below average, even borderline range or lower. Paul was brilliant in school, or in one-on-one conversations on any given number of esoteric topics, but in the real world, he had the coping skills of a Kindergartner.

Paul had a textbook Asperger's presentation in many ways, including the "little professor" cognitive style, physically and socially awkward, blunt, incredibly messy and disorganized, self-absorbed and easily frustrated. What was atypical about Paul from my point of view was the fact that he didn't particularly like LEGO. When I was interviewing his parents, they had both mentioned that it was Dr. M's idea to try him in the group, but they were both skeptical: "Paul doesn't really like LEGO. A lot of his classmates do LEGO, but Paul doesn't like to build, he says it hurts his fingers." It wasn't just motor coordination or motor planning – much later, Paul became a talented musician, and was a highly valued member of his high-school marching band – he just didn't like the process of putting pieces together.

I kept that in mind when I met with Paul for the first time and had him look over the LEGO room. He seemed to appreciate some of the creations, but didn't really see the relevance for him. I asked him my standard question: "So what do you do for fun?" Paul struggled with that one, but he eventually told me that his favorite thing to do was watch the *Weather Channel*, and keep track of world weather events, both currently and historically. He was a weather kid. There are some obsessive interests expressed by children or adults with Asperger's that are more typical or more common than others. Trains. Insects. Weather. Paul's particular interest was on-the-scene reporting – tsunamis, ice storms, hurricanes, tornados, etc. Talking about weather, weather channels, weather reporters and storm chasers got him quite excited and animated. He had considerable technical knowledge about radar tracking and, of course, about meteorology, ice flows, global warming, ocean currents, satellite signals, the atmosphere, etc.

While we were talking, and Paul was looking vaguely at some of the LEGO® creations, I took the LEGO news crew, van and helicopter (from the LEGO City collection), and started building a small news studio to go with it. Eventually Paul got interested in what I was doing, and asked about it. I said I was building a news studio to go with the on-the-scene news crew. I asked him if he thought it needed anything. Needless to say, it needed a weather reporting team. I just happened to have unearthed some of the Arctic LEGO sets, which were basically a polar expedition series, and some LEGO Extreme Team sets, both of which had vehicles, structures, gear and minifigs that could be used to create a very jazzy LEGO storm-chasing and on-the-scene extreme weather crew. (LEGO never did produce a weather station or crew directly, but not surprisingly, many requests were submitted to LEGO Corporation from fans for such a set to be produced, and a number of "build your own" LEGO weather station instructions were uploaded on YouTube.) It wasn't until I mentioned the stop-motion animation projects that Paul suddenly became interested. He liked the idea of creating and animating his own on-the-scene weather stories very much – enough, in fact, to join LEGO Club just for that purpose. He also said he could probably use "some kind of social outlet, since I don't seem to be able to develop social opportunities for myself."

Paul was very tall for his age, thin, with light brown hair and blue eyes, pale skin, and small oval glasses, John Lennon-ish. Most of the time, Paul's mood was excited and cheerful. He would run full tilt into a conversation of interest no matter where he was or with whom, talking rapidly and breathlessly while waving his hands around, and pointing in the air, as if he were using a whiteboard and you could see what he was thinking about. He had learned to feign listening. His mother, Jean, was dismayed one day when I pointed this out. She was frustrated, again, with Paul's neglect of some important event or responsibility. "How can someone who can recite the periodic table not remember to take the trash out on Wednesdays?" We talked about the motivational aspects of memory, and also how the periodic table was a system, which gave it a particular form and familiarity which Paul liked. We also talked about Paul's way of listening, which was an adaptive technique. I said, "Right, Paul?" He looked right at me and nodded his head. "Yes," he said. "Absolutely." Jean asked me, "What's that? What do you mean?" So I asked Paul, "What are we talking about, Paul?" He said, "What? I don't know. Hey, when are we getting out of here? You know Weather Center Live comes on at 4:00 and it's 3:30 already."

## LEARNING THROUGH LEGO®

Paul and I got to spend some time together in individual therapy, partly because of the issues at school, where he had been not only teased but threatened and physically hurt more than once. His parents, who were divorced but agreed about most things about Paul's needs, had insisted that the school district place him in a smaller private school, and wanted him to have therapy to address the social trauma/avoidance issues, as well as to help him learn to interact better with peers, so that he would be less likely to be targeted or rejected in the future. Paul had an engaging sense of humor, and was obviously very intelligent, but his interpersonal style was often immature and off-putting. He liked puns and pranks, and liked being provocative or annoying, especially to his parents in public places. He liked "SpongeBob SquarePants" and could do a very good imitation of the characters' voices, including SpongeBob, Squidward and Patrick, loudly, in unsympathetic company.

Despite having a lot of anxieties and a tendency to perseverate about dangers to his health – he was a bit of a hypochondriac – he could also be very rigid, assertive, demanding and right. The idea of letting someone get away with saying something that wasn't quite accurate, or using a word incorrectly, or with incorrect pronunciation or grammar, was unthinkable. With considerable effort on the part of Paul's parents and myself, we were able to get him to let people get away with a slip or oversight sometimes. So his correcting tendency progressed from all the time, to most of the time. This was not a significant enough change to keep him out of trouble with his peers, and even some adults. In Paul's view, he was just trying to be helpful. For most people, he was condescending and intolerable.

Paul and I made an initial connection by building a LEGO® weather station – with a world-traveling, disaster-site reporting crew – and we planned to do a LEGO animated film or two using these props. Paul did eventually do an animated film about global warming and the melting of the ice cap at the North Pole which was very well received by his group and others. We also talked about the incidents at school, and I had to agree with his parents' decision to have him moved, since the incidents were quite bad, and there was clearly a breakdown in supervision at his previous school. At his new school, he was away from the students who used to bully him, and he was supervised more carefully.

Once we had established a good rapport, I wanted to get a treatment alliance with Paul, which was basically having him understand that we were going to be working on some changes for him, ways for him to function better in his social environment, and maybe improve his ability to monitor himself and his impact on those around him. First, he had to accept that this was something worth working on. During our individual times, I would point out to him the times when he was being mildly offensive – which I might have let slide normally, but which he needed to be more aware of for less forgiving audiences. At times, he was intrusive, asking personal questions, or making personal statements that would not be an appropriate part of a social communication with peers, and I would note these. He would also violate personal space, make too much, or too little, eye contact, etc. I'm sure he felt set upon and nagged at times, but he did seem to accept that I was doing it to be helpful. In the LEGO Club groups, we also carried on with little whispered reminders and prompts about social behavior, about not correcting everyone on their facts and grammar, and about personal space, both physical and psychological.

Paul and I also talked about situations at home, and at school, where he may have caused some offense, or where he may have misunderstood a situation. This was a delicate subject for Paul, and for many kids like Paul, because it was right on the boundary of where their responsibility towards others to be socially appropriate and not offensive met up with their disability, and in some cases, including Paul's, the victimization that often came with having a social disability. Paul had had his share of being not only treated like an outsider, but picked on, physically hurt and then blamed for being "part of the problem," when some accountability for the situation was finally sought. It was definitely a delicate balance to help Paul find ways that he could identify for himself that he could fit in socially, be accepted and identified as an outsider.

We worked together on what I identified for him and many others like him as "tells," which are the little cues that poker players use to tell something about the other's hand. For kids with autistic/Asperger's conditions, "tells" were subtle, or not so subtle, signs of differentness that would trigger a "not from this planet," or "he's an outsider," reaction from their peers. Talking about the weather report, or insects, using a cartoon voice (SpongeBob or Patrick), correcting other people's grammar, or hopping and flapping your hands, not making eye contact when you're talking to someone, taking things from people without asking, asking personal questions or sharing personal information when you first meet someone, etc. These were all ways that Paul's behavior told others that he was different, that he had an invisible disability, and sadly, that invited others to distance themselves, or to victimize him. I made sure that Paul understood that he was not to blame for being picked on, and bullied, but he also needed to make sure he wasn't putting a "please pick on me" sign on his back every day.

After we had discussed the incidents that had happened at school, Paul and I had a good idea of the types of challenges that he would face in LEGO® Club, and I agreed to help him avoid those pitfalls. He agreed to contribute without trying to dominate, and to try to share in some of the others' interests and projects. He agreed he would try to look at people when he talked to them, and to have a back-and-forth in a conversation. He agreed not to change the subject without notice, and to check back to make sure someone was still interested if he was getting caught up in a topic. Paul understood that if he wanted others to help him with his (very exciting) projects, then he would have to help them with theirs.

For my part, I promised Paul that he would never be teased or bullied in LEGO® Club – it's one of our rules – and he could always take some time out of the group if he was feeling upset or frustrated.

## JOINING OTHERS

Paul identified with Allen, and became friends with Anthony outside of the group as well. His connection with Allen was partly because they were both inept with LEGO, but also because they shared an interest in esoteric, technical topics and spoke in rapid-fire jargon. The connection with Anthony was due to the efforts of their mothers, who took turns bringing them to the group, and also arranged some playdates and birthday parties for the group members. Allen found Paul's high energy level off-putting at times – "He's like a puppy without a leash" – but Anthony didn't even notice. Paul and Anthony both called each other out for being "drama queens," because of their tearful tantrums. All three boys discovered they had a flair for dramatic comedy, although Allen was like Billy Crystal, Anthony was more like Robin Williams, and Paul was Roger Rabbit.

Although he identified more with Allen and hung out with Anthony outside of the group sessions, inside the group Paul tended to pair up with Charlie, whose calm, quiet style was a good influence on Paul. Charlie was also less likely to get irritated with Paul's rapid-fire speaking style. Paul was the first group member to discover Charlie's creative style, and he became a devoted fan, selling Charlie's ideas and creations to the group. "Look at this, guys, it's just a crocodile and a swordfish, and they're pals but they fight. They're old friends, you know, and they just do whatever because they're bored. Anything can happen, but in the end, they're just a crocodile and a swordfish, hanging out. It's brilliant!"

At the end of one of the Crocy and Swordy episodes, Charlie had them recap the adventure – "That was cool when... Oh, yeah, did you see when I...and then that thing happened with..." – while they headed off screen, into the sunset as it were. Then Charlie ad-libbed, "Cool. That's a wrap. Let's go get a pizza." Paul was smitten with Charlie's delivery of the line, uninflected but with just a sense of relief. Paul wanted Charlie to repeat it over and over in various situations for weeks afterwards. No one else picked up on it, though, and Charlie finally had to tell him to knock it off. "We did that already, Paul. I think we need to find some new lines." Such were the gentle nudges that brought Paul into dock safely. He knocked it off when Charlie asked him to.

Whatever the group was doing, though, Paul wanted to be a part of it. He tested out his limits in the group – seeing how silly he could be, or how loud, intrusive, offensive or dark he could be before someone objected, turned away, or Sarah or I reeled him in a bit. What he found was that most of the time his contributions were valued, and he was well liked. He wasn't the leader, he wasn't the first to get every level, but he did go through the levels, and, each time, the other group members signed his certificate.

Paul eventually won the "Genius" level for creating and directing a gameshow called "Try Not to Die." Paul did the voice acting for a gameshow host who asked very difficult science questions of an audience of super-geeks. If an audience member got an answer correct, they were awarded very "lame" prizes ("A kitten!"). If they attempted and failed to answer a science question correctly, they were immediately killed in some bizarre way. The gameshow host was poised in the bucket of a cherry picker over the audience, and the camera angle on the death scenes was from there. Audience members were bombed, had chain saws rain down on them, or were plucked out and eaten by a T-rex. The season of "Try Not to Die" ended when an audience member got the periodic table symbol for potassium correct (K), and the host mistakenly corrected them. The host was immediately killed in a ball of flame (we had a special effects editor involved by then).

Paul made a lot of progress outside of the group as well. At school, he learned to avoid the danger signs, staying off the radar of the dominant types, not putting his hand up in class so much, and not sharing his good grades out loud. He resisted the impulse to break out into SpongeBob and Squidward imitations, and kept Monty Python recitals to a minimum. He and I worked on having him spy on "popular" kids at school, and he watched what they wore, how they greeted other kids, and what they were interested in. He learned to respond to a fist-tap, rather than offering a handshake, or the outdated "high five." He learned to buy his pants a couple of sizes too big and push them down low on his hips (not below his butt, which was not okay at school). He made a habit of saying "Hey," instead of "Hi" or "Howdy!" or just nodding his head.

When Paul got his hair cut, he didn't ask for the same haircut that his father had – he asked for the haircut that the stylist was giving most boys his age.

Paul also accepted my advice and said "Hey" to the popular kids by name (those who were invited to everyone's birthday parties), even if he didn't know them. I reassured him: "Paul, they're popular for a reason. They have social skills. They are going to say something back, even if they don't know you; they're not going to ignore you, and everyone else will assume you know each other." He was shocked when it worked. Even popular girls would wave or greet him back, and he was surprised how many of them knew his name. He didn't get dates by saying "Hey, Stephanie" but he was more accepted. Suddenly, he knew people, and they accepted that he should be included in the conversation, or the in-joke, instead of being the subject of it. Eventually, Paul learned to text his friends and acquaintances. Rather than having to call people and talk to them, which he found anxiety-provoking for an array of unlikely reasons, he learned he could just text them, and they were more likely to get back to him with a text than if he had left a voice message.

Paul hosted his own birthday parties for the first time, and invited some of the LEGO® Club kids as well as some classmates from school. He joined the marching band, and stayed in Boy Scouts until he finally earned his Eagle Scout badge (with help from his father). This was a very big deal for Paul and his whole family. Paul's intelligence and objectivity, which once got him into trouble with peers, eventually helped him learn to modify his social behaviors and communication style so that he was more often the one noticing social *faux pas* or violations of social norms in others than the one committing them. He also had to learn to hold off pointing out social gaffs, or to do so in a helpful way. He liked the "Rules of Cool" option of being able to identify when other group members, or Dr. Dan, were violating one of these social rules, but as we did in the group, we tried to point them out nicely and with sincere care and concern, not to be mean or belittling. Paul still had his share of tearful, angry episodes, but these were milder and less frequent – a change that was quickly apparent to both his teachers and his parents.

He continued to have some difficulties with being distractible and he could get anxious and overwhelmed in high-demand situations – band performances, exams – but he matured out of his hyperactive-impulsive phase. By the time he was a young adult, Paul was self-assured in most situations, including coming back to see me. At our last visit, I would have to say he seemed a little distracted, vaguely eccentric, but poised.

# COLIN

## INITIAL CONTACT

Colin was initially referred to me by his school district for an independent psychoeducational evaluation (IQ, academic achievement) and to clarify his diagnosis. At the time of the referral, Colin was 11 years old and in 5th grade. He was attending a private parochial school, but with special education supports funded by his school district (speech-language services and behavioral counseling), so his triennial re-evaluations were contracted out to my agency, rather than being done by the district. Colin had been diagnosed with PDD-NOS by pediatric neurologist Dr. M, in 3rd grade. He had a history of speech-language delay and toe-walking, which were identified when he was two years old, and he received one year of early intervention services before he was referred to the school district for preschool. His parents, David and Marie, had insisted on a mainstream placement, so Colin attended a private, mainstream preschool, with speech-language and physical therapy services provided on a pull-out basis. Both of Colin's parents were teachers, and they knew what they wanted for Colin: as mainstream and normal an educational experience as possible. They assumed that he was just having some mild language problems, and so they wanted to avoid the educational gully of self-contained special education settings. They weren't sure about the PDD diagnosis but they were willing to consider it as long as Colin got the services he needed.

The teacher at the private preschool had told Colin's parents that he was inattentive and impulsive, and had suggested having him evaluated for ADHD medication. David and Marie felt that this was more likely due to the fact that he was one of the few boys in his class, and that the teacher had unrealistic expectations of

Colin (and the other children) in terms of the amount of "sitting and listening." Colin's parents had gotten a private speech-language evaluation, which indicated mild general delays in language, as well as some speech articulation and speech fluency problems. Colin had a mild stuttering problem, which David admitted he had suffered from as a child as well. David and Marie didn't think the teacher was following the recommendations that the speech-language pathologist had made regarding using visual aids and other language supports in the classroom, but since it was not a special education setting, there was little they could do, other than ask the teacher to consider the recommendations. For these reasons they stalled on having Colin evaluated for medication.

Problems with inattentiveness and impulsive behavior continued to be reported by Colin's teachers as he entered elementary school. The school district had agreed to continue to fund Colin's speech-language and PT services while he attended parochial school, and they also agreed to have a behavior specialist consult with his teaching staff on improving his on-task behavior and independent learning. His parents were convinced that he would not do as well in a larger classroom, which was all the school district had to offer other than the self-contained classroom. When Colin was in 3rd grade, as a show of being willing to compromise, they had Colin evaluated by his pediatrician, who diagnosed him with ADHD in addition to the PDD-NOS diagnosis: "All she did was interview us, look at his chart, and get us to fill out this rating scale [the Conners' Parent Rating Scale for ADHD]. She didn't even interview Colin." Colin was prescribed a psychostimulant medication, and his parents had to admit that there was a beneficial effect on his behavior and attention span, although they also felt that it made him less animated and responsive: "He was paying attention alright, but he was like a zombie. I guess you do what you gotta do, but we didn't like it. He wasn't himself on the meds."

Soon after he started taking the psychostimulant medication, Colin's parents also noticed that he was getting irritable in the afternoons after school. He was getting angry and aggressive with his younger sisters, slamming doors and punching walls, and throwing things in his room when he was sent in there for a time-out. He started grinding his teeth, screaming at his mother over minor frustrations, and then he threatened to kill one of his sisters after she got into his Pokemon cards. His parents called crisis services, and then met with a child psychiatrist who felt that Colin should go back to see Dr. M for an updated assessment and medication recommendations. Dr. M saw him and recommended they wean Colin off the psychostimulant, and suggested a non-stimulant antiepileptic, lamotrigine, as an alternative. Colin initially reported some initial drowsiness on this medication, although that might have been a withdrawal symptom from coming off the psychostimulant. Colin got over that, and showed a significant improvement in his attention span and behavior at school, with no further afternoon irritability and mood changes. It was during a follow-up with Dr. M, when Colin was 11, that Dr. M recommended the referral to me for the psychoeducational evaluation and for the ADOS and ADI-R to make a more definitive diagnosis.

Colin had two younger sisters, who were both average students, and a little hyperactive, but not enough to warrant a diagnosis or special help at school. They also attended the private parochial school that Colin went to. They were both very sociable, made friends easily and had lots of playdates and sleepovers with their friends from school and the neighborhood. David and Marie both had large families and had grown up in the area, so Colin and his sisters had a lot of extended family support: both sets of grandparents, and lots of cousins, aunts and uncles. The girls admired their older brother who seemed to be good at just about everything, especially sports. Colin's parents simply adored him. It was easy to see that any discussion about difficulties he was having at school were painful for them, and when he started having social, emotional and behavioral issues that seemed to spiral from his language-based learning and attention difficulties, they were distraught. They had good coping skills, and although they didn't always agree on parenting and educational strategies, they tended to work as a team, which made a big difference for both Colin and his sisters. They also had their own parents and siblings, who helped with the shuttling of kids around to soccer and basketball practices, and watched the kids when David and Marie needed a break; the three of them together were a handful.

Although the home and community situations for Colin were busy, but pretty positive and stable, the situation at school was much less so. By the time I met Colin, he was having a lot of difficulties at school and these were being compounded by his growing awareness of his difficulties. It was not uncommon in my experience for many children with mild autistic conditions to have a spike in self-awareness around the age of 10. It was an age that I would often begin to introduce the fact that they had a diagnosis to them, in conjunction with their parents and extended family members, of course. It had been very difficult for David and Marie to accept that Colin was on the autism spectrum, and even harder for his grandparents. In fact, I got to meet a couple of his grandparents who would sometimes bring Colin and his sister to the LEGO® Club groups; both of his grandfathers expressed skepticism about whether Colin was like the other kids in the group. But Colin was starting to notice a difference between himself and his classmates, and it really bothered him. As Marie put it:

> He's getting depressed about not being able to do things as easily as the other kids. He can tell when they read out loud, or when they read what they've written to the class, he's not there. And he's very competitive. He has to be the best at everything, that's why he's so good at sports. His Dad's like that, too. You can't tell, but Colin's Dad is very much like Colin – he needs to be better than everyone else, just to feel okay. And Colin is not feeling okay, not at all. We keep telling him how smart he is, what a good athlete, and how handsome he is – isn't he handsome? But he doesn't hear it. He just thinks about the worksheets and essays, and reading assignments. He can draw you what he wants to say, he can show you – he can even build it, with LEGO, or anything. You should see all the stuff that he and David build at home, with leftover wood and wires and batteries. He's going to be an inventor someday for sure. David wanted to be an inventor or an engineer, like his Dad, and he could have been, but he wasn't very confident. He didn't even apply to engineering school. He went into education to become a science teacher. I mean, he's great at that, but you can see he wanted to do more. Colin has that, like his Dad. He doesn't want to hear about his limitations, he wants to shine, but he's almost sure he won't.

Colin's cognitive testing results showed a large split between his perceptual reasoning abilities, which were in the Very Superior range (130+), and his verbal comprehension abilities, which were average to low average (85 to 100). Although this meant he did not have a language deficit, *per se*, the difference between his visual-spatial abilities and his language-based reasoning abilities was large enough for him to notice the difference. Colin's academic testing was generally consistent with his cognitive profile, and somewhat exaggerated by this subjective awareness, that is, he tended to put in less effort on reading comprehension and paragraph writing, since he had the idea that he was not good at these, or at least, that these were difficult for him. Simpler language-based skills like word-reading and spelling were less susceptible to this effort effect, and he did well on those; in fact, he was well above average on standardized testing of word-reading, spelling and word-decoding. He was even higher, of course, on quantitative reasoning, arithmetic and math calculations. On neuropsychological tests, Colin showed a phenomenal memory for visual-spatial information (abstract drawings, patterns and shapes), at all levels, encoding, abstract reasoning and problem solving, and graphomotor reproduction.

Colin's frustration at school was starting to have an impact not only on his grades in language-based classes (English, social studies, history), but it was having an impact on his social functioning as well. Despite Colin's tendency to be rather quiet in social situations, largely due to his self-consciousness about his stuttering, he had always been fairly successful socially. He had excellent gross motor skills (although he continued to have a problem with toe-walking), and was especially good at basketball. He could dribble a ball at a gallop, and sink a basketball shot in a regular ten-foot hoop when he was in Kindergarten. He was agile and fast on playground equipment, and he was running 5K and 10K races along with his parents by the time he was 10. As he got older, though, his teammates were less happy with his freestyling style on the court. He wasn't as much a team player. He liked to take the ball and go end to end, in soccer and basketball. If his coaches made him pass, he'd get upset if his teammates didn't score. Then, there were the tantrums at school. Marie and, especially, David were very conscious of the social implications for Colin when he started to cry with frustration in class. "That's not good. I understand what he's going through, he's self-conscious now, and it really bothers him, especially reading out loud. That kills him, because it's slow, and he stutters, or stammers. He gets nervous, then he gets upset about being nervous, then everyone's looking at him, and he's crying, and he wants to run out of the room."

## LEARNING THROUGH LEGO®

Just as his mother said, Colin was a handsome boy. He had light brown hair and bright green eyes, with a wide smile; he was athletic, confident and healthy. His toe-walking was noticeable, but he had adjusted it into a confident sort of stride, as if he were about to approach a dead lift or a high jump. He had a few mild tics, a head shake and occasional exaggerated eye blinking, which weren't very noticeable at the time – he later developed more tics, which created additional complications for him. Colin looked especially athletic in the context of the LEGO Club group, who were not particularly athletic, although, as I mentioned above, that was something he had in common with Charlie. Aside from the toe-walking, the only other autistic feature I noticed about Colin was a lack of eye contact, which to me was pretty significant. As we got to know each other better, I became more aware of Colin's aloofness and his indirect social style. I eventually had a good treatment alliance with him, and he tolerated me pointing out his social differences, including the eye contact, but even when he was aware of it, and he said he wanted to get better at it, he couldn't look into my eyes.

I recognized that eye contact was important in social communication, and that its absence was not to be ignored, even in an 11-year-old boy. At the same time, I was also aware of the important differences between males and females when it came to social communication, both verbal and non-verbal. By this point, I had gotten used to the fact that most of my colleagues in child development and education were female (an observation that was not well received by mostly female audiences), and that by far the preponderance of the children being referred for treatment of mild autistic conditions were male. I had thought that if the situation were reversed – that if most children with autistic conditions were female, and most providers and educators were male – that would be an issue, but no one ever seemed to notice that the mental health and educational groups at conferences and IEP meetings were over 90 percent female, and these were the experts responsible for teaching boys how to be boys. In fact, as I learned through feedback from some of my public talks and conference presentations, it was fine to point out that most children with autistic conditions were male, but it was not acceptable to comment on the gender of the provider population, unless you're female.

I accepted that there was some justification for improving social communication styles in ways that were not gender-typical; after all, even typical males could use some improvement in communicating, especially with female partners. In my view, though, there was an important distinction to be made between social communication in intimate relationships – which might be a long-term goal for some of my older clients, and certainly for many male non-autistic therapy clients – and the type of social communication that happens in typical group settings (school, community) or work. It made sense to me to consider improving social communication as a means to address the problems of unemployment or under-employment as a priority over social communication with intimate partners. Intimate communication was something I could definitely see as a valuable goal or therapeutic outcome, especially for young adults, but I didn't get the sense that most parents and school staff – important stakeholders in the process – were really as concerned about that as they were about social communication with peers, that is, boys.

With boys, successful social interaction and com-munication with peers wasn't just different from that of girls because of the content of exchanges, it was in the form of exchanges, and a lot of that was framed by the nonverbal aspects of communication, including proximity, physical contact, and eye contact. I have three of my own children, two boys and a girl, and was able to get to observe a lot of typical interactions and styles of communication amongst them and their friends. I also spent a lot of time in classrooms and on playgrounds observing my clients, but also the typical kids with whom they interacted, both male and female. Over time, I realized that stable relationships between boys and girls developed very differently. Girls typically used more personal disclosure early on, as I've mentioned, and they made more eye contact because they faced each other, and often made direct comments about each other's appearance. They would also recall and comment about another girl's appearance and about her family life or personal habits, including how they kept their room, their handwriting, their hygiene and their clothing. Boys recalled more about what other boys brought to the interaction in terms of what they were good at, or knew a lot about, not their appearance, or home life, or even their name.

For boys, physical proximity and even physical contact (touching, rough-housing, bumping, pushing, etc.) were more incidental and unintentional, and therefore more tolerated or even ignored. The focus was typically not on each other but on something else – what they were doing together, or talking about. What I called a triangulated conversation: "You, me and the thing." I noticed this with men, too, especially young men, that they could be all over each other physically, with hugs, fist-taps, hand-clasps and bumping elbows and hips, but only rarely making eye contact, and very rarely talking about each other directly. So the social relationship aspects of the conversation were indirect, and were transmitted while the focus was elsewhere. For girls, the focus was on each other most of the time, in terms of the gaze direction as well as the topic of conversation, and interpersonal distance and physical contact was regulated much more consciously and carefully.

I had become accustomed to not over-emphasizing certain types of social communication that my particular group of clients would have experienced as jarringly alien to them and discouraging. So, I used to play some social communication games with kids like Colin, one-on-one, once we had established a good connection through some other indirect form. I would look at their eyes, and comment about the color or the patterns in the iris, and then ask them about my eyes: What color were they? Were they bloodshot or clear? What colors were there mixed in besides the obvious? I also introduced a mind-reading game, which

I played both one-on-one and in groups. "I'm going to think about either stepping on a thumbtack, or eating ice cream, and I want you to guess which one I'm thinking about." We played the mind-reading game back and forth, so we could work on both receptive and expressive sides of nonverbal communication. We also played "My lips got glued, and then..." This was a game of pantomime where we had to work on nonverbal gestures to get our point across, as in "My lips got glued, and then I lost my backpack," or "My lips got glued, and then I had to get to soccer practice."

This indirect connection way of working on direct communication seemed less threatening, and more interesting and acceptable, as well as being more effective for my clients, than simply saying, "Look at me, and use facial expressions and gestures." Behavioral strategies which used positive reinforcement for eye contact and responding to nonverbal communication were essentially doing just that – targeting and rewarding a behavior, which was actually a skill they didn't have. The method I used to get around the social avoidance, or the lack of social interest that many children with autism had, I called "triangulating." This was not specific to social communication, and was, in fact, the more typical form of social communication that I observed in boys and men.

I had observed that girls typically communicated a lot directly and even without knowing the other person very well – self-disclosure and asking personal questions were the ways they got to know each other. This very direct form of communication was not typical of boys and men, and in fact, this communication style made most of them uncomfortable. They would put up with this type of self-disclosing with girls or women, but if a male peer engaged in a lot of self-disclosure or asked personal questions at the acquaintance stage of a relationship, the conversation would end quickly, and often, so would the relationship. Disclosure between boys and men had to be more of an incidental trickle, not the firehose of disclosure that women used. And the focus of the interaction between male peers had to be a joint activity, not each other. Boys and men were comfortable with disclosure in the context of a bonding experience involving something else – a common interest or activity – a sports team, or a recent game, fishing, cars, motorcycles, jobs and the weather, or sometimes politics and money, but those were not good "starters."

Triangulated conversations I found were also useful in dealing with any difficult or anxiety-provoking situation, including disciplinary scenarios. The likelihood of emotional escalation (increasing anger or anxiety to crisis levels) was high in conflict situations when there was too much direct eye gaze and personal communication. Maintaining the focus on a common topic, whether it was what happened, or the rule involved, and keeping the emotional and directly personal aspects to a minimum, could often defuse a tense confrontation. Looking at someone, whether it involves direct eye contact or not, increases the arousal level, for good or bad. My clients often had difficulty distinguishing eye contact that indicated interest or mutuality, and eye contact that indicated hostility and confrontation. The level of arousal and intimacy involved in a situation that is already anxiety-provoking because it is not well understood often precluded direct coaching of this as a skill. Most children learn eye contact intuitively, through interaction with their parents, siblings and then peers, but children with autism often don't have intuitive eye contact and have to learn how to use it appropriately. They can learn it, though, through practice and modeling, especially with peers, but it has to have a safe context. Using a triangulated communication model, by making up a game that objectifies the eye contact or facial expression, makes it less subjectively overwhelming, and therefore allows for this to happen.

Colin really struggled with this. He could barely tolerate to look at my eyes to tell the color, and when I asked him for more details, he quickly scanned my eye area and then guessed. He got tense and irritated if I made him try harder. When I looked at his eyes, he averted them, looking up, down or to the side, or turning his head. He would be looking over my shoulder, and I would tell him to look at my eyes, and he would say, "I am, Dr. Dan." Finally, I remembered a film-acting trick I'd heard, that if you look at the other person's nose during close-up scenes, you still appear to be making eye contact, but it's easier to maintain, and your eyes don't tend to flick back and forth, focusing on one eye and then the other. So, I told Colin to look at my nose, instead of my eyes, and we had a good time laughing about our nose observations. Colin turned out to be pretty good at reading my facial expressions, but he had a lot of difficulty expressing them himself. He could also use body language and gestures when he wasn't thinking about them, but he couldn't do so when he tried to show them consciously. We kept practicing though. Colin would get impatient with this type of activity in our individual sessions, but as long as we eventually got around to doing some LEGO® building, he was willing to put up with it.

## JOINING OTHERS

Colin was very talented with LEGO, and not just for a kid his age – he obviously had engineering in his blood. One day, he came to group and he wanted to build an elevator, inside a mountain, like a mining shaft elevator. I thought it was an interesting idea, but I wouldn't have even considered trying it myself. Way too hard, and too much work. While we were working on shooting an airplane crash scene, which was a lot of fun (we wound up just throwing the airplane into the scene and letting it explode all over the place in real time), Colin was half-heartedly participating, and doing some sketches of his elevator and mountain. Before the end of the group, Colin insisted on being allowed to "sell" his idea for the next session – he wanted them to help him build it. He got red in the face, and was literally sweating as he tried to convey his idea about pulleys and cables, and counterweights, and the parts he thought we could use. Charlie just took the drawing from him, looked at it, and said, "You want to build an elevator in the middle of a mountain. Okay, we can do that." And they did.

One of the other projects that highlighted Colin's engineering talents in the group was the tower contest. We were still doing mostly LEGO sorting and building at that point, and there were three groups running per week, so each group noticed what the others were working on. The youngest group was working on building a tall tower, with the expressed goal of reaching the ceiling in the LEGO®

room from the table top (ten feet). Colin was intrigued with their tower, but was also skeptical that they could reach the ceiling. He just looked at their design, looked up at the ceiling, and shook his head: "They're not going to be able to reach." Colin pointed out that the basic design required them to stand on the table, which was against the rules, and even then, they wouldn't have been tall enough to put bricks above about eight or nine feet, without a ladder. "Even with a ladder, this is going to fall over. It's not the same on all sides, and it's too skinny. It's going to tip."

Colin got the other group members interested in the project, and they especially liked the idea of beating the other groups. There was already an implicit, and sometimes explicit, competition for resources going on between the groups, especially for minifigs and other specialized pieces that were in more limited supply. The budget decisions about what types of sets to buy, as well as how to allocate the current LEGO resources in making sets, freestyles and then stop-motion studio sets, was starting to heat up. Colin argued that if the group didn't start building now, one of the other two groups might monopolize the blocks and build a bigger tower.

Colin took charge of the project with confidence, and outlined his plan: "It has to be even, the same on all sides. And we have to build it in stages, so we can build them in chunks and then stack them together. The bottom has to be really big and solid. We can make the top parts skinnier but not too skinny. Only the very top should be one-brick." He sketched out a design, and tested out the maximum height for brick-on-brick stability, which was about two feet. The rest had to be graduated pyramids supporting hollow box towers, not solid, which used too many bricks and were too heavy. After that, it was just a matter of building it. Colin had to keep everyone focused, which was not an easy task, and it took quite a few sessions, which had to be interspersed with other projects; this made Colin very impatient, but he persevered.

Colin's talents as an engineer and designer were often called for in subsequent construction and stop-motion film projects. His own movie scripts were mostly action flicks. He did a couple of nice Westerns, and then created his own character, Stuntman Bif, who became a big hit. The Stuntman Bif series involved having the main character announce to the world that he was going to endeavor some Evil Knievel-like stunt, and he invariably crashed in dramatic and gory ways. In one of his best films, Colin – taking into consideration the age and condition of Bif after all his stunts – had Bif's announcer declaring that Bif would not attempt to "Sit in a chair!" or "Ride a bicycle!" and in each case, as usual, Bif crashed dramatically, taking out whole scenes in a domino-effect of comical crashes.

Colin's dominant modes of expression were visual and technical, and Colin's scripts were often just a page or two of brief phrases, but he did write them out himself, and he often did this at home, so he could take his time with it and not feel pressured to write with the others watching and waiting for him. The requirement to have a written script before the group would consider a film project was a serious challenge for Colin, and many other group members who were not adept at writing. Sometimes Colin and others would get someone to help them with the script. Allen and Paul both expanded or fleshed out scripts for Colin, based on his initial ideas, and in exchange for his help with designing and building scenery and other projects. These were some of the most fruitful collaborations in LEGO® Club, both in terms of the projects and, more importantly, the therapeutic experience of the group members. At one point, Colin had the insight about his writing difficulties, and he told me, "I can write good enough. When I'm a rich engineer someday, I can hire someone to do the writing anyway."

Colin was even better known in the LEGO Club scene for designing and building functional conveyor belts, escalators and self-propelled vehicles powered by pull-back motors, the electric train motor or rubber band motors that he designed and built himself. At one point, Anthony had decided that he wanted to build "a LEGO that can fly," which intrigued Colin and the other group members. When Anthony and Allen started working on some prototypes, Colin had to correct them: "You're going to build a LEGO you can throw – that's not flying." He let Anthony and Allen throw and smash many LEGO aircraft before he told them it was impossible: "You see, it's just the weight to surface area ratio – LEGO is too heavy, and they're not aerodynamic. No way to create lift." He showed them his best winged LEGO design, which was two large flat sheets firmly held together with other flat pieces, and a rubber-band motor and propeller he designed himself. This was a lot more likely to fly than the creations Anthony and Allen came up with. It "flew" about ten feet, but as Colin pointed out, not because of the propeller, but because he threw it. "That's gliding," he said, "not flying." This led to some more Monty Python recitals about swallows, and then hypotheses about whether LEGO® could float, but Colin brought them back to his assertion that LEGO couldn't fly, and that would be the end of it. We never did build a flying LEGO, but we did build an elevator inside a mountain, and a tower that reached the ceiling, thanks to Colin.

# THE SECOND MOVE

After being at the Institute for a few years, the LEGO® Club groups were relocated again to another outpatient private practice setting. We had the luxury of designing our clinic layout, and we put in a generous space for the LEGO room, with custom-built glassed-in display cases, installed high enough to keep them safe from small invaders, as well as display tables, and a kidney-shaped work table and kid-sized chairs throughout. We also included video-recording and stop-motion editing equipment, and as I mentioned above, we borrowed some time from the clinic's IT consultant to help out with the stop-motion film-making and special-effects editing. Soon after opening this outpatient clinic, we were running nine or ten groups per week; the groups were led by me, as well as a number of talented assistants, including my previous co-authors, Drs. G.W. Krauss and Sarah Levin Allen.

The groups were run pretty much as they had been before, although the space was larger, and we had access to a bigger array of both LEGO materials and stop-motion film-making equipment. Many of the group members were those who had carried over from the Institute setting, but there were also many new clients. The groups ranged in age from preschool to high school, and also covered a range of developmental levels and degrees of severity of autistic features. The less verbal, more repetitive clients required higher levels of staff input and direction, often with guidelines or choices of activity offered, as opposed to the more open-ended sessions that we held for the verbal, HFA/Asperger's groups. The large LEGO room also had a central fold-away divider that was useful for creating a smaller space, or to divide larger groups into two, if there was a need to separate the activities – for example, when one small group was working on set-building while another group was doing stop-motion filming.

For some of the groups, whether they were focused on clients with autism/PDD-NOS or HFA/Asperger's, there was still a need to have the "LEGO® Points" positive behavioral system in place. Regardless of cognitive or developmental level, there were some clients who tended to be very impulsive, or inflexible, and there were "interfering" behavioral issues including loud yelling, breaking up of LEGO sets or others' freestyles, verbal and nonverbal threats, wandering or more vigorously moving away from the activity, or even leaving the room, etc. Luckily, the staff we had were all highly trained in antecedent and positive behavioral intervention strategies, and groups typically ran smoothly. The types of "antecedent" strategies that I prefer for LEGO groups, as well as those I encourage teaching staff to use in classrooms, involve anticipating negative or interfering behaviors before they occur, and structuring the activity in advance to minimize the likelihood of these occurring, rather than waiting for the client to initiate an action and then either rewarding it (positive reinforcement for appropriate behavior) or not (contingent non-reinforcement, or "planned ignoring"). Strategies that involve "safety" maneuvers such as excluding a child from the activity (time-out), or a cost-response approach (deducting from their rewards for interfering behavior), tended to elicit escalation, or increasingly negative and disruptive behavior, as I have mentioned above in the section on Facilitating the Groups.

The LEGO Club groups tended to work well because of a combination of antecedent strategies that included active engagement throughout the duration of the group time (i.e. no "down time" during which clients were waiting for something to happen, were bored, and had decreased levels of staff supervision) – the group activities and staffing ratio (1:3) were consistently provided as planned. The staff were also well trained and experienced with "peer-mediated" intervention strategies. They knew not to make it a direct issue with them if one of the rules was being violated, but to raise it as a group issue, and to enlist the input and support of the group members. This included the distribution of the "LEGO® Points" tokens for those groups that were using them – they were administered by the staff, but, as much as possible, with the assent and input from the group members, so that a token reward was typically accompanied by positive peer attention and spontaneous praise as well. Finally, for a group member who might have caught us off-guard the previous week with an unpredictable interfering behavior, we made sure to do an ABC (antecedent-behavior-consequence) review, or mini-FBA (functional behavioral assessment), so that we could anticipate similar incidents in the next session. This applied to both the group sessions themselves, as well as issues in the waiting room area, and even negative or potentially dangerous behavior in the building lobby or parking lot.

Similar to the previous LEGO Club settings, the group influence did tend to reach out beyond the LEGO room itself to the waiting room, and then the lobby and parking lot, in informal ways. Parents and siblings of the group members naturally tended to support and communicate with each other about IEPs, issues at home, worries about the future, etc. Some of the siblings bonded with each other and became part of the "outer circle" of LEGO fans, who came to the groups and wanted to see what the groups had created that week, or watch the latest stop-motion pieces. There were the usual playdates and birthday parties, barbecues and holiday get-togethers. The LEGO Club members developed their own informal support network which performed much better than we might have done if we had taken on the task ourselves formally. Most of the parents involved were highly competent people, and a lot of them had extensive experience and self-acquired knowledge about autistic conditions and educational, behavioral, medical and other intervention strategies. There was also typically a 15–20 minute transition time, both before and after groups, when the LEGO Club staff got updates from parents, shared input about progress, and discussed behavioral and social developmental issues affecting both the group as well as school, home and community settings. Although my focus was on the groups, the parents and other family members who participated certainly deserve their share of the credit for the positive influence this was having on social development for the members.

# SEAN

## INITIAL CONTACT

My initial contact with Sean was a fairly straightforward referral for a psychoeducational evaluation – at least, it seemed that way at the time. The school district had apparently been asked by the parents to consider a change of placement based on Sean's needs, and they were referring him to me to get my input regarding his current cognitive and academic functioning, as well as behavioral issues, and to make some recommendations about his needs for an upcoming IEP review. Sean came to the first meeting accompanied by his mother – I usually scheduled an initial visit with parents for an interview and to make sure I had a complete history, as well as to establish a rapport and possibly start a working alliance with the client and their parents prior to doing any further assessment.

Sean was 11 years old at the time, attending mainstream regular education classes at a large public elementary school, but with pull-out services for language, arts and speech-language therapy. He had been diagnosed with PDD-NOS prior to preschool, and had received early intervention services and then attended an autism-specific special needs preschool. After Kindergarten, since Sean seemed to be doing so well in therapy and academically, he was given the opportunity to try mainstreaming with an aide, and he had been doing very well with that so far. Sean's parents were divorced, and his mother, Sharon, was remarried, and had another child from her second marriage. At the time of this assessment, Sean was living with his mother, step-father Frank, younger sister Cleo, and an infant half-brother, Jeffrey. He also had regular contact with his father, Robert (Bob), who lived nearby and who had Sean and Cleo with him from Thursday evening to Monday morning.

Sean's mother was a highly educated professional at the executive administration level, and she presented herself as someone who was accustomed to being competently in charge. Sean was a very tall, rangy youth, with thick, bright-blond hair that was cut short, but stuck up in every direction. He had striking light blue eyes and somewhat sleepy expression. He did not make eye contact, and he did not respond initially when I greeted him, but then when his mother told him to say hello, he said, "Hello," and put his hand out, without looking at me at all. He was dressed in basketball sweats and a t-shirt, with basketball shoes, but he did not appear athletic. His movements were somewhat inhibited and awkward. He seemed unsure of himself, and had difficulty maintaining a stable posture most of the time, sliding out of the chair, then sitting on the floor, or slouching forward, then sitting backwards in the seat, etc. He spoke with an autistic-type voice prosody, with a sing-song cadence, and flattening of the accents on syllables, and his voice ranged from a deep, adult-like rumble, to a high-pitched, childlike speech – he was speaking most of the time in scripted echolalia, with dialogue from his favorite cartoons, which included "SpongeBob," "Ed, Edd and Eddy," "Rugrats" and "Thomas the Tank Engine."

While I interviewed Sharon, Sean would frequently get up and start loudly scripting from one of these cartoons, pacing in the small room and gesturing with his hands. He seemed to be re-enacting, or almost re-experiencing, scenes from these cartoons, seemingly from beginning to end. While Sharon did her best to interrupt him and get him to sit back down, Sean sang the SpongeBob song, loudly and then quietly, and then louder and then quieter.

Sean: "Oooh, who lives in a pineapple under the sea? *SpongeBob SquarePants!*"

Sharon: "Sean, not now, you need to sit…"

Sean: "Absorbent and yellow and porous is he!"

Sharon: "…down and let Dr. Dan and I… "

Sean: "SpongeBob SquarePants!"

Sharon: "…Talk! This is important, you know…"

Sean: "If nautical nonsense is something you wish…"

Sharon: "…we're here to talk about you, Sean, about your…"

Sean: "SpongeBob SquarePants!"

Sharon: "…school. You need to pay attention to Dr. Dan, and then…"

Sean: "Then drop on the deck and flop like a fish!"
Sharon: "...we can go get an ice cream."
Sean: "*SpongeBob SquarePants!*... Ice cream? Okay. Let's go."

Sean recited whole scenes of dialogue from the cartoon, imitating the voices of SpongeBob, Patrick, Mr. Krabs, Squidward, and his favorite, Plankton, and then, laughing, he'd comment on the scene he was reviewing: "It's the SpongeBob when Plankton steals the krabby patty formula." Then in a loud, Plankton voice, "I've got it! I have the formula, ha, ha, ha!" His mother asked him repeatedly to sit down, and be quiet, and Sean would do so, briefly, but then he would start again. He also rocked in the chair vigorously – it was not a rocking chair – tipping it backwards and forwards on the back two legs, and then the front two legs, trying to balance there as long as he could, then resting on the wall, or falling forward on his hands and knees. Sharon yelled, "Sean stop that right now! You're going to break something or hurt yourself. Just sit in the chair...please!"

Sean walked over to the bookshelf and picked up a Slinky, and held it hanging down, then he swung it around in the air. "Sean!" his mother called out. "Put that back! It's not safe." Sean ignored her, swung the Slinky a second time, and let it go. It sprung across the room and hit the far wall. "Hah! Did you see that? Did you see that?" Sharon quickly picked up the Slinky before Sean could get it, and held it in her lap. "I'm sorry." she said, "He likes to throw just about anything." Sean sat down, and reached over, trying to get the Slinky from his mother's hands, and she pushed his hand away.

Needless to say, it was not an easy task getting Sean through a comprehensive psychoeducational assessment battery, but we managed. We took a lot of "play" breaks, and his mother brought plenty of snacks for me to use as rewards for completing the test items – mostly fruit rollups and gummies, Goldfish crackers, granola bars and juice boxes. I allowed Sean a lot of "out of seat" time during the testing, which seemed to help him stay on task. He was quickly able to shift his attention back and forth between the scripting he was doing while pacing in the room, and then responding to test items. Despite the obvious behavioral and social signs of autistic pathology, Sean's cognitive scores were not below average. His visual-spatial abilities were actually somewhat above average, and his language-based reasoning and problem-solving were at the lower end of the average range. He had difficulties with some of the subtests that required sustained attention, and graphomotor execution (i.e. paper-pencil tasks), since he had to sit still and concentrate in order to do those, but he was still scoring in the low average range.

Sean's academic achievement scores were somewhat lower than his IQ scores would have predicted, with math scores in the low average range, but with reading comprehension and sentence and paragraph composition in the well below average range, more than a year behind his current grade placement and age level. None of this was a surprise to Sharon, who was very familiar with his previous testing results, although Sean had previously tested in the borderline range on the IQ test, and was now more consistently in the average range. This was probably due to the fact that I was able to give Sean some more freedom in terms of his test-taking behavior (I had a soundproof testing room), and took the time to establish and maintain a working alliance with him, which included snacks. It was Sharon's contention that Sean needed to be in a more restrictive setting – a private, autism-specific school – and that a mainstream classroom was not adequate to address his educational or behavioral needs.

I could certainly see her point, given what I expected Sean would look like in a typical classroom setting – rocking in his chair, or pacing, and loudly scripting SpongeBob or Ed, Edd and Eddy. Sean had been in a mainstream setting for a while, though, and with his aide, he had apparently been able to stay there for a few years without a lot of additional supports or modifications. This was the point of view I got when I met Sean's father, Bob. He was the one who had advocated strongly for Sean to be in the mainstream setting to begin with. When he brought Sean in for his final testing session, on a Friday, Bob said, "Sharon wants him to go to that new regional autism school. I'm not okay with that at all. He's staying put. I've seen the self-contained autism classrooms, and I've been to the big institutes, and over there to the new county program. They have a lot of well-trained people there, I'm sure, but if Sean can make it in a classroom with all the typical kids, that's where he should be. When he's around those other kids, he knows how to act. He doesn't do this scripting stuff in class. That's just when he's bored, 'When you and I are talking like this, and he's just sitting there, thinking, "When do I get out of here?"'

My assessment of Sean happened over the summer between his 5th and 6th grade years, and the school district had some expectation that I would be making a recommendation for a change of placement for the fall. My results, though, did not provide strong support for either a move to a more specialized setting, or a stay-put – he needed some extra help with language arts, and a home-based behavioral consultation, but change of placement was not necessarily a priority. Sharon was definitely disappointed that I didn't discuss the placement issue in my report, but then something happened at home that changed the whole scenario.

Sean and his sister, Cleo, had not been getting along well for a while, especially since Sharon's husband Frank had come into the picture. Frank was less accustomed to Sean's eccentricities, and he had tried to be assertive with him a few times, in terms of using his authority and restricting his access to media (games, TV, computer), for being disruptive or messy at home. Cleo had also found a sympathetic ear in Frank for her complaints about Sean taking over the household and making it difficult for her to have sleepovers, etc. Sharon wasn't unsympathetic to Cleo's situation, but she also recognized that Sean had limited control over his autistic behaviors. Frank felt that Sean had been getting away with too much, and was being stricter with him. His attempts to be more assertive with Sean did not go down well with Bob, though, who really was (and still is) Sean's biggest fan.

This all came to a head one day when Sean and Cleo were in the pool together, and Sean pushed Cleo down in the pool. There were obviously two sides to this story, and I could really see both, but the upshot of it was that Cleo was pushed down in the water and held there by Sean, and she felt threatened by him. Sean claimed that he was just playing around and didn't think that Cleo should have been afraid of him. He was only a little more than a year older (he was turning 12 that summer), but was already a head taller than her and probably 50 pounds heavier. Sean thought they were both just horsing around in the pool; Cleo felt like he tried to kill her.

Frank had apparently gotten involved at the scene, and had grabbed hold of Sean, claiming that he thought he was trying to drown Cleo. That was not how Bob understood it. He was a retired police officer, and was still involved in many auxiliary duties, often wearing his uniform and regalia for police functions and funerals. He was also a former competitive weight-lifter, and still had the barrel chest and bulging biceps to prove it. Frank and Sharon had called for a crisis team to come interview Sean for potential homicidal ideation, and they wound up taking Sean to the crisis unit, where Bob went to get him. In the end, Frank and Sharon agreed to change the custody arrangements, and Sean went to live with his father full-time, with only day visits home with his mother, step-father, sister and half-brother. Both Frank and Sharon had argued that this was for the safety of both Cleo and Jeffrey, and now that Sean was getting so much bigger, he was also a potential threat to Sharon.

Following this incident, I had limited contact with Sharon, but Bob had asked for ongoing therapy for Sean, and he brought Sean in to see me for individual therapy, as well as for parent consultations and periodic updated evaluations, as well as referring him to the LEGO® Club groups. At first, I was hesitant about having Sean in LEGO Club, as I felt he might be disruptive, and I wasn't sure how he would react to the other group members. Bob thought I might be worried about the incident with Cleo, and the way that his mother described his behavior as being threatening at times. "Are you kidding me? This pussycat?" Bob said, ruffling Sean's spiky blond hair. "Look at him, he's a kitten, aren't you, big guy?" Sean looked at his father, and put his arm around his neck, hugged him and then put him in a headlock. "Yeah, I'm a kitten alright. Mee-ow. Hah!"

## LEARNING THROUGH LEGO

Bob had a lot to prove after the school district agreed to allow Sean to stay in mainstream classes for 6th grade, and then middle school. He was semi-retired – on his police pension, but also working as a security consultant part-time – and was able to spend a lot of time with Sean going to roller coasters and waterparks, which Sean really enjoyed, as well as just hanging out and learning more about his son's interests. Sean and Bob developed an incredibly close, very affectionate relationship. Bob watched all the cartoons and YouTube videos that interested Sean, and he learned to script right along with him – he could do the supporting roles when Sean broke into SpongeBob, or Ed, Edd and Eddy. He played the eye-contact and facial expression games with him that I'd started with Sean in therapy, and he used all the behavior and social skills strategies that I'd recommended.

As close and intimate as the relationship was between Sean and his father, there were still problems at times with his mother and her new family, as well as sticky patches at school. It seemed inevitable that every week Sean and Bob would be there in the waiting room, and Bob would have some news about a disaster at his ex-wife's house, or at school. At one point, Sean apparently threatened a teacher after they took some LEGO®s away from him, in order to get him back to schoolwork after a break. Bob thought the school staff had not handled the situation well, and in fact, he felt that Sean had been "set up" by this clumsy move. But as he said, "They still get to call the shots," and Sean had to be picked up at school by his father, who had to take him to undergo a homicide/suicide risk assessment before being allowed back in school.

Luckily, I was approved to do these types of evaluations, and was in fact doing them on a fairly routine basis for many of my LEGO Club clients. Inadvertent statements about wanting to kill someone, or yourself, were one of the little slips that a kid with autism or Asperger's might make, missing out on the obvious context cues – i.e. you can say you are so frustrated you feel like killing yourself at home, or in the car, or in LEGO Club, but you can't say it to your teacher, or your school counselor. About once a week, I'd have irritated parents and a confused child in my office, and paperwork to fill out for the school district.

After this initial crisis assessment, however, Sean started making a habit of it. Sean did not, as the school counselor thought, "learn his lesson" about homicidal statements. In fact, the result of the initial risk assessment visit was that Sean learned that all he needed to do to have his dad pick him up from school, and get a free visit with Dr. Dan and the rest of the day off, was threaten to kill someone or himself. He became pretty good at making believable, even graphically detailed, threats. It took us a few months to get Sean to agree that this was not a good strategy, and that he could communicate his frustration in more appropriate, productive ways. After many weeks of coaching Sean through appropriate verbal expressions, or using a stress ball, or drawing his feelings, Bob had to threaten not to bring him to LEGO Club if he did it again (Bob didn't mean it, but it worked). Sean did wind up having at least one more crisis risk assessment, after he drew his feelings in his "feelings journal" during a counseling session at school. He drew a picture of himself and his father blowing up the school, and was immediately referred for a homicidal ideation risk assessment. The school district administrator also threatened to have Sean prosecuted for terroristic threatening, but Bob and I were able to talk her out of it.

Sean and I developed a close bond, working together on improving his functional communication skills, and putting some limits on his scripted self-talk. He learned to monitor his "out loud" voice more carefully, and was able to do the scripting at first more quietly, and then just in his head. He was also able to set some time limits for himself, so that he would allow himself to engage in "playing cartoons in my head," only when he wasn't otherwise actively engaged in a learning activity, or interacting with someone else. If he was with someone else, and they weren't talking specifically about something like schoolwork, then Sean was allowed to introduce the topic of a cartoon, but he had to initiate it socially; for example, "Did you see the latest 'Rugrats' episode where…?" He also had to be cautious about his audience, not just the context. He and Bob had started watching "Family Guy" and "South Park" together, and Bob actually seemed to enjoy the heart-to-heart talks that he had to follow up with to explain some of the content. I was pretty impressed with how Bob was managing all that, except that Sean would break out into "Did you see the 'Family Guy' episode where…?" in the clinic waiting room, with preschool and elementary school children nearby.

During Sean's first year in the middle school, when he was still hanging in there in the mainstream classrooms, with pull-out for language arts and speech therapy, I got a call from Bob that sounded more ominous. Apparently, Sean had been engaging in some sexualized behavior at school, and had been suspended pending some input and intervention. I was still at the Institute at the time, and we arranged for a colleague of mine to interview Sean and his father, and to do a consultation with the school staff about how to handle the situation. Sean had made some sexual comments to a teacher's aide and to another student (sexual joking), and had also engaged in genital self-touching with others around. The consultant was able to work out a plan for home and school with regard to Sean's self-exploratory behavior which Bob and the school were both on board with. Unfortunately, I later got a call from the school administrator, who was a personal acquaintance of mine so he was being extra supportive, explaining that Sean was now engaging in self-exploration during class, while holding up a sheet of paper with the words "In Private" written on it.

Sean, Bob and I were all able to have a fairly open and honest discussion about the situation at school – which was now tenuous. Bob reported that Sean was being appropriately "private," and he was making sure that Sean wasn't being exposed to sexualized content on TV or at the movies they went to, although he said he did allow Sean to have a computer in his room with internet access, which he did not monitor. Bob did eventually admit that he and Sean had been going to the movies or renting movies, and many of them had adult content. "We're not going to watch kiddie movies, just because he's going through puberty. That's not going to help."

Needless to say, this was a major issue for Sharon, who had suspended visits with her and Cleo pending some resolution of what she referred to as Sean's "sexual acting out." Bob's version of it was, "So, he's got urges! What normal 12-year-old boy doesn't? He's physically mature – look at the size of him, and he's getting hair, you know, all over." Sean lifted his arm, giggling, to show me. Bob said he had gotten tips on talking to Sean about puberty and sexual development from the consultant, and from his support group, and he felt fairly confident that he was approaching this the right way. I spent some time with Sean building LEGO® together, and chatting about what he had learned from his father about sexual development, and he was surprisingly on point.

Sean: "There's nothing wrong with sex, Dr. Dan. It's natural. My body is doing what it's supposed to, getting me ready to be a grown up, and a dad."

Dr. Dan: "Let's not rush the dad thing, Sean. You've got quite a few years to go before that. What about girls, what did your dad tell you about them?"

Sean: "Women are different, I know that. They have a vagina and breasts, and we don't, we have a penis and balls. *Balls!* Nuts. Testicles. *Co-ho-nays.*" He laughed. "Girls are like women, but they aren't mature yet."

Dr. Dan: "Yep. Good. Girls and boys are like women and men, but they're not sexually mature. And your dad told you what sex is, how sex happens."

Sean: "The man puts his penis in the woman's vagina, and they have sex. That's how you make a baby, unless you wear a condom. Dad showed me what a condom is. It goes on your penis."

Dr. Dan: "Uh yeah. Again, I gotta say that may be a little early for you to worry about, but it's good to know I guess, for later. Did you talk about this at school, too? Like in health class?"

Sean: "We don't talk about this in health class. We talk about choosing healthy foods, and exercising, and about smoking. You shouldn't smoke Dr. Dan."

Dr. Dan: "Yeah, I know Sean, I don't smoke…"

Sean: "That's good Dr. Dan. Smoking will give you lung cancer, and Alzheimer's."

Dr. Dan: "Nope, no worries. Okay, so I guess you know about sex, and it's for later, when you're a grown up, and for now you've found out that it feels good when you touch your penis, and…"

Sean: "Yeah, no, I know it feels good but I can only touch it in private, in my bedroom or in the bathroom, but not at school, or a public bathroom. I know that part, now."

Dr. Dan: "Good, yes, I was going to say, we don't want you to feel bad, or that you can't do that, but it's, yeah, it's a personal thing you don't want to do with other people around. Sounds like you got it."

Sean: "Don't worry, Dr. Dan. I got it. Are we going to finish this? I want to show my dad – it's a really cool police station. My dad was a policeman. He's retired now but he still wears a uniform to funerals, and that. He worked at a police station, and he took me there lots of times. It didn't look like this, but it's kind of the same. He'll like it. Can we do these windows for the next level?"

## JOINING OTHERS

I had been working with Sean privately for the better part of a year when Bob heard about the LEGO® Club groups through an autism parent support group that he was attending. There was some sincere injury in his voice when he asked me about it during one of our parenting/family sessions. We had been discussing some activities that Bob had arranged with kids from school – playdates at the waterpark, the movies, Dave & Buster's – and strategies that Bob could use to get the peers to sustain their communication and interaction with Sean, which wasn't easy, even for us. He had been in the LEGO® room, and in fact, Sean and I had spent quite a bit of time in there as well, but as Bob said, "I didn't really know what you all did in there, until I heard about this great social skills program, the LEGO Club, and I put two-and-two together. Doc, you've been holding out on me, and holding out on Sean."

I didn't want to admit it to Bob, but even after having worked with him and Sean for a while, I was still tentative about putting Sean into a LEGO Club group. We had done some set-building together and even some rudimentary freestyle, but it had been a struggle. He wasn't immediately drawn to LEGO as a medium, and he was so distractible, I had to have all the materials we needed on the table ahead of time, since if either of us had to get up to get something, Sean would be off, scripting, or pacing and scripting, and it was hard to get him back to the table again. Over time though, Sean had gotten better at self-editing and limiting his "cartoon" time, and we had agreed at some point that it was only okay to do this out loud with his dad. With anyone else, he had to keep it to himself, period. I was still having doubts about whether Sean was ready for a group setting, but I also felt badly about not having given Sean a chance – and in this sense, for not having given Bob a chance.

Eventually, I told Bob to bring Sean to the ongoing group with Allen, Anthony, Charlie, Colin and Paul. The group had begun to be fairly cohesive, and the group members were interacting well. They were also focused on achieving their LEGO Club level certificates, and were active with making stop-motion films, which I thought might be a good motivator for Sean, since he was not so interested in just building LEGO. I wasn't sure how he would fit in. I didn't expect he would have much in common with Allen, Anthony and Paul, who all had Asperger's, but I thought he might get along well with Charlie and Colin, who were more on the HFA/PDD-NOS side: less verbal, but very adept with visualization. His sense of humor and his interests in cartoons, videogames and YouTube were likely to help him, since those were common interests for them all.

Once Sean started in LEGO Club, he and Bob never missed a session. Sean and Bob were both nervous and excited when they came to the first group. Sean was pacing in the waiting area, and as I heard later from some of the other parents, they were making everyone else nervous, too. It was like having two Vikings suddenly arrive in the clinic, and then be playfully affectionate and goofy with each other. In the LEGO® room, once I had introduced Sean to everyone, Colin stepped up and greeted him, and then everyone else followed. We were working on the LEGO Tower at the time, as well as a Cindy Brickberg film, "Batman vs. Godzilla," and Colin wanted us to work on the tower, but Allen wanted to shoot more of the movie. Anthony, who really wanted the tower built, but was also invested in the movie (he was the voice of Batman), suggested getting the tower done so we could use it in the movie.

Colin was also enthusiastic about having an extra helper, especially one with Sean's height, which he knew would be an advantage in getting the tower to the ultimate height, the ceiling. Sean was happy to help out with the tower building, although he wound up spending more of his time trading SpongeBob quotes with Anthony and Paul. Sean started scripting a few times while Colin was trying to get everyone focused on the tower – he was doing his best, but aside from Charlie, most of them were not contributing much. Colin ignored him, but the others seemed to appreciate the distraction, and were impressed with Sean's memory and his voices. This also set off a SpongeBob imitation competition, in which Paul had the best SpongeBob, but then Sean did an amazing Mr. Krabs, outdone only by Anthony's Patrick imitation, which cracked everyone up, even Colin.

The next week, the other group members started interacting with Sean in the waiting room, and Bob wanted to join them. "Sean, introduce me to your new pals." Sean didn't remember their names, but he was clearly glad to see them, and to do more comic spoofs. Colin and Charlie told Bob about the tower project, and beating the other groups to the ceiling, and Bob was excited about that, and was clearly proud when Colin told him that they would need Sean to help them assemble the tower when the sections were done. Anthony piped up that they were working on the Batman vs. Godzilla movie, and that was even better news – Bob and Sean were big Godzilla fans. Bob did a very credible Godzilla in the waiting room, and Sean joined in, giving a loud shriek, and yelling, "I'm Rodan!" Sean and Bob roared and screeched at each other and positioned themselves for battle, which impressed the LEGO Club gang a lot, except for a couple of the mothers who had anxious little ones with them.

Sean got to do his share of voice acting on the stop-motion movies of the other group members, while he was still working on getting his LEGO® Builder and Creator levels. Although he continued to have difficulty staying focused long enough to do much building, he was good at finding parts, and he was an essential asset in the final tower assembly. During the film recording, Sean was not only able to remember all of his lines after reading through the script a couple of times, he also remembered everyone else's. This was a problem at times when he would repeat others' lines along with them on the recording, but the group members were able to get him to stop that. Another issue became more serious, which was Sean's tendency to drift off and pace and script while the others were working on a stop-motion scene.

Sean was happy to be a part of anyone's project, usually doing some of the stop-motion and voice-overs, as well as helping to build the sets, but his focus on the activity never lasted much longer than about five minutes. Still, after the group, he would always point out to Bob which voice he had done or which part of the scenery or animating he had done. During one stop-motion film sequence, on a movie led by Paul – an arctic weather station is over-run by angry polar bears who are upset about global warming – Sean was pacing and scripting when he was cued to say his line. He didn't respond right away, and the group was in a hurry to get the scene done, so Anthony said his line for him, "Come on, let's make sushi outta these guys." Sean heard him say it, and stopped pacing, turned towards the group and said, "No! That's my line! I have to say it." Anthony said, "You weren't paying attention, so I said it for you, so next time pay attention."

Sean reacted immediately in a loud, high-pitched voice: "You have to go back! Go back, I'm here. I want to say my line. You said my line!" Suddenly, he was howling, rushing at the table where the computer and other equipment was, and lunging at Anthony. I jumped and got there just in time to squeeze between Sean and Anthony. Sean was trying to grab him, and Anthony was ducking and backing up to the wall behind the table. Sean stopped pushing at me, and he let me guide him back towards the door, while he was still yelling and pointing at Anthony. "He took my line! I was supposed to say, 'Come on, let's make sushi outta these guys.'" He was pushing at me and trying to get past me to get at Anthony. "He said my line! It was my line, and I was waiting to say, 'Let's make sushi outta these guys,' and they didn't cue me. It's my line..." He was crying and yelling, and I had to get him to sit down by the door to try to calm him down. I had little doubt at that moment, that if I hadn't gotten in between Sean and Anthony, Sean would have grabbed him and probably made sushi out of him.

Once that was over, we were able to talk about it. Sean was calm enough eventually, and Anthony didn't seem particularly fazed, so I encouraged Sean to tell him why he was so angry, and then Anthony, Charlie, Allen and Colin were able to explain to Sean how his self-talk was interfering and delaying with the stop-motion process. They all agreed that they would not usurp Sean's parts in the future, but he had to stay on cue and not wander around the room gesturing and talking to himself. The motivation for Sean to stay as part of the group, and to contribute – by building or moving features during a shoot, or by doing voice-overs – was strong enough to make him inhibit this very longstanding behavior pattern, which had persisted at home and at school for many years, despite many behavior plans and medications.

I had seen similar situations with many kids with autism who had well-entrenched repetitive, stereotyped movements (hand-flapping or twirling, hopping), or more complex action sequences (scripting, putting LEGO® pieces around the room, or stacking similar pieces in long chains), suddenly decide to suppress them because there was something they wanted to do that was more important to them. In a couple of younger nonverbal boys with autism, it was the LEGO electric train – getting to play with it, or use it in a film sequence, or make modifications to it, etc. – which was motivating enough to get them to stop the repetitive behavior long enough to participate. Once this "crack" in the well-armored stereotyped behavior appeared, we were often able to use the new interest, and accompanying behavioral repertoire, to start using a Differential Reinforcement of Incompatible (DRI) behavior model in other settings, which had previously been unsuccessful. The DRI approach (Vollmer and Iwata 1992) was one of the few behavior change strategies that I had seen work with stereotyped behaviors, which are especially difficult to change because they are "automatic," or self-reinforcing – they are not necessarily maintained or supported by secondary gain or reinforcement, and therefore, changing the reinforcement schedule for that "behavior" does not always work. Some stereotyped movements are so entrenched and nonfunctional that they do not seem as much like behavior as they do tics or other involuntary movements. Because Sean and others were so motivated to engage in the LEGO® activity, they were voluntarily willing to suppress the behavior, and once they experienced that for themselves, it was fairly straightforward to convince them (and their parents and teachers) that they could do likewise in other settings. Most importantly for Sean, the decline in his pacing and gesturing with self-talk led to an increase in his involvement with the creative process in the group. As a result of that, we all got to experience more of his great visual humor and action sequences, many of which became classics in the LEGO stop-motion collection we were building. Needless to say, Bob was his biggest fan.

When Sean started directing his own LEGO movies, Bob was thrilled. He had a bit of a flair for acting himself (he had a commanding presence, and booming voice), and was very animated and theatrical with Sean as the two of them acted out their favorite scenes in the waiting room. "If he's going to be doing this stuff, he might as well do it right. And just like you taught me to do, Dr. Dan, I'm not trying to stop him, I'm joining him. Making it social, right? Now we've got half the clinic here in on the act." Now, instead of the two of them repeating scenes from movies they'd watched or cartoons, or videogames, they'd be in the waiting room with the rest of the LEGO Club members and their parents, rehearsing or "blocking out" action scenes for another of Sean's movies. Sean turned out to have a Chaplinesque gift for slapstick and knowing what would make something funnier in a LEGO scene. In his own films, he was always striving for the big laugh, and he would stalk it patiently, and try out different visual images to see how it came across to the other group members: "No, no, no, wait…he stands there, he doesn't say anything, and then, he hits him with…a turkey leg! Yeah, ha! Ha! Never mind, not funny enough. You didn't laugh. A pizza? No, not a pizza. How about a cow? He throws a cow! You get it, he's throwing a cow! Ha! Okay, that's funny."

I continued to see Sean periodically for updated assessments and consultations as he got older. He and Bob remained very close, and although they often clashed, they were generally on the same team about most issues. Sean participated in a peer-mentoring program and attended his local community college, taking courses in electronics and media, and he worked part-time for this father, who had started a private media production consulting firm. Sean had become much more aware of his personal appearance – including the fact that he was very tall and a bit intimidating, which he used to his advantage at times – and had his heart set on having a girlfriend. At the last visit I had with Sean and Bob, he was taking driving lessons, after Bob had finally admitted that he should "let the professionals handle it." The driving course was specifically for students with disabilities who were attending the college, and Sean was an avid, if timid, driver. They both continued to have a fascination with filmmaking, and acting, and eventually joined an amateur theater group. I had always thought they would make a wonderful Prince Hal and Falstaff.

# VICKY

## INITIAL CONTACT

As was the case with many clients who later became LEGO® Club members, Victoria, or Vicky, was initially referred to me for a neuropsychological assessment by her parents, who were in a dispute with their school district about Vicky's IEP. Vicky's parents, Gina and Donald, were young, well-educated professionals who had grown up in the area and had considerable family and social support. Vicky had been diagnosed with a rare neurological disorder that affected some aspects of her motor functioning shortly after birth. It was not until Vicky was in elementary school that they started to notice difficulties with her social adjustment. Despite the neurological condition, Vicky, like her parents, was exceptionally bright. The independent assessment was requested in order to help clarify Vicky's educational and developmental needs, as well as any possible co-morbid mental health issues in addition to the congenital neurological disorder.

Vicky's cognitive testing results were fairly remarkable: she had visual-spatial abilities in the average range, with some clear evidence of interference from the neurological condition, but her language development was in the very superior range, well above the cut-off level for "gifted." Her vocabulary, syntax and sentence structure at the time, in early elementary school, were very adult-like. It was eerie to hear such language coming out of a young child. Vicky was also utterly adorable. She had long curly auburn hair and bright blue-green eyes, a smattering of freckles, and a tendency to dress in a cacophony of colorful layers (she kept that style through adolescence). She was matter-of-fact to the point of being quite pedantic, and literal.

Vicky had a dry sense of humor, of the type one appreciates in jovial university professors, and was very observant and insightful about certain things, but completely clueless and impractical in other ways. She noticed my face was unshaven one day and said, "Dr. Dan! You forgot to shave this morning. How will you develop a successful practice if you come to your office looking so shabby?" She herself was wearing mismatched socks and muddy shoes, and had blue paint all over her hands and her t-shirt. She loved animals, and was often involved in rescuing injured birds or rodents, and worried about the semi-domesticated species that lived in her gentrifying suburb: "We're the ones who messed up their ecosystem, so we should take the responsibility to make sure they are able to find food and shelter." About school, she used words like "tedious" and "mundane."

Vicky's parents understood that she was gifted, which was not the usual outcome for children with her neurological diagnosis, but weren't aware of how atypical she was socially until her younger sister was born and started to develop – her sister was also bright, but was much more animated and naturally childlike in her emotions and attachments. Vicky seemed other-worldly, and had many idiosyncratic traits that were endearing, for a while, but then became more ominous as she got older, more verbal and more assertive about her habits and rituals. While she was fascinating to her parents and family members, and to me, of course, she was less so to her classmates. In preschool and early elementary school, her peers (and teachers) didn't seem to notice the difference so much, but by the time Vicky was in 3rd grade, and eight years old, she was speaking in paragraphs with a post-graduate vocabulary, and was often correcting her teacher's input rather than just doing her own schoolwork. No doubt, she was bored to tears.

Vicky's dry humor and interpersonal observations seemed to come from her father, who was also a bit aloof and clearly an intellectual sort, but she couldn't have been more different from her mother, Gina, who easily engaged with others and was emotionally expressive. Both Donald and Gina were passionate about Vicky and her sister's care and education, but they were also careful not to try to overpower them with their parental concerns, and wanted them to feel free and uninhibited about exploring the world. Because of this they were quite unhappy with the feedback they were getting from the school regarding Vicky's "inattentiveness" and "disruptive behavior." Vicky's parents started to worry that the school was not prepared to provide her with the necessary modifications and supports that they knew she would need. After my assessment report was completed, which included a diagnosis of Asperger's Disorder and which documented her unusually high IQ and academic achievement scores, they felt better armed to argue for some flexibility with regard to her eccentric behavior, and her curriculum needs. They were disappointed by the school district's response, which was an offer of a weekly half-hour group counseling session with the school psychologist, and some OT sessions to improve Vicky's handwriting, which was well below her other academic achievement levels.

The school district seemed to virtually ignore Vicky's neurological diagnosis, possibly because she was doing so well academically, which infuriated Gina. She felt they should be more focused on the areas in which her disabilities did impact her – visual-motor functioning and social adjustment – rather than on her academic achievement scores. Again, the Vineland assessment tool was useful in convincing the IEP team that Vicky should continue to be eligible for special education supports – as noted above, despite her high IQ and academic scores, Vicky was very impractical, had significant difficulties with peer relationships, and was highly dependent on her parents for most activities of daily living. She was highly disorganized and was just as likely to lose her homework as do it, and it was a daily chore getting her to keep track of her backpack, cell phone and glasses.

## LEARNING THROUGH LEGO®

As was mentioned earlier, Vicky was not initially referred for any kind of treatment, but for a comprehensive assessment, but in the review and discussion of the evaluation results, Donald and Gina were interested in hearing my input about Vicky's needs as a young girl with Asperger's who was also gifted. There is a sub-literature (as well as a sub-culture) about the gifted Asperger's students who are especially difficult to program for, since they have such a wide range of needs – from learning materials and curricula that are appropriate for students with very high cognitive abilities and academic skills, to social and behavioral interventions to help with very immature social and coping skills. This is not an easy combination to program for in terms of both an IEP and an appropriate learning environment. How do you offer appropriate peers to someone who is functioning academically many years in advance of their age level, but has the daily coping and social skills of a much younger child? As a result of this combination, and the fact that they are also often rigid, unilateral and self-focused, they can also be off-putting or annoying to their peers, as well as to some teaching and support staff.

The good news was that Vicky fitted right in with LEGO® Club. Initially, we weren't sure if this was going to be a good fit for her, as she showed little interest in LEGO, and both Vicky and her parents were skeptical about the potential benefit of engaging with other children with social learning difficulties. This was an objection I had heard many times before from parents when I described the groups to them – what I came to refer to as the "mind-blind leading the mind-blind" argument. I could see both sides of this issue, since I often utilize typical peers as mentors and supports for students with autism/Asperger's in school and community settings, and have coached them and siblings to be helpful with feedback and social coaching for the affected individual. In those instances, I have also noticed the tendency for the relationship to be more of a fiduciary one, with an individual with autism/Asperger's perceiving their peer mentor as more like an adult than a well-informed peer.

In other words, the affected child tends not to identify with the mentor as a peer, *per se*, but more as they would a young therapist or teacher. The recognition of a core difference in worldview (autistic and mind-blind versus neurotypical and socially intact) also causes the affected child not to identify with the other in challenging situations but to compare the differences, in a way that puts themselves in a negative light: "Yeah, that works for you, because you're good at this stuff. I'd rather just stay home by myself." This was certainly becoming Vicky's response more and more to her parents and her aunts and uncles when they tried to get her more involved with peers, either at family functions, or in township soccer, or other activities.

Vicky's initial reaction to the LEGO room was not typical, though. She was curious, but did not at first see the creative potential there, and was more focused on the fact that it was all LEGO: "That's all you have in here?" Her parents also perceived it as somewhat limiting: they wanted Vicky to have the freedom to choose a medium for expressing herself, and not be limited to interconnected bricks. Her father, Donald, was more enthusiastic, especially after he saw all the Star Wars LEGO® on display, and the camera equipment and laptop with stop-motion software. Gina was not convinced. She asked, though, if I would consider working individually with Vicky on improving her social coping and communication with peers, and addressing some of her developing school avoidance and OCD tendencies, which were getting worse and creating more issues at school than the staff seemed able to handle (there was talk about disciplinary action for missing school, and for losing her assignments and books, etc.).

I agreed to work with Vicky on some self-monitoring and self-management goals, using cognitive-behavioral therapy (CBT), as well as consulting with her parents and her school staff about putting together an effective school-based program for her. Vicky and I often met in the LEGO room, and over time she became more interested in the activities in there, including the scripts and storyboards, film sets, hand-written titles and credits, etc. She began to realize LEGO Club was a lot more than just putting LEGO sets together, and she asked Gina about it. At the time, we were in the process of building up a second, younger LEGO group at the Institute.

Vicky eventually joined that group – there were also two other girls in the group at the time – and she fitted right in. She was, of course, much better at script-writing and voice-acting than LEGO building, but she also had some very creative and "outside-the-box" ideas about building. She used LEGO platform sheets, for instance, as a canvas on which she "painted" two-dimensional pictures using small LEGO pieces (this was before the LEGO artist Nathan Sawaya had become very popular). She also stepped up to lead a group project, after suggesting building a LEGO zoo, to accommodate all the LEGO animals we had on hand, as well as some we later built or acquired specifically for the project.

## JOINING OTHERS

The LEGO Club experience was good for Vicky in a few ways. Initially, she was a bit overwhelmed by the activity, since most of the other members were boys, and they were more familiar with the materials, and had more clear ideas about what they envisioned happening in the group sessions. So, at first, Vicky was just along for the ride, and spent most of her time either chatting with the other girls in the group – who found her a bit teacherly and condescending – or with Sarah. In the later groups, after we'd made the move from the Institute to the new clinic, Vicky was by then an "old hand" at LEGO® Club and was much more willing to step up as a group leader. In the first group, there were initially some "boy vs. girl" issues which we straightened out right away (the girls could definitely hold their own on the LEGO Helper, Builder and Creator skill sets). Vicky was also a bit busy correcting her peers' grammar and adding a lot of tangential details to our conversations, or fussing about the occasional rule violations. Over time, though, she got more focused on the activities, and engaged her creative side.

The positive relationship I had built with Vicky prior to her starting in the group was a help in getting her to join and be willing to participate. She trusted me and seemed to accept that I wouldn't give her bad advice, or put her in situations that might overwhelm her; however, this connection also tended to backfire a bit when the social interactions in the room got a bit stressful for her. When there were strong emotions expressed by the other members – most often anger and frustration, but there were also some times of over-excitement and giddiness, or sadness and tearful withdrawal – Vicky would seek me out to talk about it. It seemed like she needed an objective person to act as a barrier to what could have become an intense interaction. In any case, whenever someone was upset or behaving a bit unpredictably, she would come stand near me, sometimes tap me on the shoulder, and say something like: "Erm, Dr. Dan... [pointing] ...that boy is, err, how do I say this politely? He's having a complete snit, and, well, he's freaking me out! Do you think you could do something about him?"

> That was not an uncommon reaction from group members when there were emotions being expressed, either by one individual, or more than one. It was not unusual for two or three group members to have an issue that could end up disrupting the entire group session. And just as Vicky would approach me and ask me to address the issue in her lovely, articulate way, the normal reaction from group members

was to look to me, or the other adults in the room, to solve the problem. We did not. This was the most difficult part of the group process that group members, new therapists and even parents (who often could hear the ruckus from the waiting room, or would hear about it later from the participants) had to cope with. As I told the graduate students and others who came to participate in the groups over the years, unless there appeared to be an imminent threat of physical aggression, or someone was doing something potentially dangerous, the group members were coached to solve their own social conflicts – we would not solve them for them. This was the only way, in my view, that they would feel comfortable and confident about solving social conflict situations in their own lives outside of LEGO® Club. The situations had to be allowed to escalate to the point of being personal, and strong emotions were a part of that experience.

Of course, there were also exceptions to this basic concept. The main guideline I used, which was not always an easy concept to implement, was that I would allow any social interaction and affective expression to engage the members and have them resolve it, as long as it was of the sort that they might experience in their daily lives outside of here. Just as I recommended to school staff with whom I consulted, it did not make sense to have group members learn to cope with a social situation or someone else's behavior which was not likely to occur at school, in the community, at home or, eventually, in the workplace. Teasing and bullying were good examples of these exceptions, and these were explicitly identified in the rules. I would typically identify what I thought was teasing or when a group member was being domineering towards others (or when two members or even a small clique would form and dominate a group), and then encourage the others to address the issue. But this was not a "normal" social conflict situation – teasing and bullying are not tolerated at school, and they typically don't occur in most other settings – and the fact that they were occurring in LEGO Club was usually the result of group members having been exposed to unusual teasing or bullying situations and re-enacting these scenarios in the group. Whether this was a "working through" or "identification with the aggressor," or just inappropriate social modeling, I was much less likely to let the group members work this out on their own – there was little point to having them learn to deal with a situation that they were not likely to encounter outside the group. Since my direct input into social conflict situations was used very sparingly, the group members tended to respond fairly quickly when it happened. Being calm, identifying the situation and then using humor, we were usually able to get past the issue.

Occasionally, we had group members who were probably misdiagnosed and who had more oppositional or conduct disorder traits, or a combination of ADHD and oppositional behavior. These members were more likely to be included in a group in later iterations of LEGO® Club when there were a lot of groups running and I was less directly involved in selecting the group members. This was also partly due to the increased use of autism/Asperger's/ASD diagnoses by colleagues less familiar with this population who were taking a more literal, quantitative view of the criteria, rather than having a clear sense of what constituted the core features of an autistic condition. Many children and adolescents were diagnosed with ASDs who had some rigid, repetitive behaviors that were more like typical childhood habits, who were also impulsive and had social difficulties due to problems with poor frustration tolerance, and often a lack of response to authority due to parenting or other family issues. Children with these issues, who have been described as having "externalizing" behavioral issues, were much more difficult to manage in the LEGO Club setting. They also did not interact well with the socially anxious, inhibited, idiosyncratically rigid and eccentric population of "internalizers," for whom LEGO Club was developed. They were clearly not from the same planet.

The LEGO Club group process was in some ways similar to the process of LEGO building: slow, but steady and systematic, with gains expressed through small increments of adaptive social coping, one piece added to the others.

Both the therapeutic process of the groups, and the tangible analog of that process, the LEGO® creations themselves, were also very fragile. One destructive minute could cost the group many sessions of re-building the safety and integrity of the relationships, as well as the creative works that reflected the process that built those relationships. Many times, a destructive impulse could be worked through productively. A member would express frustration with themselves, or with the others, or both, and smash a creation, or dump out a tray, yell, bang on the table, slam a door, etc. It would inject a sense of not feeling safe, and a need for adult intervention – the pull was strong on both sides for me to step up and resolve the issue. But, if the group members were able to discuss the situation and amongst themselves come up with a reasonable solution, the bond between them became stronger, and their conception of how to cope with a social conflict, and how to respond to an emotional crisis, improved.

For new group members, I would sometimes inoculate them to the potential for disinhibited strong affect and destructiveness, which I anticipated they would not expect to experience in the group. Sometimes, in an assessment session or in the group, I would become playfully petulant, and I would purposely destroy one of my own LEGO sets or creations. I would knock it to the floor, or toss it at the wall. It was dramatic. But then, I would model what would be expected to happen in LEGO Club: I'd pick up the pieces, put them in a tray, and either reconstruct the set, or set it aside and re-build it later. LEGO materials are very forgiving that way. We can express anger in a destructive way, but there is always the opportunity to redeem ourselves later by reconstructing it. The bricks are very resilient, as is the creative process. These "acts of redemption" became an important part of the group process, especially as the group members became more heterogeneous, and there was a need for members to be able to redeem themselves with the group for having been offensive – intrusive, domineering, selfish, etc.

If one of the LEGO Club group members came in to group following a frustrating event elsewhere, just having a bad day or maybe just a bad car-ride, or they had a disappointing experience in the room, they might respond by becoming loud, insistent and demanding. It was what I would commonly describe to the group members as "wearing the microscope." In that analogy, when a frustrating event captured their attention and was strong enough to elicit some adrenaline, there was a tendency for that event to become fixed in their thoughts, and to become exaggerated, to seem larger and more important than it might otherwise. It became difficult for them to consider alternatives, or to just "let it go," as we the other members often said to microscope-wearing peers. When group members were very upset, they had a hard time changing their focus to anything but the immensely huge issue they saw looming before them, and apparently no one else in the room could see. They rigidly and doggedly argued that we should be able to see how urgently important it was, and somehow we had to resolve this issue for them.

What we learned to do together as a group was partly "active listening" (Carl Rogers' (1951) concept) – we would help them feel understood. Even if we couldn't understand what they were talking about – it was only usually only the microscope wearer who had this particular view of things – we could sometimes identify with having felt that way at some point about something, and we'd try. Just trying to help someone feel understood and heard was half the battle. Then, once the person felt heard, we'd stall a bit with rational problem-solving, which almost never worked since this wasn't a rational problem, but we'd kick some ideas around so that the microscope wearer could shoot them down. Then, when the adrenaline was down a bit, I'd encourage a bit of insight and group participation in getting the microscope away from the person, often using humor. Sometimes, I'd try the paradoxical approach by suggesting an exaggerated and silly solution – "Maybe we should just disband LEGO® Club, and donate the LEGO to charity. It's not working out at all. Oh well, we tried. So who's going to tell the parents?" or, "Yep, Mitch really was being pushy there. I guess we should all take him out in the parking lot and beat the heck out of him. Does anyone have a crowbar or baseball bat we could use? Maybe we can find an old two-by-four, or some big rocks. A two-by-four with some nails in it would be good. Okay, come on Mitch, and the rest of you, let's go." I'd be calm and apparently sincere about this, so the group members would have an initial sense of shock, followed by relief and, hopefully, laughter, at the incongruous and farcical suggestion.

Vicky was one of the group members who almost never got into the microscope trap. Part of the reason for this was her calm disposition – she had an observer-participant style in most situations, and her emotional reactions tended to take a while. She was also not so driven to achieve anything that she became frustrated or disappointed with and so was not inclined to have adrenaline-driven rants if she didn't get her project done, or someone else was interfering with her. This became a bit of an issue a few times, when I felt she was not being assertive enough. An important goal of the LEGO® Club approach was to create an atmosphere that allowed children and adolescents who might otherwise not contribute their ideas and talents to the rest of us to do so, and to learn to be effective communicators and self-advocates in the process. Vicky is an excellent example of someone who clearly had a lot of unique talent and ability that we could all benefit from, but who would also happily keep it all to herself if the barriers to her participation were too high. She was someone I would encourage to persist and to be more assertive in communicating her ideas, to stay engaged in the process, even if others were getting animated; her more creative, sensible idea could be held out there, and could withstand the heat and blows of weaker, less rational opinions. This, I felt, was an important capacity for all the group members, but especially for someone with such rare gifts as Vicky.

Vicky did learn to wait out the microscope moments. Some of them blew over in an instant, especially once the groups had been running for a while, and the group members learned that getting loud, or menacing, or tearful, would not necessarily elicit an adult intervention. But some of the outbursts could be prolonged, and there might be multiple serial episodes of it, sometimes carrying over from one session to the next, as was the case with Anthony when he was trying to get his LEGO® Master and was routinely frustrated. There were often vicious cycles that could spiral up when a mild frustrating event elicited a negative reaction which then resulted in negative attention from others and a negative self-assessment, followed by more frustration and self-condemnation, resulting in more negative feedback from peers, and so on. In either case, whether it was a momentary blow up, or a long, drawn-out eruption, Vicky tended to stay out of it, somewhat aloof.

Over time, though, as the relationships with the other group members became more important and personal to her, Vicky felt more compelled to stay involved even when there were strong emotions – she wasn't so inclined to leave the situation and come seek out an adult for advice and security. She quickly picked up and started modeling the "active listening" part of our de-escalation efforts. In fact, Vicky became very adept at defusing conflict situations with peers using the combination of listening, problem-solving and then humor and deflection. She rarely accepted responsibility to solve the other person's problem, and while she would be assertive in leaving the responsibility with them to sort out an "act of redemption," she might point out how the rules may have been violated, or that an individual or the group as a whole might need to be compensated for their actions. There were no explicit directions about how to handle these situations, but Vicky, like the other group members, was exposed to enough of them that they soon learned how they were typically handled: we listened, we engaged in problem-solving, then quickly moved to humor/distraction, and an opportunity for redemption was found and presented. By learning this routine, or at least the active listening and rational problem-solving parts, Vicky was quickly able to become a peer mentor, and it gave her the confidence to stay "in the moment," or to stay engaged in affect-riddled, irrational and turbulent interpersonal interactions.

Vicky's neurological condition did affect her ability to create using LEGO to some extent, but her narrative ability more than made up for it with her peers in the group. She was generous to a fault with her time and energy as a script editor, and could give a more adult-like direction to some of the more rudimentary dialogues. She was also willing to participate as a voice-over actor, and ad-libbed more than she used the script. She was also very patient and tolerant, often taking on the role of peer therapist. Her pedantic style slowly morphed over time into something more like a big sister role – she was tall for her age, and was very much like LEGO® Club's own Wendy Darling from "Peter Pan," with her pseudo-adult speech, maternal attitude and storytelling ability.

Eventually, Vicky hit her teen years in full stride and became an oppositional handful for everyone. She was still charming, delightful and brilliant, but her disorganization, forgetfulness and tendency to be tardier than most was putting her parents and supporters at school to the test. The staff at her school did eventually learn to appreciate and engage her, but that was in high school. I don't think her middle school staff ever quite got over her. Somewhere around 7th grade she became her own lawyer, and would argue her way out of or around just about any rule, at home or at school. At least, she gave it a sincere try. To some extent the increase in argumentativeness was fueled by a blossoming of self-consciousness, which was a development that had become very familiar to me by then.

The concept of "mindblindness," which has been well described and researched by my colleague, Simon Baron Cohen, is a core autistic characteristic that renders especially young individuals with autistic conditions opaque to others' thoughts, feelings and ideas, but also obscures to some extent the notion of a self or identity, an awareness of one's own thought processes, attachments, habits of mind and emotions. Many individuals with autistic conditions, even very intelligent people like young Vicky, are concrete and externally focused. They have a hard time understanding concepts like subjectivity and constructivism. They're naïve realists to the core. Vicky would not have accepted that "reality" was a social construct comprised of the related but separate, overlapping viewpoints of individuals communicating together about their experiences. She did, however, seem to be able to grasp that an individual's view of reality might be distorted by their past experiences or emotions, with her as a notable exception, of course. So, she wasn't completely "mind-blind," but she was more consistently "self-blind."

Vicky was lucky enough to have parents who understood and accepted this. Vicky could not blossom into a fully capable, creative person without first exploring the self-other separation – the separation-individuation process – which was soon followed by her identity achievement, which included a lot of trying out of different hats, so her attitudes, values and commitments changed on a more-or-less daily basis for a while. With Vicky, because of her insight and her wonderful communication abilities, much of this process was transparent and she shared it with me and her parents.

Vicky hadn't quite made up her mind about boys at that point, but she was fairly well committed to being "alternative" in her style and work ethic. Talking to her about "romance" still tended to make her anxious, and she would just chew on her lips or her fingers, and look blankly at me. She wasn't ready. She was devoutly non-conformist, though, and also, like her parents, very conscientious about the environment and its impact on critters of all sorts. While this was a bit of a social problem at times in middle school, by the time she was in high school, she had a lot of company and she developed a social circle of friends who were also conservatively anti-conservative, with a penchant for dark, quirky humor. Retro-hippy was definitely "in," and Vicky found herself, possibly for the first time, feeling in sync with her peers. She was a budding intellectual, and probably destined to be a playwright or a journalist. At the point of writing this, that story is still unfolding, and for her parents and others involved in her life, I'm sure Vicky is just as mesmerizing and awesome as ever.

# ZEKE

## INITIAL CONTACT

Zeke was one of a number of LEGO® Club members who arrived at our clinic via an adoption agency support group. There were quite a few, including Zeke, who were adopted by local families from former Soviet bloc countries where there were many orphaned children living in very compromised settings. Zeke was a bit of an anomaly in that context because of his size – he was off the growth chart for height from the time he was adopted at just a few months of age. He continued to grow quickly and was a head taller than his classmates in preschool. This tended to obscure the developing social difficulties he was starting to show, since his parents and teachers tended to ascribe anything atypical about Zeke either to his early childhood challenges as an adopted orphan, or to the fact that he was simply awkward because of his size, or that people may expect too much from him because he appeared older than his age. After the transition to Kindergarten, however, and during some of his follow-up visits with Dr. M, who was a consultant to the former Soviet adoption groups, it became clear that there was something more affecting Zeke than just social adjustment and his height.

Like many of the children with autism/Asperger's who came to LEGO Club, Zeke was initially diagnosed with ADHD, and was put on medication for that. He continued on ADHD medication throughout his elementary school years, in fact, and was still on them when I last had contact with him as a high school student. Zeke presented with a combination of anxiety issues, including social anxiety – a shyness that verged on selective mutism – and more typical ADHD features of distractibility, forgetfulness, impulsivity and difficulty self-monitoring. Zeke also had a combination of difficulties sustaining his attention on non-preferred learning activities, and excessive focus on his own topics of interest that was clearly obsessive and intrusive. He was quite typical in his tendency to steer any conversation towards topics of his interest – eventually he did this in subtle ways, but initially he would just interrupt and start talking about his interests, which were mostly video and computer game related. Zeke's inattentiveness and hyperkinesis were very evident if he was not on his medication – he literally bounced in his seat, or bounced his legs, scribbled or fidgeted with pencils or anything else he could get his hands on, and would be talking out loud to himself, or to anyone around him in class.

Zeke lived in an intact family home with his parents, who were both successful business people – his father, Abe, was an accountant and his mother, Tina, was a small business owner. Zeke had an older brother, Nathan, who was also adopted from Russia, and was not genetically related. Zeke and his brother were quite different physically and socially, but they got along well, mostly because Nathan was a very kind and supportive older brother, and because Zeke looked up to him (although eventually, Zeke was a lot taller than his brother). Nathan often poked his head into LEGO® Club and came in to interact with Zeke there a few times – he was a LEGO fan – and like many siblings, he was envious of Zeke's experiences there, but he also understood that this wasn't just a club. Nathan knew his brother had problems and was on medication, and he knew that coming to the clinic, to see me for evaluations, and Dr. M, and then LEGO Club, were things his parents were doing to help his brother. Abe and Tina were model parents. Although they were both busy with their work commitments, they brought Zeke, and often Nathan, to many appointments at our clinic in addition to the group sessions, and they had Zeke involved in many other physical and social activities, including yoga, OT, swimming and martial arts.

Zeke was often noticed by other parents or school staff for his height and athletic physique. He also had bright blond hair and light blue eyes, with a square jaw and handsome features. He looked like the stereotypical budding Olympic athlete, maybe a swimmer or decathlete. As Zeke and his parents became quickly aware, however, he was very uncoordinated. It was not just his size, either, as many hopeful basketball coaches would offer. He was clumsy, and he had no interest in sports, anyway. His brother Nathan, and his father Abe, were both serious tennis players and would have killed for Zeke's height and strength, but Zeke couldn't hit a tennis ball, and didn't want to learn.

While Zeke's aloofness in social situations and his ADHD seemed to be potentially due to factors in his social history (possible substance exposure in utero was common in Russian adoptees, as well as features of attachment disturbance), his rigid, idiosyncratic interests and physical coordination difficulties (dyspraxia) got Dr. M thinking about possible Asperger's Disorder. Zeke was also not doing that well in school, and he had begun to show signs of dysgraphia, as well as possibly dyslexia, so Dr. M referred him for a comprehensive neuropsychological assessment, including cognitive, psychoeducational and psycho-diagnostic testing. The results showed that Zeke had intact general language abilities, but with reading fluency and comprehension difficulties. His cognitive and neuropsych results also showed that he was in the gifted range for visual-spatial and perceptual reasoning abilities – he'd be an engineer or scientist, not a novelist. His graphomotor execution was also very poor – consistent with what we would later describe as a generalized dyspraxia. He had well below average scores on fine motor, gross motor and oral motor tasks.

These motor issues as well as his social and performance anxiety also had a negative impact on his adaptive functioning. At the age of about eight years, he was already three to five years behind on communication, socialization and daily functioning skills. One of the contributing factors here was a lack of social modeling or imitation, and a lack of motivation for acquisition of skills in these mostly "self-taught" areas. He had been very slow to pick up on toilet training, for instance, and it never seemed to bother him that much that he wasn't fully toilet trained like his peers in 1st and 2nd grade, as much as it vexed his parents and even his older brother. So, just as he was with sports – he didn't have the coordination for it, and didn't care – he was with a number of daily things, like putting his books and papers away in his backpack, or using utensils to eat with and a napkin to wipe his mouth, or folding and putting away his laundry, or making his bed, or brushing his teeth and hair, or tying his shoelaces. He was very loveable, but a mess.

I worked with Tina on some home-based strategies to encourage Zeke to be more motivated, and Tina diligently took him to private OT sessions as well. Zeke definitely made some progress, although it seemed to cost Tina some relationship points with him at times, and she wound up having to choose her battles – brushing teeth and personal hygiene: definitely worth working on; making the bed and folding laundry: not worth it – close the door to his room when guests are over; and tie shoes and button up shirt: not worth it – shop for Velcro shoes or slip-ons, t-shirts or hoodies. Nathan and Abe were also a big help here, since they were able to give Zeke some more man-to-man feedback about his appearance and communication style when Zeke had relegated poor Tina to "nagging" status.

Zeke's anxiety in social situations was exacerbated by the attention he often got for being tall, and then was made even worse by his having some mild articulation difficulties. His speech was clear and fluent most of the time, but he would often rush to get a thought out, and he would begin to stammer and his words would get jumbled together, which made him self-conscious and frustrated. He often seemed preoccupied, and somewhat distant, and as I learned, this was because he was there with you but thinking about something else. He was another one whose parents had to learn to ask him to repeat back what was told to him, otherwise, he was happy to say, "Yep, unh-huh, sure," in an automatic and uncomprehending way. He was also not very good at noticing when others didn't understand what he was saying – either because his speech was rushed, whispery and poorly articulated, or he was talking to the wall, or he was just saying incomprehensible things that made sense to him, but just about no one else.

## LEARNING THROUGH LEGO®

I had a good rapport with Zeke from our first meeting – which was in the LEGO room, and Zeke was definitely intrigued by the LEGO room – and so I had not seen much of his social anxiety, until the first LEGO group. He was a different kid entirely when he first came in to the group setting. I hardly recognized him. One-on-one with me in the LEGO room, Zeke was chatty, animated and focused on his interests of course, but also curious about the other themes and creative works on display there. He liked superheroes, and wasn't particularly stuck on Star Wars.

Zeke had a somewhat uncharacteristic need to share – either by physically sharing, for example with gestures to show or demonstrate something, or by verbally sharing in a narrative, telling a story about an experience. I had experienced many children with autism/Asperger's as making me feel quite alone even when we were talking. There was a distinctly one-sided quality to the communication, as if we were sending each other messages by telegram. Very little joint communication took place in those scenarios. But with Zeke, he really seemed to want your attention, and he wanted to share something with you, something exciting or interesting to him, that he thought you would enjoy. He didn't always have the best timing, or a good idea about what other people were individually interested in, but his motive was sincere and it was clearly a social one. He wasn't just looking for an audience so that he would have an excuse to engage in self-oriented scripting.

One of the difficulties affecting Zeke that became more evident during our interactions in the LEGO® room, and then through my evaluation of him, was that he had difficulty dividing his attention. Shifting attention back and forth between two or more foci is a characteristic of mature "executive functions." In fact, there were some specific tests for this type of ability in the neuropsychological assessment battery that Zeke completed (e.g. the Delis-Kaplan Executive Function System, D-KEFS). Although he did well on measures of fluency, and being able to focus on one thing at a time, when he was required to shift his attention back and forth, he became much slower and more inefficient. This was evident when we were having a conversation and did some LEGO building together. He could do either very well, but really struggled to do both. He would either be engaged in an animated conversation, but not able to concentrate on the LEGO project at all, or he would be completely absorbed by the LEGO and completely unresponsive to communication.

I knew this would be a weakness that would slow him down in LEGO Club, but also that it would be an issue for him in a variety of other settings as well, including higher academics and vocationally. Even in social situations, most people are able to combine eating or playing a board game with social conversations; Zeke could not. This was also a reflection of a particular characteristic that I had seen in the mental processing of many children and adolescents with autism/Asperger's, which was a difficulty with maintaining a contextual mental set. Mental set is a term that refers to something like an intention or an attitude towards events that gives a continuity and meaning to them. Most people lose mental set periodically, as in walking out the door and forgetting where you're going, or watching a baseball game and forgetting the score, the inning, or even who's playing. You get absorbed in your thoughts or something else in the environment, and you lose the context of what you were doing, the "why" of the activity that explains your interest or your role.

Being able to divide attention between multiple sources is necessary for maintaining mental set. You need to focus on the forest and then the trees, and back on the forest again. Or the number of strikes and balls, and then back to the inning and who's on base, etc. In social situations, there is the topic of conversation, or the facial expressions and body language, and then the context: this is a work-event, a Christmas party, a barbecue, a hallway in my dormitory, a shopping mall, and then, back to the person and the conversation, and so on. With Zeke, and many children like him, he was either focused on the environment, or he was focused on the conversation, or some other type of interaction, or his phone or Gameboy®, or his own thoughts, and he couldn't integrate them very well. It gave conversations with Zeke a strange quality, like switching back and forth from a telephone to a TV, or using Skype when it fades in and out; he was there, then he was gone, then he was back.

We worked on this together, building LEGO®, while I cajoled him about responding to conversation and reminded him about the topic, etc. He also was willing to try during the LEGO Club groups, which was good practice for communicating with peers, while engaged in a distracting activity. His parents and brother were very kind and accommodating, so it was easy for Zeke to get away with being self-absorbed at home. In fact, he was quite irritable with his parents when they tried to be intrusive with him in the ways that I did. He wasn't used to it, and it took mental energy to shift his attention back and forth. He was also a very tolerant and accepting person, so he was willing to put up with it once he understood that his parents and I weren't just messing with him to be annoying.

Zeke finally did some homework I'd been recommending – homework for school, I called it – which involved him observing other students in his classes. Zeke was still in public school at this point, and he was able to identify some peers who were "the cool kids," the ones everyone wants at their birthday party (or on their list of Facebook friends, or whom others follow on Twitter). With some kids, I'd have them observe a particular way of gesturing or their gait, or style of dress, and for Zeke, I wanted him to see what they did while they were having a conversation. Zeke immediately noticed that "cool kids" could multi-task.

Zeke had a hard time walking, or even, as I noticed later, being in an elevator, while carrying on a conversation. He had to concentrate on walking, or he'd bump into things, or he had to focus on being in the elevator, otherwise, he'd keep talking and forget to push the button, or not get off when the doors opened. "Cool kids" could talk and walk, or dribble a ball, ride a skateboard, or work on a science project and keep up a conversation. Zeke got motivated to do that, too, which was not a far stretch for him; as I mentioned, he was a generous sort of person, and saw this as a necessary way of not being rude or self-absorbed. Eventually, Zeke was able to carry on a conversation with me while we built LEGO® together, or we went through his backpack and re-organized his books and papers, or he showed me something amazing on YouTube, or we walked together out the doors and to the parking lot.

## JOINING OTHERS

Zeke was in the group with Vicky, which started at the Institute and carried on into the new outpatient clinic. Those two got along well, partly because they were both calm and not demanding, but also because they were both tall and quiet. When Zeke arrived for his initial LEGO Club session, the first thing he tried to do was disappear. We let him stay in a corner, fiddling with some freestyle parts, for a while, but eventually I knew I had to get him engaged. It was a good time for him to demonstrate his LEGO Helper skills, which I knew he had. We were getting near Hallowe'en and the group was interested in making a Hallowe'en scene, with a dark castle, witches, skeletons, snakes, spiders and webs, etc. Zeke was happy to help look through the bins for pieces, and this then necessitated his communication with some of the group leaders who were busy building the LEGO castle, including some trap doors, and a dungeon full of snakes and spiders. Zeke dug out black and gray bricks and architectural pieces, and then collaborated on building the castle and designing some of the features.

Zeke was like Vicky in that he tended to get quiet when other group members were getting loud or upset, but he would not gravitate towards me or other staff members. He would just withdraw. He never tried to leave the room, as some might have – we often had to go rescue members from their parents' laps in the early days – but he would find a quiet corner to hide in. There was no doubt that he was socially avoidant, especially in performance/demand situations, but he was also clearly conflict avoidant. In a way, he was lucky to have a very accepting and kind family, including his older brother who would never have bossed him around or taken things from him, so the occasions of inappropriate acting out that some of the group members engaged in were very unfamiliar to Zeke. Despite his size, Zeke was never intimidating, and he didn't use his size to back up being dominant, belittling or even verbally aggressive. He rarely criticized or pointed out others' faults. He was usually too focused on his own.

Unfortunately, because of this, as Zeke moved from early to later elementary school and into middle school, he was often the target for teasing and inside jokes. Zeke was big enough that he was not subjected to outright physical bullying, but some of his peers were willing to taunt him or try to get him flustered. Mostly, Zeke was just impatient with what he perceived as immature bantering and posturing, and the staff were not always very vigilant about it, which Zeke resented. Later, Zeke was simply excluded from a lot of social interactions. It wasn't necessary to actively exclude Zeke. If he wasn't being encouraged, or even required, to participate, he would find something else to occupy his time. He was perfectly happy being on his own. His teachers and other staff at his public school had noticed this, and eventually, his parents and his IEP team agreed to try him at a private special needs school which was designed for children with Asperger's Disorder. Zeke was more or less an instant hit at this school, where his quiet, idiosyncratic style made him very much mainstream. Zeke wasn't sure what to make of suddenly being popular, but he didn't mind it, and no one was making a fuss if papers were falling out of his backpack, or if he had stains from breakfast on his t-shirt.

Zeke was also starting to blossom in LEGO® Club. He had managed to become much more adept at communicating while also engaging in a parallel activity, and he was excited about the opportunities for sharing his creativity and goofy sense of humor with like-minded peers. In LEGO Club he became comfortable and confident enough to show off his real interests and his style – quirky, zany, self-referent. He especially liked spoofs, which was a common theme in LEGO animated film work. He liked doing recognizable but twisted versions of popular game characters – Super Mario, Sonic, Sub-Zero, etc. – which were a hit with the other group members and the LEGO Club community at large.

At his new school, and through LEGO Club, Zeke learned to accept himself and he was much less anxious and inhibited as a result. His parents would have liked to see him more motivated to continue to develop and change. This was an issue for a number of LEGO Club members at some point, especially in the later years, when the "geek syndrome" concept had caught on in the public media. As I mentioned before, it became much more acceptable to be part of a counter-culture that eschewed "style," and being "popular," or even "socially appropriate." These were terms that adolescents like Zeke and Vicky learned to rebel against. It was us neurotypicals, the "NTs," who set up these more or less arbitrary social norms and expectations, and expected the Aspies (people with Asperger's Disorder) to conform.

Some parents and teaching staff supported this view – that society simply needed to be more accepting of this social difference we were calling "autism." My view was more skeptical, since I was involved with both the early childhood diagnosis of autistic conditions – characterized by impediments in language development, deficits in social reciprocity, and atypical, rigid and repetitive behaviors and play evident before the age of two years – as well as transition-planning for young adults entering college or the workforce. As I indicated earlier, this was not a cultural movement, and it was not a choice. It was a lifelong disabling condition. Regardless of the more subjective, stylistic issues that were not a key issue, this was a condition that severely limited these individuals' abilities to function independently in the world, including getting a job, getting married and having friends. Zeke's parents, Abe and Tina, were well aware of this, especially since, like many other families, they had a typically developing son and could easily see the differences between Nathan and Zeke's development and adjustment.

The last time I saw Zeke, he was in high school. Still a gentle giant, and with a quirky, idiosyncratic sense of humor, and still with a generous nature, wanting to share his pleasure and creativity, and still with a messy, overstuffed backpack. Tina and Abe were concerned about his complacent attitude about his future. He had some vague ideas about going into the gaming industry, but no more immediate goals in terms of his college education, or skill set. Zeke's parents were still hardworking business owners, and Nathan was now at college and working at a part-time job to support himself and help pay for college. The school that Zeke was attending had a post-secondary transition program which was a collaboration with a local county college. His parents were also considering trying Zeke in a mainstream public high school for this last couple of years to see if that would help motivate him, and give him a better chance at getting into a competitive university.

Zeke's school didn't require him to do homework, and he could barely keep track of his assignments, although he was still an above-average student. He spent a lot of time on-line with friends chatting about videogames and YouTube videos. He had slight remnants of his former speech-articulation difficulties, but his communication patterns were generally appropriate, and you'd have to interview him pretty carefully to detect any features of Asperger's. In a group of millennials on a college campus, which is where I envision Zeke will be soon, he wouldn't stand out, except he'd probably be the tallest. At least now, he would not be alone.

# MATTHEW

## INITIAL CONTACT

I first met Matthew when he was in 2nd grade, and I continued to be involved with him and his family – updating his assessments, providing individual, family and behavioral consultations, and seeing him in the LEGO® Club groups – for the next six years. Like many of the LEGO Club participants, Matthew had two very accomplished parents, Walter and Jess. He also had an academically and socially successful older sister, Jana. He was, and is, a very handsome boy, with dark curly hair and black-brown eyes, slender and athletic. In 2nd grade, he was neatly groomed and stylishly dressed, wearing glasses. He showed minimal, if any, interest in or responsiveness towards other children his age, including his classmates at school. Most people coming into contact with Matthew at that time would have been struck with his aloofness, and unpredictability. He would be cooperative and focused on completing school work for a while, then he would suddenly yell "No!," knocking his paperwork to the floor and throwing or breaking his pencil.

In public school, prior to his being referred to a private autism school program, Matthew's behavior was even more out of control, and the rates of aggressive, destructive and disruptive behaviors were very high, at more than ten per hour. The difficulty in programming for Matthew was that, although he was clearly autistic and did not seem to be responsive to social norms and the expectations of his teaching staff, he was also very intelligent. Matthew was hyperlexic and could read and comprehend well above his age and grade levels, and his math abilities were even higher. At the same time, he required careful monitoring, a 1:1 aide throughout the day, and a consistently applied positive behavioral support plan just to get him through the day. He was not manageable in most classroom settings because of his calling out and unpredictable outbursts, going after staff directly, and occasionally even putting his peers in harm's way by throwing or smashing things.

Matthew's parents were both busy healthcare professionals, and so from an early age, Matthew had a nanny at home, and he was well cared for in that setting. He demanded a lot of attention from his parents, and family life definitely revolved around Matthew's schedule and Matthew's needs. His sister, Jana, like many siblings of children with autism, became very adept at accommodating and supporting Matthew, while also resenting him at times for the impact that meeting his needs had on her life. When Matthew was young, it was not easy for the family to go out for dinner, or to a movie, or have friends or relatives over to the house, or go on the occasional vacation trip. Somehow, they managed to do all of these things, but all three family members had to do their best to anticipate and adjust to Matthew's complicated demands.

Like so many children with autism, Matthew showed an interest in systematic, orderly things, including the sciences and math, and LEGO®. When Walter and Jess first heard about LEGO Club they were hopeful about it, but not sure that he would be able to refrain from disruptive behavior. By the time he was formally referred to the group, I had had the opportunity to observe him in school, and it was clear that he would have difficulty participating in group activities, especially peer-led activities. He didn't make eye contact. His speech was halting and had an unusual, flat prosody, and he usually made statements, or engaged in verbal scripting – repeating phrases or sections of dialogue from his favorite cartoons or TV shows. He showed very little reciprocal communication, and it took a lot of effort to get him to respond to straightforward factual questions, let alone social questions or social cues. He was not used to sharing materials, or participating in a give-and-take process with peers.

## LEARNING THROUGH LEGO

In order to prepare Matthew for the challenge of being a LEGO Club member, I spent some time with him in the LEGO room, just to get a sense of how he would react to the process, and also to have him feel more familiar and comfortable in that setting. What struck me immediately about Matthew was how well he remembered each of our encounters. He remembered not only that I had visited his classroom, but every detail of what had transpired while I was there. He had a phenomenal event memory, and later, I learned he also had an exceptional memory for visual information in general – such as where every LEGO® set was the last time he was in the room. Initially, we built LEGO sets together, something he had done with his father, Walter, many times. He was very fast with building, and would even become impatient with me if I wasn't getting the parts to him quickly enough. He wouldn't say anything, but he would reach over and start taking the parts he needed from the tray in front of me, and I'd have to move the tray out of his reach. Then he'd be petulant and slap his hand on the table. "You're too slow, Dr. Dan. I need the next piece, this one [pointing at the directions], it's right there [pointing at the tray]," then holding out his hand for the piece, without looking at me once.

Matthew was impulsive at times and willful, but he could also be tolerant and patient when he was motivated. With me, his motivation was to finish the LEGO set. Once he had started a set, he normally wanted to finish it in one sitting – leaving an unfinished LEGO set until next week was not something Matthew was prepared to do at this point. When he was done with the set, which he understood as the main or only reason for being in the LEGO room, he was done. He'd want to put the set up on a shelf with the other sets, and he liked the idea of having his name posted with the set to indicate who had built it, and then he'd just walk out the door to the waiting room.

Dr. Dan: "Matt! We're not done yet. Come here. You didn't even say goodbye."

Matthew: "I'm done. Goodbye."

Dr. Dan: "Woah. I thought we could talk about next week. You're going to be coming to LEGO Club."

Matthew: "Yes." Then he walked out.

Jess: "Are you all done, Matthew? I think Dr. Dan still wants to talk to you."

Matthew: "I'm done building, let's go."

Jess: "I think Dr. Dan wants to get you ready for joining the LEGO Club."

Matthew: "No, I'm ready for the LEGO Club. Let's go." His voice had taken on an urgent edge to it, and he had put his hand on his mother's arm, tapping it, and then lifting it.

There was obviously something else he wanted to do. I had observed Matthew enough in school to know when he wanted to move on to something else. It would take a while for LEGO® Club to become rewarding enough to compete with the Cartoon Network or YouTube. It did happen, though. I had seen many children like Matthew, whose characteristics were more consistent with autism than Asperger's, who tended to have very full and rigidly adhered-to schedules. Something new like this was always going to be a bit of a struggle at first. I was willing to be flexible with him at first with regard to any compliance issues. It was a rare situation that a child did not want to be in LEGO Club, and most of the time, if they didn't want to be there, we tried to find another way to meet their social development needs – another group, or peer-based strategies at school. The main benefit of the LEGO Club approach for many participants was the fact that it was inherently rewarding. Sometimes, though, as with Matthew, it took a while for that to happen.

The following week, which was supposed to be his first LEGO Club session, I decided to have him in for one last individual session. I wanted to spend some more time working on his collaboration and communication while engaged in LEGO activities, and I wanted to see if he would participate a bit in the pre- and post-group check-in and review activities, which were often the most overtly social parts of the group activity, and also gave the group members a sense of ownership with regard to the activities and the materials – we decided what to build, what new sets to purchase, and voted on the LEGO level system certificates.

That next week, Matthew was irritated that he was not in LEGO Club yet, but he was willing to hear me out. I explained to him again about the level system and the benchmarks for achieving the different levels, and I showed him examples of projects that other group members had worked on to achieve the different levels, including some stop-motion films. One of the films that was still being worked on was a SpongeBob spoof, and the set included the Krusty Krab restaurant set, and Matthew was definitely intrigued by this. He even looked at the script and storyboard for the film, and asked to see the first minute or so of the stop-motion animation over and over. He was smiling and laughing, and repeating some of the lines from the SpongeBob scene over and over. Of course, he wanted to make his own SpongeBob movie, and he immediately started trying to create a set for the movie, including some of the set pieces from the other scene.

Dr. Dan: "Matthew, that set is still being used by the LEGO® group that built it. You can look at it, even move some parts around, but we have to leave it all there on the tray – that's the scene for the movie they're making."

Matthew: "I want to make my own SpongeBob movie."

Dr. Dan: "That would be very cool, but you'll have to practice a bit first. And in order to make a movie in LEGO Club, you have to earn your way up to it. You haven't even joined a group yet. Then you have to be a good LEGO Helper, and then a Builder, and then become a LEGO Creator, before you can start writing your own scripts and directing your own movies. We just talked about this. Do you understand how this works?"

Matthew: "Yes, I have to be a helper, then a builder, then a creator, and then I can make movies on my own and become a master."

Dr. Dan: "Not quite. We do everything in LEGO Club together. It's a lot more fun that way. You'll have to watch and learn from the other kids, and they'll show you how to become a Creator, and then you can be a leader in making movies, but you won't be doing them by yourself."

Matthew: "Can't I just make a movie now?"

Dr. Dan: "We can do individual projects like that when we're not in the group, yes. We can even do that today, but I think we need to practice a bit. It's not as easy as it sounds, making a movie."

Matthew: "I know how to do it. I can see how to do it," he said, pointing at the scene and the camera.

So Matthew and I went through the process of what was likely to happen in his first few LEGO Club sessions, the check-in, deciding whose project to work on, assigning roles, completing tasks, then reviewing, etc. I also reminded him about the sorts of activities that he would be engaged in at first – helping clean, sort and store LEGO, finding pieces and working on other members' set-building and freestyle projects, etc. He was patient and listened. I made sure he was getting it by having him repeat back to me – paraphrasing, not parroting – what he would have to do to become a LEGO Master. Then I described to him what a LEGO Genius was, told him about some of our LEGO Legends, and showed him some of their films and construction projects. He was excited and still wanted to get going on some stop-motion filming, so I let him use some of the SpongeBob characters from the set. I required him to give me a verbal description of the action sequence and physical setting, camera angles, etc., and then helped him learn to use the camera and software. He was absorbing the information quickly, but the slowness of the stop-motion process and complexity of the editing software were frustrating.

Matthew: "This is a lot, Dr. Dan. This is a lot for me. It's not easy."

Dr. Dan: "Yes, Matthew. Like I said, it's not as easy as it sounds. But you'll get it."

Matthew: "Yes, I can do it, but it's very slow. It's hard."

Dr. Dan: "Well, it's a lot faster when you have friends to help you. You'll see when you come to the group. When everyone works together, it goes a lot quicker."

Matthew: "Will they help me make my movie?"

Dr. Dan: "Of course, but first, you'll have to help them. You're still going to be a LEGO® Helper when you start, but you'll move up fast, if you don't just do your own thing. You can't get to Master by doing your own thing. You help out others, then they'll help you. They'll help you build sets, work with you to write scripts and storyboards, camera work and editing, and even do voices and move the characters in the scenes."

Matthew: "Okay, I'm going to be a good helper." He smiled at me and headed for the door. "I'll be here next week. Goodbye."

## JOINING OTHERS

Matthew joined the group that included Zeke and Vicky, as well as a number of others. The group sizes had begun to grow, and were now more consistently about nine, as opposed to six, as the usual size. At that time, we had three adults in the room, and usually the groups were divided into three small groups of three, but there were also many other configurations, depending on the ongoing projects, and the needs of the participants. The room was also sometimes divided up physically with a divider, or there were also two smaller rooms attached to the main LEGO room, which we used as mini sound and editing studios at times, when the voices or just the LEGO bin-searching noise was going on.

Jess had brought Matthew to the group early, so he had a chance to meet some of the other group members in the waiting room. Matthew was playing on a game system in the waiting room when one of the other boys, Brandon, came in. Brandon was nine years old, about Matthew's age, and had similar autistic features, with probably less fluent speech and more echolalia than Matthew. Matthew had engaged in scripting, often combined with repetitive hand and arm movements such as thrusting his arms out, rubbing or clapping his hands together, or twisting his hair. He tended to do these repetitive movements in combination with scripting. Brandon also scripted, but he also just repeated sentences or questions that he'd heard, or he might say the same sentence over a few times, first out loud, then whispering it to himself, then loud again, with his voice tone rising each time to a higher pitch. Brandon's background was almost identical to Matthew's: successful professional parents, an athletic and bright older sister, and excellent academic skills, including hyperlexia, but very poor functional communication and virtually no capacity for social engagement with peers.

Brandon stopped in front of Matthew and looked down at his Gameboy®, with his head almost touching Matthew's. Brandon was also carrying a Gameboy®, but for some reason, he wanted to see what Matthew was playing. Matthew didn't seem to notice, but then he reached up, without looking at Brandon, and moved his head gently to the side. Brandon seemed to take this as a cue to sit next to Matthew, which he did, and then leaned in, obscuring Matthew's view of his game. Again, Matthew didn't react angrily – he just moved the Gameboy® over, and up, so he could see. Brandon stayed there, with his head more or less in the middle of Matthew's chest, and then sat up and looked at his own Gameboy®. They sat together like that, each playing their own games, until it was time to come in to the group. We knew Matthew was here for the first time, so one of my assistants came out to get him, asking him to leave the Gameboy® with Jess. Then he brought him in with the rest of the group members, and introduced him around.

There was usually a lot of excitement in the first few minutes of LEGO® Club, with loud voices coming down the hall from the waiting room, then some excited chaos in the room while everyone checked out what had been happening in the room since they were there last, and looking at their own projects from the past weeks. Vicky introduced herself to Matthew.

Vicky: "My name is Victoria, but everyone here calls me Vicky. I don't mind, since Victoria is such an old-fashioned name, but I haven't decided yet if I'm really suited to being a Vicky or not. What's your name?"

Matthew didn't respond, and was looking around the room.

Dr. Dan: "Matt. Vicky is introducing herself. Do you want to tell her your name?"

Matthew: "My name is Matthew." He didn't look at her.

Vicky: "He said his name is Matthew. You called him, Matt, Dr. Dan. Do you think he minds being called Matt? He might not like that you know, since he said his name was Matthew."

Dr. Dan: "I don't think he minds. Matt? Do you prefer Matt or Matthew?"

Matthew: "I don't know." He was looking around and noticed Brandon was near the camera, with one of the assistants and Zeke, setting up a scene. He walked over to watch Brandon and Zeke rebuilding a movie set, which was a deserted island with a palm tree, sand and a monkey.

Vicky: "I guess he's not that interested in names."

The assistant, Greg, prompted Matthew to join them, and modeled it for him.

Greg: "Hey there, I've met you before. I'm Greg, and this is Brandon and Zeke. We're working on a movie we started last week. It's Brandon's project."

Brandon: "It's Brandon's project. *Brandon's project.*"

Greg: "Yes, it is! And this is Zeke, he's helping us. He's new to LEGO® Club like you, been here just a few weeks, and he's a LEGO® Creator already."

Zeke: "Hi. I'm helping Brandon with his movie. It's about a little monkey on an island."

Vicky: "I want to help, too. Can I help on your movie, Brandon?"

Greg: "Brandon?... Get his attention, Vicky."

Vicky moved over to Brandon and got in his line of sight and smiled.

Vicky: "Can I help you on this movie, Brandon?"

Brandon: "Sure. You can. You're the. You can be the. You're going to be the tree. Can you move the tree? When I show you?"

Greg: "Brandon, where's the script? The storyboard, so Vicky and Matthew can see what we're doing."

Brandon held up a two-page cartoon strip-style storyboard, outlining a sequence in which a monkey tries to climb a palm tree, but the wind blows the tree and he falls out repeatedly, then the monkey gets an axe, but the tree dodges him, then he gets a chainsaw and cuts down the tree, and climbs onto the stump and looks out to sea with a telescope. On the other side of the room, another small group was working on a pirate scene, with pirates aboard a ship at sea, which was headed towards the monkey's island.

Matthew: "What can I do?"

Zeke: "I'm the monkey. I mean, I've got the monkey. I'm moving him in the scene, and I'm making the monkey sounds." He demonstrated his monkey squeal, and laughed.

Brandon: "We need more sand. More sand, *more sand*, and an axe, and a chainsaw. Can you find us more sand? A flat, some flats, like this that look like sand. And an axe, a big one, and a chainsaw. *Chainsa-aw!*" He shook his hands in the air and tensed his body, making chainsaw sounds.

Matthew looked at Brandon for a second, apparently recognizing the gesture as very similar to his own. Then he went off in search of the props. In the meantime, the group worked with Greg on the scene they had, moving the monkey into the scene and then onto the tree, climbing it, then the tree swaying and the monkey being pitched off. The island in the scene kept moving around, and we had to re-do a number of scenes, using the "onion skinning" option on the stop-motion software to reposition the island after the tree was moved – Vicky was struggling to get the tree to move without moving the whole scene. Zeke's head and hands were also in the scene frequently when Brandon would say "Clear the set," and Zeke would have to finish his last movement of the monkey, but then he'd forget to get all the way out of the camera shot.

Matthew came back with some more sand-colored bricks, and a couple of sand-colored flats, and gave them to Brandon. Greg prompted Brandon to say "thanks," which he did, and then Brandon tried arranging some of the new sand around to make his island bigger – he had wanted to have the camera pull back slowly from the island when the monkey climbed on the stump. Matthew looked at the camera shot on the computer and immediately understood what Brandon was after, so he helped him align the sand pieces to make the shape of an island, then went to find the axe and chainsaw.

Greg had got some blue masking tape that matched the blue plates we were using for the sea, and he and Vicky were taping the island to the table when Matthew came back with an old-fashioned Knight's battle axe, and a chainsaw.

Brandon: "Axe, axe and chainsaw. *Chainsaw!* Okay, okay, okay. We need the tree by itself, *clear the scene!*" He took a shot of the island with the palm tree in the foreground, then: "The tree sees the monkey coming."

Somehow, Vicky knew what he meant, and she leaned the tree back and away for the next shot, then had the palm fronds stand up, as in fright, for the next one after that.

Vicky: "Terrified palm tree! I love it."

Brandon: "Cue the monkey, with axe. Zeke! Monkey with battle axe, moving in."

Zeke: "Monkey with battle axe." He started making cheerful monkey sounds, and step by step brought the monkey back into the scene carrying the battle axe, and then swung it at the tree, which Vicky had dodge the swings, and the monkey left the scene. Vicky did her best to have the tree sigh in relief, lifting then dropping its fronds. Then, the tree shuddered again and went straight and fronds up, in fear. The monkey returned, with Zeke making cheerful monkey sounds, and Brandon doing his best chainsaw.

Matthew was watching carefully, and when Brandon made a chainsaw sound, Matthew did a better one.

Zeke: "Good chainsaw, Matt. But it's Brandon's deal, he's got the..."

Vicky: "I like it. That was a scary chainsaw, Matt."

Brandon: "Yes, he's the chainsaw. Matthew, do the chainsaw again, on cue: *Chainsaw!*"

Matthew made the chainsaw noise, loudly, into the mic. The kids on the other side of the room poked their heads around the barricade, curious about the noise, which was very lifelike.

Zeke: "Yeah, that was definitely the better chainsaw. Good."

They progressed with the scene, and then Brandon needed the telescope, which was not an easy part to find. Matthew tried the bins, and couldn't find one, then he noticed that the other group were using most of the pirate-related LEGO® for their scene. He came

back and told me, "They're using all the pirate LEGO®. I don't know if
they'll let us have the telescope or not."

Dr. Dan: "Well, we're all working together on the same movie, and
we need it for our scene. Why don't you ask them?"

Matthew went over and asked the assistant, Brittany, for the
LEGO telescope, but she deflected the question to the group
members working there. They weren't sure if they had one or not,
and Vicky went over to help out. She and Matthew scanned the
pirate ship and the pirates. Matthew dug into a few treasure chests,
and eventually found one. He held it up in his fingers to show that he
had found it, then turned away.

Vicky: "Hold on, Matt. You better ask them for it."

Matthew: "Okay, can I have this for our scene? I'll bring it back."

Vicky: "Good, Matt. That's one of our rules, right? If someone
else is using it, you don't take it, you have to ask."

Brittany: "Yep. That's the rule, and you did the right thing asking,
but you didn't wait for an answer." She looked to the group. "Can he
borrow it?"

Peter: "We're not using it now, so yeah, he can borrow it."

Matthew, Vicky, Brandon and Zeke finished the monkey scene,
which was one of the best moments in the pirate movie. Matthew
got to tell his mother about the project, and she got to watch the
scene – a little more than a minute long – at the end of the session.
Matthew told her that he had helped build the island, and found the
props, and he seemed pleased with himself. Then he said, "And I was
the chainsaw. *Chainsaw!*" – and made the sound, held his fists up
and shook them.

Matthew continued to struggle at school having periodic
outbursts, scripted speech and hand/arm movements, especially
when he was not engaged or during transition times. In LEGO
Club, we had initiated a peer-modeling approach for many types
of stereotypies, which we noticed often persisted even after we
ensured that we were not inadvertently rewarding them with social
attention, i.e. we implemented "planned ignoring" by both the staff,
including me, and the members, for what we identified as an autistic
"tell," or other potentially stigmatizing behavior, which we would
agree to call "shaky hands," or "self-talk," etc.

In the LEGO room, group members would be prompted to
model a more socially appropriate form of a stereotyped gesture

or vocalization. I would model a socially typical gesture and nonverbally cue a peer to do it with me, such as shaking our fists as a victory gesture in response to a group member flapping their hands. Or, I would put a hand to my chin as a "thoughtful" gesture, and get others to model it, when someone put their fingers or thumb in their mouth or some other atypical hand-to-face gesture. I also modeled and had the peer group "echo" using a high-five, and later, a fist tap, rather than a stiff body-shaking or arm wiggling, when excited about something. Then, the group members would be cued to encourage the target member to try the modified gesture, rather than the stereotyped, potentially stigmatizing one, and if they modeled it, we'd praise them with "Yeah, that looks better," and I'd thank my helpers. Eventually, there was a clear sense of group cohesion and of helping each other as they would spontaneously respond to autistic, stereotyped behaviors with more typical-appearing alternatives.

Although I did not emphasize making eye contact – it involves subtle and complex social judgment – we did make it a habit to look at each other when we spoke, especially when conveying functional information, as opposed to just chatting. "I don't know who you're telling that to if you don't look at me?," or, "How do I know you're hearing this if you're not looking back at me?" etc. We also often modeled voice prosody and age-typical diction and syntax at times – for instance, with Vicky, who still spoke like the queen she was named for. My assistants and I used colloquial speech, and would rephrase pedantic speech, or flat, monotone speech, using appropriate inflection. Then, more importantly, we would have the group members model it for each other as well. Sometimes, this was the blind leading the blind, but there were lots of opportunities to practice. As I noted earlier, one of the benefits of using LEGO® building as a therapy modality is the repetitiveness of it, and the high rate of opportunities for practicing appropriate communication.

LEGO Club was only one source of influence on Matthew's social communication style, though. He was also getting speech-language therapy at school, and privately outside of school, his parents were working with him on effective communication at home, and he had many opportunities outside of school since his parents kept him involved in a range of activities, including swimming and tennis lessons. Although Matthew's communication and speech patterns improved significantly over the years, he continued to have a somewhat atypical voice prosody, which is a qualitative autistic feature that is very difficult to change. Matthew was aware of this issue, of course, and he did make an effort to both notice and imitate typical speech prosody, but it's a very subtle feature, like having a foreign accent. The amount and quality of eye contact was another characteristic that Matthew improved on a lot, but it was still somewhat of a "tell" that he could not quite moderate eye contact in a neurotypical way.

Matthew was able to shape repetitive hand-smacking and hand shaking into a quick couple of claps, or fist shakes, with a "Yeah!" or other contextually appropriate vocalization, rather than engaging in a stereotyped and idiosyncratic scripted phrase. Although, at first, he only did it when prompted by an adult, not peers, he eventually became more responsive to his peers, and would model the prompted gestures or vocalizations. Then, he started anticipating the modeling, and would do it just before he got the prompt, but was still initiating the stereotyped movement or phrase first. Eventually, after months of coaching in the room, Matthew was using more socially appropriate gestures and vocalizations most of the time.

One of the other "tells" that Matthew was somewhat aware of, but had little direct help with, was his facial expressions. Although he could self-observe his own gestures to some extent, facial expressions, like eye contact, are very difficult to normalize if they do not develop in the typical way. Matthew's facial expressions were muted, and difficult to read. When he was very emotional – either very sad, or happy, or very angry – he would combine a facial expression with vocalizations and other behaviors which made it easier to tell what he was experiencing. Most of the time, however, another person would have to know him very well in order to have an accurate sense of what he might be experiencing. Without knowing his interests and his usual habits and routines, and without knowing his past responses to particular situations, Matthew's behavior could be mysterious and unpredictable. This was not an issue to his parents, but it did become a problem at school as his teaching staff necessarily changed every year or so, and then they'd be learning how to read him all over again.

At that time, Matthew was also working on decreasing the frequency of these sorts of gestures and vocalizations at school.

They had not identified his pedantic speech or monotone prosody as educationally relevant issues at all. Of course, that was something he was working on in private speech therapy sessions. He was also working on some other behaviors, which included persisting episodes of getting angry and throwing things, cursing and threatening staff, etc. We didn't see much of that in LEGO® Club, and our in-house de-escalation strategies were working well any time Matthew got frustrated, or came in upset about something else. I had suggested trying the peer-modeling strategy at school, but the behavior specialist involved had recommended planned ignoring. I tried letting the teacher know that this wasn't likely to be effective (planned ignoring works for behaviors with a social attention reinforcement history, but not so well for automatically reinforced or non-contingently maintained behaviors, including stereotypies, tics and many avoidance behaviors).

Somewhat surprisingly, although Matthew was in a special needs classroom with other peers with mild autism or Asperger's, there was very little interaction among the students in that setting. I had encouraged the behavior consultant and teaching staff to consider peer-mediated social learning and behavior change strategies, and they accepted my input, but never implemented it. This was becoming a familiar scenario for me. It seemed that the classroom order, including behavioral compliance, and covering the core curriculum materials, took precedence over social development, even in classrooms where the main identified problem was social development. Matthew and most of his classmates were actually highly motivated students, at or above age level in most areas of academics, but the staff were still focused on making sure they were "doing their work" rather than interacting with each other during class time. Rather than allowing students to share their ideas and learn together, they preferred to have them either sit quietly and listen to the teacher, or work individually, with headphones on, using the computers in the room.

What was somewhat surprising to hear from Matthew's teaching staff, and to observe directly, was that he had become so self-conscious – about people observing him, about this aide helping him, about his appearance, and about his autistic stereotyped behaviors. While his irritability and negativity in response to having unwanted attention could be a problem at times, from my perspective, it was also a very good sign. Matthew had become self-aware. He was particularly sensitive about being perceived to be autistic. It was like he didn't want to be reminded about it. In fact, Jess had commented that he didn't like to be around other children or adolescents who exhibited autistic behavior, especially more overt forms of repetitive stereotyped movements or vocalizations. Matthew had told her that it reminded him of how he used to be, and he didn't like to remember that. It made him feel inferior and helpless somehow, to be reminded that he once exhibited such overtly autistic behavior.

Although this self-consciousness was a good sign in terms of his cognitive and social development, it did make helping Matthew with some of his "tells" more difficult. No very self-conscious adolescent would like to have others carefully scrutinizing their every move, and giving them corrective feedback about their gestures, eye contact, facial expressions and voice prosody. That would be torture for anybody, really. The irony of it was that Matthew really wanted to get better at these things – he wanted to pass for normal, and he would even state sometimes that he wasn't autistic anymore, and didn't need the speech therapy or the special school he was attending. He hated these reminders that he was not quite there, that his autism was still apparent, still making him different. My rapport and treatment alliance with Matthew had gotten to be quite good over the years, so he would tolerate feedback from me about these issues up to a point.

If it was something that he could observe about himself, and then immediately change, such as when he was perseverating on a topic, or making stereotyped movements, he would take the feedback with a sullen nod. But then he would get frustrated, growl at me, literally, and walk away, when the feedback made him feel helpless, or when it was mysterious to him, like it would be for a person trying to learn to speak a new language and speak it like a native speaker – there were so many subtle nuances to learn and practice. Matthew wanted to get better at it, he wanted to improve his self-monitoring and capacity to inhibit his autistic behaviors, and this motivation kept him at it. He was certainly capable of that level of insight, but then he would also growl and get irritable when one of his classmates or a peer in another setting exhibited what he perceived to be overt autistic behavior – like an ex-smoker smelling tobacco smoke, he had developed an intolerance for whiffs of autism.

The last time I had contact with Matthew and his family, he was almost 14 years old, and was towards the end of his 8th grade year. He was still at or above age and grade level norms in all subject areas, especially math. He was struggling a bit with some of the subjective aspects of English literature, but was not significantly behind his peers in this area. One of the main issues for Matthew at school was this intolerance of his own disability: he didn't like having a classroom aide, and the aide had had to back off and pretend to be working with other students most of the time, or Matthew would become surly and rude to him. "Go away! I don't need help. I can do it by myself." He hated being corrected, but he was rude and critical to his teacher at times. For instance, she had written something on the overhead and asked if anyone had any questions, and Matthew said, "You forgot the 'a' in *monastery*."

It was difficult to give feedback to Matthew about his social behavior in a way that he would understand. He was tall, dark and handsome, a good tennis player, and very intelligent, but he was coming across as rigid and self-absorbed. He was petulant and easily frustrated, and he could be cold to his peers, and even ruthless and cruel to his aide. Matthew was responsive to feedback, but it had to be presented in a very objective way and, as much as possible, without social judgment. This was not a simple task: we needed to give Matthew ongoing feedback about his social behavior without making him feel criticized or self-conscious. Matthew's parents and I discussed having Matthew learn a self-monitoring and self-management approach, which I had used successfully with a number of kids like him – with high functioning autism or Asperger's Disorder – in order to improve social and other behavioral issues.

The strategy involved, first, identifying a few target issues, behaviors that Matthew would agree that he wanted to change, either decrease or increase the rate or duration, etc. Then Matthew wore a signaling device, a Motivaider®, which would prompt him to make a record based on his self-observations of the target behaviors. Then, there was a point or token system by which Matthew was rewarded for both improving on the target behaviors, as well as for consistently doing the self-monitoring record. In this way, Matthew could get consistent feedback about some of the autistic behaviors that were bothering him, without generating a reaction to being observed and criticized by someone else. It was a good strategy for

Matthew, and one which I used many times over the years in very similar circumstances. This level of cooperation and insight from a youth with autism is not typical – many do not have the motivation to change, or the capacity to participate independently in such a strategy, which does require considerable effort and motivation – but for those who could do it, and who had the necessary support from parents and their teaching staff, it worked extremely well. For Matthew it was a great relief. Finally, he could be the judge of his own behavior, and the one in charge of changing it.

# CONCLUSION

I am hopeful that this book has given the reader some view of what transpired in the process of developing LEGO®-based therapy, and why it seemed to be worth writing about. There were obviously a variety of personalities and clinical issues considered, often simultaneously, so this was far from a homogeneous, cookie-cutter approach. I have tried to choose a balance of case histories that were both representative of the process, but also which covered some of the range and diversity that was evident during the initial foundation of the LEGO therapy process. I have also not steered away from cases that presented with significant amounts of complexity and challenge.

One of the other themes that I have tried to stress here is the extent to which children with autism are able to grow and develop if we give them the opportunity and the freedom to do so. The LEGO Club approach would have been superfluous if there had been flexibility and acceptance offered by these children's schools. The situation has improved dramatically, of course, and now, thanks to colleagues like Gina Gomez, G.W. Krauss and Sarah Levin Allen, LEGO-based therapy itself is more accessible to teachers, school counselors and related professionals (e.g. occupational and speech-language therapists). It was my hope that LEGO-based therapy would be provided in schools, both public and private, and perhaps that there might be some utilization of this method with other populations of special needs students, other than those with autism/Asperger's. As I have previously argued here, social competence arises from such a natural and almost miraculous force in the learning process for most children, it is easy to overlook it as a fact of normal and even autistic development.

Similar to language, most children just pick it up out of the air around them, play with it, whirl it around, stamp on it and bend it, and then tune it to their own ears. For many children and their families, social development, like language and motor development, is a fairly mysterious and mostly autonomous process that is marked by 'developmental milestones' which register the progression of a variable but progressive path. As parents, we try to teach our children some social rules – play nice, share, use your words, don't push, say please, thank you and sorry, pass the ball, pass the peas – but the rest just happens. And 'the rest' is an enormous field of reciprocal action sequences, verbal and nonverbal communication, alliances and shared experience, moral reasoning and ethical dilemmas, sacrifices, selfishness, sexual and aggressive impulses, posturing, acknowledging, joining and excluding.

Although there is no general curriculum for social development, what is such an effortless process for some, like walking or riding a bike for the athletically gifted, is still accessible for those less blessed. Some of the other approaches to helping autistic individuals learn to be social that I have tried seemed artificial and overly structured. The results inevitably seemed that way to the others in their lives who mattered: their peers, parents, siblings and teachers. Anyone can tell the difference between the sounds created by a musician who understands the deeper meaning of a tune and someone who is just playing the notes, or worse, letting a computer do it. Most of us can also tell the difference between someone who is inspired by visual beauty to recreate it in art, and someone painting by numbers, or according to a lesson plan, or again, using a graphic printer. Just as easily we can tell the difference between someone who is genuinely happy to meet us, and someone trying to sell us something, or someone who sincerely shares our grief versus someone who is trained to express phrases of support.

There is something about authenticity in social situations that is exceptionally difficult to replicate without some sincere engagement: you have to mean it. The same is true for children with autistic conditions who are learning in a rote, structured way to be social. If there isn't a sincere, intrinsic motivation to be part of a social interaction, regardless of the detailed level of behavioral conditioning and shaping involved, the result will not be authentic – it will be stilted and strange, possibly even off-putting. The social awkwardness that seems harmless and endearing in a young child with autism is much less cute in a young adult. This is even more evident when it comes to children with autism trying out their newly acquired "social skills." An eight-year-old boy can insist on shaking hands with people in a situation that doesn't call for it, or make too much eye contact, raise a toast, or wear a tie in a way that goes against the grain – no one will take offense. But take the same set of faux pas and apply them to a 32-year-old looking for his first job, and the cuteness is gone. The problem is, most therapists working with eight-year-olds never see 32-year-old autistic adults.

What I have tried to convey in this book is the spirit and quality of LEGO®-based therapy, as opposed to the systematic aspects. Part of the reason for this approach is that a large part of why LEGO Club has been successful in improving social functioning for children with autistic conditions is that it increases the participants' motivation to participate. Participation was also not just engaging with the LEGO materials, although that was often the case in the beginning. At the core of the LEGO-based therapy method is the requirement that participants join others in engaging in creative activity – assembling LEGO – that they would normally do on their own or in parallel play. I use the term "join," as opposed to "interact," or "communicate," because there is something more to the process than simply interacting or even engaging. "Joining" implies becoming part of a group, not just having an interaction with others. And it is an active process, one in which the child initiates and sustains because they want to, not because we want them to.

When I first evaluate a child or adolescent to determine if they are appropriate for one of my groups, I take them for a tour of the LEGO room, to see their reaction. Most children see that there is a lot of fun going on – the room is full of it. It just looks like a lot of fun. And, yes, they want to join this club. They want to be part of whatever is going on in there. Once they have taken that step and made the decision to join, then the therapy process has begun – now they need to learn how to really join, how to be part of a social unit, to benefit from the group's successes, and suffer along with the other group members when there are disappointments, or disasters. Without first capturing that motivation to join, however, there is little momentum to sustain a child through the challenges of sharing, miscommunication, committing to being there every week, settling disputes, and acknowledging others' accomplishments.

LEGO® groups were little studios of focused effort, but they could also be chaotic and highly emotional settings: it was definitely personal, and whether we were tediously reviewing the details of a complex Star Wars set, or ready to go to blows over a missed opportunity in a stop-motion film, the experience was authentic. No one was pretending to be good at social skills; we were all bumbling along trying to communicate and work together without creating too much offense or hard feelings, and sincerely trying to get better at it, for the sake of our art, the group LEGO project. Simply by setting up a social and physical environment which brought out and encouraged the motivation to have this interpersonal experience, LEGO-based therapy allowed children who had minimal social interest, and even less social talent, to want to participate and to get better at it. As a result of these experiences, most of the participants not only got better at interacting with their peers in the group, they became interested in having social experiences outside of the group. Simply put, they had become convinced of the value of creativity in the context of social relationships.

# FUTURE DIRECTIONS

What started as a strategy to get children with autism/Asperger's interested in participating in a social skills group evolved over time into a treatment approach in its own right, and the publication of that method inspired a number of other providers and researchers to consider its merit. At this point, groups using this method with this particular population are actively being run in a wide range of settings, and researchers in the US, Canada and the UK are continuing to examine the efficacy of the original methodology, as well as alternative formats (e.g. MacCormack, Hutchinson and Matheson 2015). It is my hope that this trend will continue and other providers and researchers will utilize the basic principles of LEGO®-based therapy to expand on or explore variations of this approach. The basic idea, as I have indicated previously, really came from the participants themselves, as I have tried to capture in the first few case histories of this book.

The subsequent replication of the method with other groups, and then in another cultural and geographical setting, was important in convincing me that this might become more than just a one-off successful but unique venture. At first, I do recall thinking that it was just a nice coincidence that I had found a few kids with a common interest, LEGO. I had no idea at the time how widespread this common interest was going to turn out to be. Once there were a number of groups running, and it was clear that the interest in LEGO was more than just a few unique cases, the next step was to establish that the groups were effective in improving social functioning, and not just an enjoyable pastime.

Once my colleagues and I had agreed that there seemed to be a valid and measurable impact of this method on social functioning, it was just a matter of describing what we had done in a way that could be replicated by others. In the LEGO®-based therapy manual (LeGoff *et al.* 2014), we expanded a bit on the manual that I had originally written for Gina's replication study (Owens *et al.* 2008), and tried to include enough advice and details about running the groups to help steer other providers or researchers in the right direction, and minimize the chance that they would make some of the same mistakes that I had made in the early days. Some of the advice was really core to the group process, like not letting participants do individual projects, and requiring them to participate in the interactive process, and other advice was simply helpful, and somewhat commonsense, like not having parents in the room, or not eating during sessions. What we had not been able to give others advice about was how to do this with other populations, i.e. other than kids with autism/Asperger's, since we had not done that ourselves (I have had kids with other diagnoses involved, but I have not systematically used LEGO-based therapy as a treatment approach for students or patients with non-autistic conditions).

Since the publication of the manual, there has also been considerable informal feedback from other providers who have been using the manual to guide their implementation of LEGO-based groups. These other providers, in a variety of countries and agency settings, have had a variety of professional backgrounds, from school psychology to psychiatric nursing and speech pathology, to lay persons with no background in healthcare or education. What has not been undertaken so far, however, is to use the LEGO-based therapy approach with other populations, such as anxiety disorders (social anxiety, for instance), mood disorders or externalizing conditions (ADHD, ODD, etc.). It seems reasonable that the benefits in terms of social and communication skills for participants with autistic conditions would also benefit those with social inhibition and low social self-efficacy. Alternatively, the therapy might also be a good source of social support and positive experience of accomplishment for children with depressed mood, or grief and loss issues.

For externalizing conditions, which I have not felt as hopeful about, the methodology would need to be modified, with more of a focus on interfering behaviors. The LEGO®-based therapy approach does offer ample opportunities for the practice of key executive functions, such as sustained attention, sequential processing, planning, freedom from distractibility or maintaining mental set, impulse control and affect tolerance, etc. In my experience, most children with ADHD and ODD also have significant deficits in social functioning, partly because of these difficulties with executive functions, but also due to some intolerance of their disruptive behaviors by peers. Just as it is difficult for peers to accept and support students with autistic conditions because of their social difficulties, it is at least as difficult for peers to accept and work around the impulsivity and disruptive tangents of children with externalizing disorders. Perhaps a good option would be to have peers who have similar issues and to acknowledge this amongst themselves and work together to improve both their impulsive, tangential thinking, as well as their disruptive interpersonal style.

It has also been suggested by colleagues that we consider offering LEGO-based groups to adults as well as children and adolescents. As Daniel Junge and his colleagues have aptly shown with their documentary film, "A LEGO Brickumentary," many adults are just as fascinated and involved with LEGO as are children. This could create a format for adults to improve their social and communication skills, whether in the context of remediation for a psychiatric or autistic condition, or simply as a personal improvement or organizational management strategy. Many individuals who have participated in the LEGO-based therapy training over the years have commented on how useful this approach might be for corporate or self-improvement settings. Of course, being a child psychologist, I have limited time with and even less access to, populations of willing participants other than children, so that will have to be up to someone else to explore.

# REFERENCES

American Psychiatric Association (APA) (2013) *Diagnostic and Statistical Manual of Mental Disorders, Fifth Edition (DSM-V)*. Washington, DC: APA Press.

Chorpita, B.F. and Donkervoet, C. (1995) *Implementation of the Felix Consent Decree in Hawaii.* Available at http://childfirst.ucla.edu/2005%20Felix%20Decree%20(Chorpita,%20Donkervoet).pdf, accessed on 05 December 2016.

Gray, C. (1994) *Comic Strip Conversations.* Arlington, TX: Future Horizons Press.

Gray, C. (1998) 'Social Stories and Comic Strip Conversations.' In E. Schopler, G. Mesibov and L. Kunce (eds.) *Asperger Syndrome or High-Functioning Autism?* New York, NY: Plenum Press.

Koegel, R.L. and Koegel, L.K. (1995) *Teaching Children with Autism.* New York, NY: Paul H. Brookes.

Kohler, F.W., Strain, P., Hoyson, M. and Jamieson, B. (1997) 'Merging naturalistic teaching and peer-based strategies to address the IEP objectives of preschoolers with autism: An examination of structural and child behavior outcomes.' *Focus on Autism and Other Developmental Disabilities 12*, 4, 196–206.

LeGoff, D.B. (2004) 'Use of LEGO® as a therapeutic medium for improving social competence.' *Journal of Autism and Developmental Disorders 34*, 5, 557–571.

LeGoff, D.B. and Sherman, M. (2006) 'Long-term outcome of social skills intervention based on interactive LEGO® play.' *Autism 10*, 4, 1–31.

LeGoff, D.B., Gomez de la Cuesta, G., Krauss, G.W. and Baron Cohen, S. (2014) *LEGO®-Based Therapy: How to Build Social Competence through LEGO®-Based Clubs for Children with Autism and Related Conditions.* London, UK: Jessica Kingsley Publishers.

Lepper, M.R., Greene, D. and Nesbitt, R.E. (1973) 'Undermining children's intrinsic interest with extrinsic reward: A test of the "overjustification" hypothesis.' *Journal of Personality and Social Psychology 28*, 1, 129–137.

MacCormack, J.W.H., Hutchinson, I.A. and Matheson, N.L. (2015) 'An exploration of a LEGO® based social skills program for youth with autism spectrum disorder.' *Exceptionality Education International 25*, 13–32.

McGinnis, E. and Goldstein, A.P. (1997) *Skillstreaming the Elementary School Child: New Strategies and Perspectives for Teaching Prosocial Skills.* Champaign, IL: Research Press.

Murray, H.A. (1943) *Thematic Apperception Test Manual.* Cambridge, MA: Harvard University Press.

Owens, G., Granader, Y., Humphrey, A. and Baron Cohen, S. (2008) 'LEGO® therapy and the Social Use of Language Programme: An evaluation of two social skills interventions for children with high functioning autism and Asperger Syndrome.' *Journal of Autism and Developmental Disorders 18*, 10, 1944–1957.

Rogers, C. (1951) *Client-Centred Therapy: Its Current Practice, Implications and Theory.* Boston, MA: Houghton-Mifflin.

Vollmer, Timothy R; Iwata, Brian A (1992). "Differential reinforcement as treatment for behavior disorders: Procedural and functional variations.". *Research in Developmental Disabilities.*

Schopler, E. and Mesibov, G.B. (1992) *Social Behavior in Autism.* New York, NY: Plenum Press.

# INDEX